Professional Decision Making in Social Work

Post-Qualifying Social Work Practice – titles in the series

To order, please contact our distributor: BEBC Distribution, Albion Close, Parkstone, Poole, BH12 3LL. Telephone: 0845 230 9000, email: **learningmatters@bebc.co.uk.**

You can also order online at **www.learningmatters.co.uk.**

Professional Decision Making in Social Work

BRIAN J TAYLOR

Series Editor: Keith Brown

LearningMatters

First published in 2010 by Learning Matters Ltd

British Library Cataloguing in Publication Data
A CIP record for this book is available from the British Library.

ISBN: 978 1 84445 359 7

Cover and text design by Code 5 Design Associates Ltd
Project management by Swales & Willis Ltd
Typeset by Swales & Willis Ltd, Exeter, Devon
Printed and bound in Great Britain by TJ International Ltd, Padstow, Cornwall

Learning Matters Ltd
33 Southernhay East
Exeter EX1 1NX
Tel: 01392 215560
info@learningmatters.co.uk
www.learningmatters.co.uk

FSC
Mixed Sources
Product group from well-managed
forests and other controlled sources
Cert no. SGS-COC-2482
www.fsc.org
© 1996 Forest Stewardship Council

Contents

Foreword to the Post-Qualifying Social Work Practice Series

All the texts in the Post-Qualifying Social Work Practice series have been written by people with a passion for excellence in social work practice. They are primarily written for social workers who are undertaking post-qualifying social work awards, but will also be useful to any social worker who wants to consider up-to-date practice issues.

The books in this series are also of value to social work students as they are written to inform, inspire and develop social work practice.

Keith Brown
Series Editor
Centre for Post-Qualifying Social Work, Bournemouth

About the author

Brian Taylor is Senior Lecturer in Social Work at the University of Ulster where he has lead role for post-qualifying education and training. His research and teaching interests are in decision making, assessment, risk and evidence-based practice. He has published widely and had a lead role in developing the Northern Ireland Single Assessment Tool for the health and social care of older people. He previously spent twelve years as a practitioner and manager in social work, residential care, primary school teaching and youth work. He worked for fifteen years in social work education, training, and organisation development in health and social care, including three years as project manager implementing new children's legislation. His doctorate was on risk and decision making in community care and he has taught for ten years on the topic of risk and decision making on post-qualifying courses for newly qualified social workers. **www.ulster.ac.uk/staff/bj.taylor.html**

Acknowledgements

Firstly I would like to thank my father, Bernard Taylor, for his example of integrity in every decision that I ever saw him make. I am grateful to many of my family, friends and colleagues – too many to mention – for their support and encouragement during this endeavour. Thanks too to our dog for putting up with my absent mindedness on recent walks.

I am indebted to Dr Michael Donnelly, Reader, Centre for Public Health, Queen's University Belfast for his inspiring encouragement of my research on decision making and to Mr David Carson, Reader in Law and Behavioural Sciences at the University of Portsmouth for his invigorating enthusiasm in his work on the interface between law and professional decisions.

I would like to thank the social workers on post-qualifying courses and other colleagues in practice who have shared examples of their judgements, decision making and dilemmas with me. I am very grateful to a member of the general public and colleagues who have commented on draft chapters, exercises, bullet lists of pointers and questions, etc. from the perspectives of clients, education and training, information technology, law, management, regulation, and research as well as professional practice. I would particularly like to thank Garth Agnew, Taralisa Allen, Patricia Casey, Eithne Darragh, Helen Gault, Marc Harvey, Jan Houston, Campbell Killick, Marie McCann, Oonagh McGivern, Eileen McKay, Rita McKelvey, Helen McVicker, Jacinta Miller, Stephen Russell, Debbie Stringer and Richard Taylor. Any errors or omissions are, of course, the responsibility of the author.

Very many thanks to Miss Janice McQuilkin, Assistant Subject Librarian at the University of Ulster for her help and patience in accessing and referencing legal documents. Many sincere thanks to Mrs Siobhan Irwin, Mrs Sharon Lucas, Mrs Sue Gamble and Mrs Janice Clayton for loyal administrative support over the years.

I apologise for any omissions to these acknowledgements.

Last but not least, heart-felt thanks to my wife Mary for her never-failing support not least during these months of pulling together a decade of teaching, research, writing and reflection for this manuscript.

Introduction

Much of what social workers do concerns decisions about future courses of action, which puts decision making at the heart of social work as a core professional activity.

Sarah Banks (1995) *Ethics and Values in Social Work*, 2nd edn.
Hampshire: Palgrave, p9.

The place of decision making in social work

Social work involves making decisions that impact on the lives of vulnerable people. These decisions have traditionally been about whom amongst so many fellow-citizens in need should receive scarce resources, whether these have come from charitable or government sources. As social work has developed an increasing role in protecting the most vulnerable on behalf of society, we have become involved in crucial decisions hinging on the role of the state in intervening in the lives of families to protect individuals. Such decisions may involve high risks such as continued abuse or death of a child or a vulnerable adult. These decisions are never easy! Some of the media may be quick to highlight instances where it seems in hindsight that social workers or other professionals might have prevented some harm inflicted by one person on another. There are also lower profile decisions such as where social workers are supporting someone with a disability or on hospital discharge to take steps towards more independent living. Social work decisions span a wide range from safeguarding through to allocating services and advising clients and families on courses of action to improve their lives.

This book draws together various theoretical aspects of *decision making* in order to develop a supportive approach to guide professional practice. We must draw upon various sources of professional knowledge – such as law, policy, research, theory, standards, principles and practice wisdom – to inform complex and sensitive judgements and decisions in uncertain situations where harm may ensue. Values of the client, our profession, your organisation and our society are an intrinsic part of decision making, and must be related to these other aspects in decision-making processes. These various strands must be brought together as we participate in organisational and societal decision-making systems including child protection case conferences, decisions about capacity to consent to care and treatment, panels within organisations to allocate care resources and court hearings.

This textbook is written to provide a framework of knowledge and skills relevant to judgement and decision making with all client groups. The text is illustrated with examples from family and child care, older people, mental health, disability and criminal justice. The focus is on concepts, principles and processes that are transferable across jurisdictions and organisational arrangements so specific legislative and government policy references for particular client groups have been kept to a minimum. All chapters are written to be applicable to all client groups, and written to help the reader to apply the concepts to their own context. The focus is on empowering front-line professionals through reflective practice to integrate multiple factors and perspectives into sound problem-solving judgements so as to support client decision making and safeguarding and gate-keeping decisions. It is increasingly important for social workers to be able to articulate the rationale for their judgements and decisions, drawing on research evidence, theory and the use of robust assessment tools, and relating these to relevant parameters of law, policy and principles. This book assists in that process.

Knowledge and skills for professional practice

This book is written for professionally qualified social workers undertaking post-qualifying education and training, where effective professional decision making is a key area of knowledge and skill. It is assumed that the reader has a foundation in the roles and tasks of social work in a democratic society, and knowledge and skills in the basic social work helping process (Taylor and Devine, 1993; Shulman, 1999) applied in a variety of contexts including counselling and care planning. This book has been written specifically to address requirements of social workers undertaking awards within the post-qualifying frameworks for social work in the UK, such as the following.

- Work effectively in a context of risk, uncertainty, conflict and contradiction (The Post-Qualifying Award in Specialist Social Work (Generic Level Requirement vii.), General Social Care Council [England], 2004).

- Work effectively as a practitioner, researcher, educator or manager in a context of risk, uncertainty, conflict and contradiction where there are complex challenges and a need to make informed and balanced judgements (The Post-Qualifying Award in Higher Specialist Social Work (Generic Level Requirement vi.), General Social Care Council [England], 2004).

- Work creatively and effectively as a practitioner, researcher, educator or manager *and take a leading role* in a context of risk, uncertainty, conflict and contradiction or where there are complex challenges and a need to make informed and balanced judgements (The Post-Qualifying Award in Advanced Social Work (Generic Level Requirement vii.), General Social Care Council [England], 2004).

- Competence in working effectively in complex situations (Post-Qualifying Award, Requirement PQ2, *Scotland & Wales (= UK Framework 1990–2007)*).

- Competence in exercising the powers and responsibilities of a professional social worker, including the appropriate use of discretion and the management of risk (Post-Qualifying Award, Requirement PQ3, *Scotland & Wales (= UK Framework 1990–2007)*).

- Ability to make informed decisions (Post-Qualifying Award, Requirement PQ4, *Scotland & Wales (= UK Framework 1990–2007)*).

- Demonstrate consistent and sustained sound judgement and decision making in the context of complexity, risk, uncertainty, conflict and contradiction (Specific Award Requirement 3, Northern Ireland Post-Qualifying Education and Training Partnership, 2007).

- Use a range of skills and methods of intervention, work effectively and creatively and with initiative in a context of risk, uncertainty, conflict and contradiction where there are complex challenges. Make informed and balanced judgements in the context of relevant policy and legislation (Specialist Award Requirement 5, Northern Ireland Post-Qualifying Education and Training Partnership, 2007).

- Work creatively, innovatively and effectively, taking a leading role in the context of risk, uncertainty, conflict and contradiction or where there are complex challenges and a need to make informed, independent and balanced judgements (Leadership and Strategic Award Requirement 5, Northern Ireland Post-Qualifying Education and Training Partnership, 2007).

This book addresses skills specified in the National Occupational Standards for Social Work in England (TOPSS, 2005), in particular: Key Role 4 Manage risk to individuals, families, carers, groups, communities, self and colleagues. This book addresses aspects of Units within all of the Key Roles, as indicated at the start of each chapter.

For social workers in other countries, broadly similar considerations will apply. For other professions parallels may be drawn as there are many similar issues and areas of knowledge and skill even though some aspects (such as the active interface with the law and engaging family and community resources) may have a higher profile in social work.

Structure of this book

There is a challenge in writing a book (which has a linear sequence of chapters, paragraphs and sections) on this topic where many dimensions and aspects influence each other in complex ways. The chapters have been sequenced in what seems to be the most logical order, but each chapter is better viewed as illuminating a different aspect rather than as sequential steps in a process. Topics are included where they seem the most appropriate, but the reader needs to be aware that there are many inter-connections. As an example, the issue of making a decision on limited information relates to legal aspects of standards of care in emergencies (Chapter 3), the suitability of assessment tools and processes (Chapter 8) and satisficing decision theory about the cost of gathering more information for a fuller assessment on which to base a more robust decision (Chapter 9). In places, the inter-connection between topics has been indicated but to avoid this becoming tedious the reader will need to be alert to the connections.

The basic structure of the book is that we begin with core concepts, client focus and legal aspects. We then consider collaborative processes and the nature of individual judgement before considering particular dimensions of social work decision making such as safeguarding, taking risks, assessment and dynamic decision processes. We conclude by considering the organisational context of decision management. A chapter summary is provided at the end of each of the ten chapters.

Reflective practice and continuing professional development

This book has been written to support professional social workers in making the best judgements and decisions possible in carrying out their roles in relation to clients, families and the wider society. The aim is to support the reader in a process of learning by doing, by providing concepts and examples that enable and prompt reflection on your practice. Case studies, research summaries and activities are included to illustrate and support the application of concepts. You will gain more from the book if you take the time to apply the concepts and principles to your own experience. Reflection on your practice – informed by theoretical insights derived from research, theory, models, statutes, case-law, standards, values, guidelines, inquiries, policy and principles – is a key tool for continuing professional development (Brown & Rutter, 2006) and refining skills.

This book provides conceptual models to assist the professional to integrate the multiple complex strands inherent in making decisions. This involves both re-conceptualising tasks that have always been carried out by social workers and also seeking to learn from and apply more recent research and theorising. When I first felt the urge to write this book (more than 10 years ago!), I hoped that I would be able to present a unified model for decision making in social work, parallel to that which I presented on assessment and care planning in an earlier book with a colleague (Taylor and Devine, 1993). No such unified theory of decision making exists in social work or in the wider world of research and theorising on decisions. So, a range of concepts and tools to aid reflection on practice are presented here, drawn from wider decision theory and applied to social work. Part of professional knowledge and skill is in selecting an appropriate model for a particular practice situation. This is a source book of key ideas for a creative journey, involving contributing to developing our professional knowledge base as well as creativity in finding ways to engage with and help clients.

Caveat

This book is for general education, not to provide guidance in specific cases. The purpose of this book is to provide a framework for reflecting on professional practice that will support you in purposefully integrating the diverse aspects of making judgements and participating in decision-making processes. Any change in practice that you intend to implement cannot be undertaken in isolation. You need support to implement a new approach, and an organisation requires a degree of uniformity so as to fulfil its duty to ensure quality of decisions and resource allocation that is appropriate to needs and risks. Ensure that you make good use of professional and line management supervision, and proper use of the policies and procedures of your organisation. References to legal aspects in this book are for general education on principles only, written by a non-lawyer for non-lawyers. In any situation where legal action might be a consideration (of your client or of your organisation) you should consult with your line management and professional supervisor and seek legal advice through appropriate channels.

Terminology

Key terms are discussed in the text at appropriate places; a list is included in the Glossary on page 164.

Some social workers in the UK prefer the term *service user* to *client*. Looking at the best evidence I have been able to find, research suggests that this is not a preference of people who come to social workers (Lloyd *et al.*, 2001; Keaney *et al.*, 2004; Covell *et al.*, 2007). It may be that the current vogue for the term *service user* in the UK is driven by politicians rather than by people who come into contact with social workers (Heffernan, 2006). The traditional and international term *client* seems to convey better the professional responsibility of the social worker for his or her actions (see Seal, 2008, page ix) which is a key focus of this text. On a more personal note, my internet service provider refers to me as a *service user* and for me the term has connotations of a faceless organisation to which I am known primarily by a 30-digit number! To get my needs met, I have to struggle through a fog of jargon and alien procedures. By contrast, the aroma-therapist and solicitor that I see on occasion refer to me as their *client*. They have helped me through various stresses and crises of life, and within their own discipline they are each competent and caring about my welfare. I still make the ultimate decision about treatment or action, but as the client I have the support of a confidential professional relationship with each of them. The professional relationship, where the social worker contributes a particular area of knowledge and skills within an ethical framework, remains at the heart of effective social work practice. I would argue that this is better conveyed by the term *client* so this is normally used here, although *patient, survivor, tenant, resident, service user* and *customer* may be used occasionally.

Concluding comments

A short book can give only an overview of this vast and exciting topic. The references to material have been limited to readily available texts and articles that are likely to be of interest to a wide range of social workers. For further study consider also related topics such as those that apply these principles to your own client group; clinical and social care governance; evidence-based practice; social welfare legislation and the statutory duties and powers of social care organisations; standards of central and local government, service commissioning bodies, employers of health and social care staff and professional bodies; health and safety legislation, policy and procedures; decision-making processes, including case conferences, panels, courts, the legal system and legal processes; inter-professional working as it relates to decision making; and decision aids including assessment tools and computerised systems. This book is to support you in that crucial process of conceptualising your professional role and task in making judgements and decision making so as to continually improve the service we offer for the ultimate benefit of clients, families and the wider society.

This book has been developed specifically for social workers undertaking post-qualifying studies. It has been developed from sessions that I have organised or delivered over the past decade for health and social care professionals, in particular newly qualified social workers undertaking post-qualifying education and training. As decision making within professions is a relatively new and expanding topic, this textbook may raise questions about research, evidence, theory and models for practice. Comments (particularly about the application of theoretical models in practice) that might contribute to improving professional practice are welcome and should be sent to me at bj.taylor@ulster.ac.uk or care of the publishers.

Chapter 1

Roles, concepts and frameworks for decision making

CHAPTER OBJECTIVES

This chapter will help you to meet the following National Occupational Standards for Social Work.

- Key role 4, unit 12: Assess and manage risks to individuals, families, carers, groups and communities.
- Key role 6, unit 18: Research, analyse, evaluate, and use current knowledge of best social work practice.

This chapter will help you to meet post-qualifying requirements for social work in the UK such as the following.

- Work effectively in a context of risk, uncertainty, conflict and contradiction (The Post-Qualifying Award in Specialist Social Work (Generic Level Requirement vii.), General Social Care Council [England], 2004).
- Competence in working effectively in complex situations (Post-Qualifying Award, Requirement PQ2, *Scotland & Wales (= UK Framework, 1990–2007)*).
- Competence in exercising the powers and responsibilities of a professional social worker, including the appropriate use of discretion and the management of risk (Post-Qualifying Award, Requirement PQ3, *Scotland & Wales (= UK Framework 1990–2007)*).
- Ability to make informed decisions (Post-Qualifying Award, Requirement PQ4, *Scotland & Wales (= UK Framework 1990–2007)*).
- Demonstrate consistent and sustained sound judgement and decision making in the context of complexity, risk, uncertainty, conflict and contradiction (Specific Award Requirement 3, Northern Ireland Post-Qualifying Education and Training Partnership, 2007).

Good judgement and quality decisions are two of the marks of the competent professional in any field.

(Simmonds, 1998, p175)

Introduction

This first chapter introduces concepts of *judgement* and *decision making* in both everyday life and social work practice. A framework for professional judgement and decision making is outlined, drawing on a range of decision models such as helping clients to *envision the future, balancing benefits and harms* and making a *criterion-based judgement.* Key terms are discussed and defined. This chapter provides a foundation for later chapters by introducing theoretical concepts about judgement and decision making that are then expanded in later chapters where they are applied to practice.

Everyday decisions

We all make decisions every day, such as what to eat, what to wear and how to spend our time. We make judgements every day, such as about the anticipated tastiness of some food in a shop, about the likely weather today, and about the value or pleasure that we expect if we use our time in a particular way. We also take risks every day, such as the risk of food poisoning, the risk of embarrassment or getting wet because of choosing the 'wrong' clothes to wear or of feeling we have wasted our time on an activity. Decisions, judgements and risk taking in the face of uncertainty are everyday activities of life. Life without risk would be dull, and lacking in the stimuli that lead to learning and growth. Making choices in the face of uncertainty is part of the challenge and joy of being human; it is part of normal development for children as they grow in knowledge, skill and confidence in dealing with the world.

As social workers we make many judgements and decisions daily. Our judgements cover diverse domains, such as whether a child should be regarded as in need or protection, assessing the risks inherent in a proposed care arrangement following hospital discharge, or selecting a practice method for work with a particular family. Some decision making (generally where consequences are more serious) is formalised into group or organisational processes, such as court hearings, strategic planning meetings, case discussions, family meetings and reviews. Some collaborative decisions are more informal, such as a practitioner checking a decision with the team leader as he or she is dashing down the corridor to a meeting!

Decision making in situations of uncertainty is a central professional activity in health and social care services. We are making decisions in uncertainty, or *taking risks*, every time we support a person with a disability to achieve greater independence, plan the discharge of an older person or psychiatric patient from hospital, support a family in a state of dysfunction or intervene to protect an individual from abuse. The fundamental professional task of assessing needs and planning care (including psychosocial interventions such as counselling or group work) is given added complexity by our pivotal decision-making role as social workers in assessing risk as well as needs (Taylor and Devine, 1993; Parton *et al.*, 1997) and the professional judgement that is required.

Our professional judgement and decision making takes place in a variety of contexts including the client, family and the wider society; the professional task and role; and the organisation within which the professional is employed. We consider these in turn as we build up a map of concepts to guide our journey through the rest of the book, at the same time as defining key terms and integrating these considerations with the social work helping process. The frame of reference by which we conceptualise and articulate a problem situation is crucial to turning need, distress or chaos into a manageable decision process where we can help clients and families to change and where we can undertake safeguarding and service gate-keeping functions on behalf of society.

ACTIVITY *1.1*

Meanings of words about uncertainty

What do these words mean to you in the context of your work?

How does their usage differ among your peers at work and in the wider society?

- *Dangerousness.*
- *Fate.*
- *Risky.*
- *Risk taking.*
- *Vulnerable.*
- *Gamble.*
- *God's will.*
- *Harm.*
- *Hazard.*
- *Judgement.*

Engaging stakeholders

Professional social work practice normally takes place within an organisation, whether statutory or voluntary, although a few social workers provide counselling and therapeutic services as self-employed practitioners. The most important decision making will not be left to the individual but will be part of a process within the organisation. By *important decisions* we mean those with the most impact on people's lives (such as taking a child into care) or those with the greatest resource implications. Thus the most important social work decisions will not be made unilaterally, but will be subject to various checks and balances involving other people. Your line manager or professional supervisor will be involved in these decisions; the most serious decisions will go further up the line management. Other professionals should be involved as and when appropriate in accordance with their area of knowledge and skill in relation to the needs of the client or family. It frequently falls to the social worker to co-ordinate the multi-professional process. In terms of our training this seems appropriate, as our strength is often not so much as a specialist in any particular area, but as the profession with the most holistic, user-centred view of the needs, risks, resources and options. The contributions of different professions need to be co-ordinated effectively and efficiently, and this is discussed more fully in Chapter 4.

Terminology: 'judgement' and 'decision making'

The terms *judgement* and *decision making* are often used interchangeably. In this book, where they are to be distinguished, the term *judgement* focuses on an individual *assessing alternatives* and the term *decision making* focuses on an individual or group *choosing between alternatives* (Dowie, 1993, p8). We define a *professional judgement* to be *when a professional considers the evidence about a client or family situation in the light of professional knowledge to reach a conclusion or recommendation.* We use the term *evidence* rather than *information* to highlight the fact that the range of data that we have about a client, family and situation has varying degrees of reliability, just as our professional knowledge has varying degrees of reliability. The number of days of school attendance may be reasonably factual; the *reasons* why the young person has missed so many days of schooling may be a rather less reliable composite picture put together from perceptions gathered through interviews with the child, parents and school teacher. In this definition we use the term *professional knowledge* to include all varieties of sources of knowledge that we rely on in our work, such as statutes, case-law, policy, theory, research, standards, principles, protocols, procedures, values and experience.

We define a *decision* to be *the selection of a course of action as a result of a deliberate process by one or more people.* Sometimes, judgements and decisions merge into each other; in other situations they are more distinct. A decision may be made by one person, or it may be the result of a *decision process* involving a number of people.

The social work role in society

The protective role of social workers acting on behalf of society now extends beyond seeking to protect children from abuse to include protecting vulnerable adults from others and themselves. The task has become more complex as more knowledgeable and skilled approaches are demanded. Social workers in most countries have the lead role in relation to child protection and are often blamed by the media if a tragedy occurs (Pascoe-Watson and Wilson, 2008), despite the multi-professional nature of the work and the impossibility of predicting harm by a particular individual with any great degree of accuracy. Do we make rational decisions based on objective facts? If our decision making is *rational*, on what facts is it based? If it is not rational, how are our activities justified to society, the tax-payer or the contributor to the employing charity? How do value issues, legal parameters and political pressures fit into the decision-making process?

- Do we consider the situation in the past as in the traditional social work emphasis on taking a social history in such fields as child protection, mental health and criminal justice?

- Do we consider the situation now as in functional assessment of older people and those with complex health and social care needs?

- Do we consider predictions about the future as in recommendations about returning home a child who has been abused in the past, or the discharge of a person who has been violent or suicidal from psychiatric hospital?

- Do we consider the likely impact of an intervention as in using evidence of the effectiveness of specific health and social care interventions in a situation with particular features?

A key issue is *who is at risk* and *who is taking the risk* in decisions about care planning issues, such as safeguarding a vulnerable person, seeking greater independence and choosing to take the risks that enable rehabilitation and recovery from mental and physical illnesses. A key issue is *who is at risk* and *who is taking the risk*. We can consider major categories of possible harm as being:

- by others e.g. abuse, whether physical, sexual, emotional, neglect or financial;

- to others e.g. violence, aggression, accidentally setting fire to housing, etc.;

- to self e.g. self-harm, suicide, self-neglect, etc.

CASE STUDY 1.1

Clarifying your role

A key part of my social work role is to enable any vulnerable adult to access support to enable him or her to live a life free from abuse, exploitation or neglect. My work entails investigating alleged or suspected situations of abuse, exploitation or neglect; assessing and managing the risk to the higher-risk vulnerable adults within the multi-professional team; working with individuals and families to seek to resolve issues underlying the abuse or neglect, and put in place safeguarding measures; fulfilling statutory functions; and working with the police and other agencies as appropriate particularly where criminal prosecution is a consideration.

- *Do you have a clear statement of the scope of the work undertaken by your team or unit or department?*

- *If you have a particular role within the team or section, do you have a clear statement of your role?*

Risk-taking decision making

Our judgements and decisions are made in situations where the outcome is uncertain. As the outcome is uncertain, there is always the possibility that a less desirable outcome will ensue, possibly some harm or loss. Such losses or harms are sometimes referred to as *risks*, such as in phrases like *the risk of further abuse* or *the risk of falling*. Where the term *risk* means simply *the likelihood of* or *the probability of*, we shall use here these phrases instead as they are more precise. Hence we would refer to *the likelihood of further abuse* or *the probability of falling* rather than *the risk of falling*. For rational human behaviour we assume that the decision is made in order to achieve some sort of *benefit*, interpreted broadly to include not only good health or financial gain but also such qualities as social independence or moral integrity. Taking risk is intrinsic to human decision making, and hence to social work practice in advising and supporting clients to make decisions. Thus we use the term *risk* as *a decision-making situation where the outcomes are uncertain and where benefits are sought but undesirable outcomes are possible.* In general, the term *risk* can lead to unnecessary confusion as it has so many meanings (Dowie, 1999), so we will normally use alternative expressions. It is often better to use a term such as *probability* (when referring to the likelihood of something undesirable happening), *harm* to refer to the undesirable consequence of an event, and *hazard* or *danger* to refer to the foreseen circumstance or object that may lead to harm. Undesirable events are not equally undesirable and in this respect the term *risk* relates closely to values. The contexts where the term *risk* seems most useful are in *risk taking*, and in organisational *risk management*. The term *risk factor* (common shorthand where we are considering factors that influence the likelihood of something undesirable occurring) is so well established that we have retained it here.

The law and protecting people's health and safety

Within the UK there is legislation regarding health and safety at work that embodies stringent protective measures introduced across the European Union. The statutes (Health and Safety at Work [etc.] Act, 1974; Health and Safety at Work (NI) Order, 1978, both as subsequently amended) deal with responsibilities of employers and employees, and provide protection towards employees and visitors to employer premises including public buildings such as hospitals and social work offices. This legislation requires employers and employees to take reasonable steps to protect others from harm. There are tensions in that this legislation does not embody any concept of *risk taking* such as we are discussing here, even though it is intrinsic to the professional role of health and social care staff. This is discussed further in Chapter 3 in the context of the law relating to *reasonable decisions*, and in Chapter 7 in the context of balancing possible gains against possible harm or loss.

The helping process

We consider the professional helping process to have four main aspects: *assess – plan – implement – evaluate* (Taylor and Devine, 1993). This professional practice process of assessing needs and planning care is defined broadly to include the functions of assessment and planning inherent in any psychosocial intervention (such as varieties of counselling, family work and group work) as well as co-ordination of a range of health and social care services, now generally known as *case management* or *care management*. This basic framework is expanded here to give particular attention to decision making.

In terms of the helping process, *judgement* focuses on the stages of assessing and planning an intervention. *Decision making* might be regarded as following on from a judgement (Figure 1.1) or might be viewed as encapsulating all of the stages, including the evaluation of the effectiveness of the decision.

Assessment, judgement and the helping process

Assessment is considered here in terms of three key functions: gathering, ordering and analysing information. These three aspects are considered in greater detail in Chapter 8,

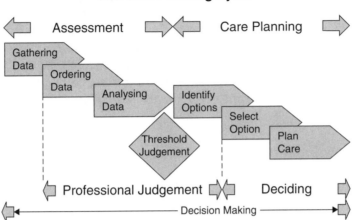

Figure 1.1 Professional judgement and decision-making process

which considers the use of assessment tools to support professional judgement and decision-making processes. The assessment stage leads on to the planning stage, which includes identifying options, selecting an option and care planning, which are discussed in greater depth in Chapter 9.

Professional judgement, bias and knowledge

Assessment takes place at a critical point where knowledge derived from research, theory, law, standards and policy are brought to bear on the facts of the client situation. A professional has a body of knowledge, skills and values that a typical member of society will not have. However, this does not mean that we *know it all*, even in relation to our own domain of expertise. We all have blind spots, particular enthusiasms and a perspective that reflects our professional journey to date. There is a long history of research in psychology on potential bias in decision making (Beach and Connolly, 1997; Hardman, 2009); we consider this further in Chapter 5 in relation to reflective practice, the professional judgement process and the task of using knowledge to inform judgements.

Types of decisions

Social workers make many judgements and decisions. We consider four major types of decisions here: supporting client decisions; eligibility for services; safeguarding decisions and care planning decisions.

1. Supporting client decisions

Our starting point is the client and family with their hopes and fears, their relationships and the crisis or need that has brought them to the attention of a social worker. Our starting point is that *normally* clients should be supported to make their own decisions (Department of Health, 2007) in accord with their own values. The professional role in this case might focus on providing information (including service contacts and voluntary organisations), challenging assumptions and helping the client to think through the implications of the choices that are available. This type of decision process might be characterised as *envisioning the future* or as *balancing benefits and harms* (Taylor, 2006b). In Chapter 2, in particular, we consider in more depth supporting the client decision-making process, the values of the client and the *risk culture* and values in the wider society.

2. Eligibility for services

The trigger for a decision is a referral to a social worker by whatever route this comes. The professional must make a judgement about action to be taken, even if the decision is ulti-mately to take no action. The referral may be for a social care service for which the social worker is the professional gate-keeper. We characterise this type of decision process as a *criterion-based judgement* (Hammond, 1996). The situation of the client and family are being judged in relation to the criteria for eligibility for a particular service at this point in time, however these are determined. We consider this type of decision further in Chapters 2 and 6 particularly.

3. Safeguarding decisions

In some situations – such as where the client lacks capacity to decide or where there is a mandate from society to protect a child or vulnerable adult from abuse – the professional may have to act to safeguard an individual, often in opposition to the views of some family members or others. This type of decision process might be characterised also as a *criterion-based judgement*, and also as an *ethical decision-making process.* In essence, the client or family situation is being judged against some criteria or thresholds at which the organisation should intervene on behalf of society to protect an individual. Such decisions often carry with them an expectation of predicting possible harm, such as in the ques-tions: *Is it safe to return this child home?* and *How safe is it for this patient to be discharged from the psychiatric hospital?* We discuss these types of decision particularly in Chapter 6.

4. Care planning decisions

The assessment phase is not an end in itself, but is normally the starting point for plan-ning an intervention, whether care service provision or some form of counselling or other psychosocial intervention (Taylor and Devine, 1993). Even where there has been a *crite-rion-based judgement* regarding eligibility for a service, or in relation to a threshold for implementing compulsory safeguarding measures, there then follows a decision about planning the next step. The *balancing benefits and harms* model may be helpful at this stage of the process, as the professional seeks to weigh up the possible alternative courses of action. We consider this type of decision further particularly in Chapters 7 and 9. These four types of decision are illustrated in Figure 1.2.

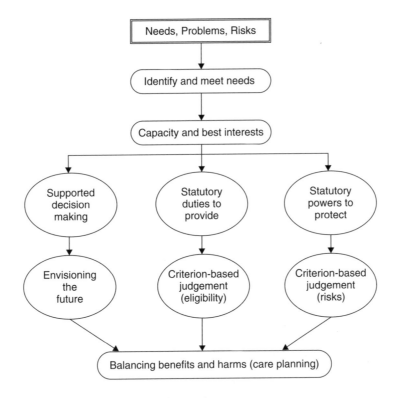

Figure 1.2 Decision types in social work practice

Decision management

The main focus of this book is on the activities of the professional social worker with his or her client and colleagues. However, the duties carried out by social workers are normally on behalf of an employing organisation, whether they are statutory functions carried out by a publicly funded body, or aspects of social helping on behalf of a voluntary (not-for-profit) organisation. This organisational context is essential for understanding the role of social work in the 21st century, and the employing body has a crucial role in supporting and managing decision-making processes. In recent years increasing investment has been made in governance processes, which are systems put in place so that the senior staff and Board members of an organisation (whether public, private or charitable) know the major hazards facing them. They are thus more readily held to account for decisions about addressing these. Within social work we have a long history of many of the key elements of good governance, such as professional supervision and seeking feedback from the users of our services. These various activities, and some new approaches to addressing risk issues and ensuring quality of services, are now being drawn together under the umbrella of social care governance (Simmons, 2007). The focus to date has tended to be on risk management activities, such as risk registers and the management of complaints. However, managers need a broad focus to reflect wider developments in terms of decision management. Each inquiry into a child abuse tragedy brings increased pressure on senior managers and greater clarity about roles and responsibilities. The focus will increasingly be

Figure 1.3 Judgement and decision framework for professional practice

on how resources have been managed, what policies, support and governance systems are in place, and what training has been provided for staff. *Defensive beliefs and reactive approaches to risk (managing the harm once it has occurred) will increasingly be chal-lenged by developments in risk assessment and risk management. The emphasis is moving to decision-making processes and their management* (Carson, 1996, p4).

The activities of the individual social worker are illustrated in their broader organisational context in Figure 1.3. The main contributions to the judgement and decision process regarding individual care are identified under the headings of *client*, *professional* and *society*. The assessment, judgement, decision-making and care planning process is under-pinned by the policies, systems and procedures of the employing organisation. These latter aspects are discussed more fully in Chapter 10.

Chapter summary

- This chapter has introduced concepts of judgement, decision making and risk in both everyday life and social work practice.

- As social workers we support clients in decision making as well as having to make pro-fessional judgements ourselves in such roles as safeguarding, gate-keeping access to publicly funded social care services and care planning.

- Three basic decision models have been outlined: *envisioning the future*, *balancing benefits and harms* and making a *criterion-based judgement*.

- Key concepts have been discussed and defined in this chapter, and these are listed in the Glossary together with other useful terms.

Banks, S. (1995) *Ethics and Values in Social Work.* 2nd edn. Hampshire: Palgrave.

This is an excellent book on ethics in social work, providing an essential reference point for professional decision making.

Beach, L.R. and Connolly, T. (1997) *The Psychology of Decision Making: People in Organisations.* California: Sage.

This is a very readable book giving a balanced overview of theories of decision making including: (1) those beginning from an assumption of rational decisions and then considering how true to life these are (normative models); (2) those beginning from studies of real-life decisions (descriptive); and (3) more recent attempts to integrate these through naturalistic decision-making models.

Carson, D. and Bain, A. (2008) *Professional Risk and Working with People: Decision-Making in Health, Social Care and Criminal Justice.* London: Jessica Kingsley.

This is an excellent book on the legal aspects of risk and decision making, particularly the tort of negligence and 'duty of care', and discussing the way that the law supports reasoned, reasonable decision making by professionals.

Taylor, B.J. and Devine, T. (1993) *Assessing Needs and Planning Care in Social Work.* Aldershot: Ashgate.

This is a very readable book outlining the basic social work helping process – assessing, planning, intervening, evaluating – and is a widely used textbook on qualifying social work courses. The present book builds on this basic model by considering in more detail the judgement and decision-making aspects.

Chapter 2

Crises, emotions and supporting client decision making

CHAPTER OBJECTIVES

This chapter will help you to meet the following National Occupational Standards for Social Work.

- Key role 1, unit 3: Assess needs and options to recommend a course of action.
- Key role 2, unit 4: Respond to crisis situations.
- Key role 2, unit 9: Address behaviour which presents a risk to individuals, families, carers, groups and communities.
- Key role 4, unit 12: Assess and manage risks to individuals, families, carers, groups and communities.
- Key role 4, unit 13: Assess, minimise and manage risk to self and colleagues.

This chapter will help you to meet post-qualifying requirements for social work in the UK such as the following.

- Work effectively in a context of risk, uncertainty, conflict and contradiction (The Post-Qualifying Award in Specialist Social Work (Generic Level Requirement vii.), General Social Care Council [England], 2004).
- Competence in working effectively in complex situations (Post-Qualifying Award, Requirement PQ2, *Scotland & Wales (= UK Framework 1990–2007)*).
- Competence in exercising the powers and responsibilities of a professional social worker, including the appropriate use of discretion and the management of risk (Post-Qualifying Award, Requirement PQ3, *Scotland & Wales (= UK Framework 1990–2007)*).
- Demonstrate consistent and sustained sound judgement and decision making in the context of complexity, risk, uncertainty, conflict and contradiction (Specific Award Requirement 3, Northern Ireland Post-Qualifying Education and Training Partnership, 2007).

Two things fill the mind with ever new and increasing wonder and awe: the starry heavens above me, and the moral law within me.

(Immanuel Kant, quoted in Peter, 1980, p173)

Introduction

Chapter 2 starts from the needs and crises that bring clients to social workers. We consider the position of a client or family making sometimes difficult choices, their values and how they might engage with information about hazards they face and options that they have. We consider the place of emotion in decision making, confidentiality and resilience. We discuss the professional engaging with clients and other family stakeholders in decisions, *game theory* to help us understand the dynamics of the decision-making process between professional and client, and the role of the social worker in (normally) supporting reasonable and informed client decisions. We utilise UK guidance on *supported decision making* and image theory as models for the professional in supporting clients and families in *envisioning the future.*

Crisis and needs

Voluntary clients come to social workers because of a sense of *need*. Theories of need usually begin by considering basic biological drives, such as for food, clothing, shelter and a safe environment (Doyal and Gough, 1991). Maslow's hierarchy (Maslow, 1943) suggests that these more basic needs must be satisfied before we can strive to meet higher order needs, such as for emotional, sexual and intellectual fulfilment. Other approaches focus on moral imperatives and the rights of individuals to basic essentials required for a reasonable life, such as the right to family life, to be free from persecution or torture and to hold your own beliefs provided they do not actually harm others. Such rights depend on another person or group of people (usually a society) accepting that they have the corresponding duties to allow or provide these rights. In social work a combination of these approaches seems to be common. *Needs* are distinguished from *wants* by some consideration of their universal nature and the seriousness of the harm to the well-being of the person if they are not meet. *Needs* are often considered to be those which might reasonably be met, subject to available resources, by the public purse or the charitable

---

RESEARCH SUMMARY 2.1

Older people entering long-term care

With the increasing pressure on social and health care resources, professionals have to be more explicit in their decision making regarding the long-term care of older people. This grounded theory study used 19 focus groups and nine semi-structured interviews (99 staff in total) to explore professional perspectives on this decision making. Focus group participants and interviewees comprised care managers, social workers, consultant geriatricians, general medical practitioners, community nurses, home care managers and occupational therapists. The emerging themes spanned context, clients, families and services. Decisions were often prompted by a crisis, hindering professionals seeking to make a measured assessment. Fear of burglary and assault, and the willingness and availability of family to help were major factors in decisions about living at home. Service availability in terms of public funding for community care, the availability of home care workers and workload pressures on primary care services influenced decision 'thresholds' regarding admission to institutional care. Assessment tools designed to assist decision making about the long-term care of older people need to take into account the critical aspects of individual fears and motivation, family support, and the availability of publicly funded services as well as functional and medical needs. (Taylor and Donnelly, 2006b)

giving to the organisation (Taylor and Devine, 1993). We often make judgements about the eligibility of the presenting needs for the provision of publicly funded services.

Decisions in crisis

Some of the situations where needs are presented and judgements have to be made are situations of crisis for clients and their families. The decisions that they might make may not be their *normal* decision. They may be willing to share their feelings more and welcome a trusted professional who understands their sense of panic, dread or pressure. The client and family may be more open to change than normal and thereby open the possibility of supportive professional help to make changes to such major issues as lifestyle and relationships (Roberts, 2000; O'Hagan, 1991). We may help by partialising the problem-solving and decision-making processes into manageable steps. This may be an opportune time to offer to support family problem-solving interaction. Depending on the degree of urgency, a *holding decision* may be made while further assessment is undertaken.

Emotion in decisions

When we make decisions, we may (with varying degrees of consciousness) get in touch with deeper feelings and perhaps share them with others before making the decision. We may be reluctant decision makers, *beset by conflict, doubts and worry, struggling with incongruous longings, antipathies and loyalties, and seeking relief by procrastinating, rationalising or denying responsibility for [our] own choices* (Janis and Mann, 1977, p15). Decision making can be tough; emotions and avoidance behaviours are to be expected.

The context for social work involvement in client decision making may be emotional, involving crisis, stress, tension, and sometimes a lack of understanding, effective problem-solving skills or capacity for action. Clients and their families may have a variety of emotions because of their life situation, because of the crisis that has brought them to our attention, and in relation to accessing help. Clients may over-react to circumstances. They may hope for help but may also feel fear, anxiety, hostility, or concerns about what sort of person they will be dealing with and his or her values and manner. Clients may have a

---

CASE STUDY **2.1**

Client emotion in decision making

Mr Doherty is a 90-year-old man who was referred to the community social work tea or older people following a fall and a period of rehabilitation in a residential home. Doherty has mental health problems and did not think that a care package was nece for her husband, and was refusing to follow the safety recommendations of the m professional team. It was only through building a good working relationship with N. Doherty that I was able to understand her own physical and mental health issues, and hence to encourage them both to engage with a care plan for the benefit of both of them.

- *Consider a recent case in which the emotions of a client have blocked a decision that otherwise seemed sound and sensible?*
- *What unanticipated factors might have been at work in the situation?*

wide variety of emotion as we engage with them in decision making, such as panic, anger, blame, frustration, regret, over-confidence or resentment at being obliged to do certain things or at needing to ask for help.

People seeking social work help may be in a state of loss of control. An individual or family crisis whether abuse, illness or a crucial decision about greater independence, may be the emotional context for approaching a social services department. Knowledge and skills drawn from such as crisis theory (Roberts, 2000) may be appropriate in responding to an emotional decision situation. They may come with a sense of unfairness (such as the stigma of disability) or a feeling that their choices are severely limited (such as by illness, disability, or compulsory safeguarding measures). Emotion in decisions should not be seen as entirely negative. On the positive side, people in crisis may be more open to the possibilities for change. This is particularly relevant to considering the client contact as a decision point for the client.

> It is as if each human person constitutes a committee constantly sitting to decide life's questions and the behaviour desired in a given situation. This committee has many members within, each voicing a particular slant – our fears, feelings, dreams and hopes, our history and relationships, our memory, our various sub-personalities and our reason. Hopefully the chairperson of that committee is reason, deeply influenced and guided by affectivity. Descriptively the task of a human person appears to become more and more integrated, whole, 'together' within that on-going meeting. All the voices need to be heard and listened to. Ultimately, at their best, people make choices that chart the direction and, over time, develop the person.
>
> (Dyckman and Carroll, 1981, p33)

Emotion may enhance or inhibit decision making (Pfister and Bohm, 2008). In their conflict theory of decision making, Janis and Mann (1977) pose four basic questions that the decision maker may be asking if emotional conflict is playing an important role in the decision.

- Are the risks serious if I do not change?
- Are the risks serious if I do change?
- Is it realistic to hope to find a better solution?
- Is there time to search and deliberate?

CASE STUDY **2.2**

Conflicting emotions in decision situations

Lucy Brown (aged 4 years) was referred to our team by the playgroup because of a number of concerns that might indicate neglect. I visited her mother Sabrina, a single parent of 23 years, because of these concerns and to explore what support we might offer. As I spent time with Sabrina it was apparent that she had many conflicting emotions, not least wanting to care well for her daughter but struggling in her relationship with her partner and with the threat of redundancy from her work at the local supermarket. I was also aware of my own feelings of inner conflict, not least as a mother myself.

- Identify the emotions underpinning a recent decision situation for the client, other family members and for you as the social worker.

Our own emotions may detract from our decision making and helping. Too little emotion may be inhuman, suggesting a lack of engagement with the client and limited ownership of the problem or its solution. Too much emotion may suggest being overwhelmed with stress, the bias of over-identifying with a client's problem or the confusion of excessive fear or anger from personal issues that are not sufficiently resolved.

ACTIVITY 2.1

Emotion in professional decision making

- *What types of decisions in your role affect you emotionally?*
- *Why do you think these decisions particularly affect you emotionally?*
- *What emotions do you have when engaging with clients in situations such as:*
  - *supporting clients and families in making their own decisions?*
  - *deciding on eligibility for publicly funded or charitably funded services?*
  - *making safeguarding decisions to protect an individual from harm?*
- *What impact might your feelings have on you and on the decision?*

Engaging with clients

In some respects, care aims to minimise risk to the individual, families and society. But how does this fit with clients choosing to *take risks*, not only in morally contentious areas such as drug misuse, but also in everyday matters such as an older person in a home choosing to go for a walk alone contrary to the advice of the staff (Brearley, 1982)? What is the professional role in encouraging, discouraging, preventing or condoning such varieties of risk-taking?

CASE STUDY 2.3

Engaging clients – using an interpreter

I am a hospital social worker. I am working with Mr Cheng who is terminally ill with nasal cancer towards discharge. Mr Cheng and his family are from the Chinese community. Communication with Mr Cheng has been difficult due to fluctuating confusion; Mrs Cheng has limited English. They were reluctant to involve an interpreter due to the nature of the issues to be discussed, preferring instead to involve their son aged 11 years. However, as Mr Cheng's illness progressed and the nature of the issues became more personal I thought that it was not appropriate for their son to be involved. I carefully explained this to Mr and Mrs Cheng as well as I could. I tried to get an interpreter for the next meeting but none was available at the short notice, but Mrs Cheng brought along a trusted friend who could interpret. The meeting went well, even though the use of an interpreter presented a challenge for me in discussing sensitive issues.

- *What are your employer's arrangements for when you need an interpreter?*
- *What knowledge, skills and practical arrangements do you need in order to use an interpreter most effectively?*

The social work principle of empowerment involves seeking to maximise the power of clients and give them as much control as possible over their circumstances (Banks, 2001). In the context of decisions, empowerment might be viewed as *the entitlement to take risks and to exercise choice* (Ross and Waterson, 1996). Our social work role includes such dimensions as engaging clients in understanding and assessing risks to their health and well-being, helping them to clarify their values regarding options and helping communication and negotiation between family members where values and opinions differ. Does the client welcome or resent the choices available with their inherent dangers?

We have a key role in helping clients to verbalise potential gains in possible courses of action (such as quality of life, normalisation, independence, etc.) as well as possible harms in decisions as a rationale for taking risks. In responding to clients we need to try to assess severity and complexity of problems and their intent and motivation to change. We may need to promote an awareness of dangers, to help clients to consider the long-term effects (health, relationships, financial, etc.) of a decision, to address risk issues including conflict with social norms, to consider the responsibility of roles that they have (e.g. as a parent or employee), and to help them to reflect on the appropriateness of spontaneous decisions in terms of the implications for themselves and others. *To make good choices people need to understand the consequences and take some responsibility for them. So we want to promote a culture of choice that entails responsible, supported decision making* (Department of Health, 2007, p1).

CASE STUDY 2.4

Client capacity to choose

Brendan (aged 27 years) has a learning disability and lives in a supported housing scheme. He decided that he wanted to buy some brightly coloured shorts. The care worker did not think that they suited him and said that he should not buy them. She later discussed this with me in supervision as the social worker managing the scheme. The care worker came to recognise that Brendan had capacity to make this decision. At the end of the day there was no substantive reason why he should not buy these shorts, such as, for example, a level of immodesty that might cause offence to others. Brendan lives in a holiday town and this style of shorts was being worn by other young men.

Person-centred approaches are central to social work (Taylor and Devine, 1993; Department of Health, 2001 and 2009). However, our values as individuals or as a profession may not concur with those of our clients. We have responsibilities as a profession to make judgements about the provision of appropriate services, to be able to stand over any decision to support risk-taking by an individual client, to undertake statutory safeguarding responsibilities, and to prioritise services across clients as public and charitable resources are not sufficient to meet the needs of all those seeking them. These various dimensions, and their interplay with any particular client and family, require knowledgeable and skilled professional approaches.

CASE STUDY **2.5**

Engaging clients in decisions

Mr Smith, an 89-year-old man, had a prolonged hospital admission caused by fractured neck of femur, and complications caused by heart failure. When referral was made to me to make plans for appropriate discharge, assessments had already been undertaken by a range of professionals who had reached a consensus that Mr Smith's physical health and care needs had changed significantly enough during hospital placement that he would require long-term nursing home care.

An important part of my task involved exploring Mr Smith's perception of the benefits of taking the risks involved in his wish to be at home. These could be summarised as his sense of emotional well-being, sense of independence and control of his life. Mr Smith said that he placed greater importance and value on the independence of living alone in his own home above more support with his physical needs which he recognised that he may receive in a care home setting.

The outcome was that Mr Smith was fully aware and understood the impact of the changes in his health and the limitations that this placed on his ability to be fully independent at home. He openly acknowledged and accepted that he would have to change his routine and lifestyle at home to reduce risks. Mr Smith and his family were taking responsibility for the risks and their decisions. The strengths in this situation were that Mr Smith's family fully supported his decision to take the risk and at least have a trial period at home. This was completely successful; Mr Smith continues to live in his own home with a mixture of support from statutory services, family and voluntary agency. Part of the social work role in this case was also bringing along others in the multi-disciplinary team with the outcome and helping them understand the reason for Mr Smith's decision.

As an adult with full capacity to make decisions, Mr Smith always had the ultimate decision about his discharge plan. However, engaging in the risk assessment process not only fulfilled agency requirements and ensured that risks were not ignored, but it also enabled Mr Smith to make an informed decision. The involvement of his family in the risk assessment process led to them being committed and involved in the risk management plan, which included:

- *a care package with four structured daily calls by a home care worker;*
- *a daily visit by a family member (which was taken in turn);*
- *visit fortnightly by district nurse;*
- *use of an aid call button which would be worn at all times by Mr Smith (to be used in the event that he fell or was unwell); and*
- *regular review and monitoring by the community social worker.*

Collaborative decisions and games people play

In common with other citizens, our clients may be more sceptical than in previous generations about the expertise of professionals (Slovic, 1999). With the ever-expanding volume of potentially useful knowledge, it is important not only that professionals keep up to date but also that we recognise our limitations. With our consistent approach to being person-focused and listening to the client, social work does not lag behind other professions in this regard. Social workers have a key role in helping to provide security and protection for individuals in society, even though it is impossible to predict or prevent all harm. Making effective decisions that minimise the probability of unwanted harm is most effective as a collaborative exercise between professional and client wherever this is possible. Measures to promote respect and effective communication are central to our professional task of creating trusting relationships (Alaszewski, 2000) where dangers can be discussed openly and honestly, and decisions made that are most helpful in enabling, safeguarding and advising clients.

As social workers we sometimes make judgements about the most desirable course of action in the best interests of the client and family. We then try to bring clients and families along with these proposals. There may be varying levels of support from different family members. In the study of decision making, such situations are called *game theory*. This does not imply that the consequences do not matter or that the content is purely recreational. Game theory is essentially about power, relationships and interactions that occur in decision making. *Game theory attempts to mathematically capture behavior in strategic situations, in which an individual's success in making choices depends on the choices of others* (Wikipedia, 2009, **http://en.wikipedia.org/wiki/Game_theory**). There may be active competition to *win* this serious *game*, with very different views of what is a desirable outcome! Other *players* in the decision (clients, family, other professionals and organisations) may be seeking their own concept of a fair outcome (which may be different from your own) or may deliberately sabotage your attempts at *reasonable* decision making (Beach and Connolly, 1997).

Clients may be less familiar with the *rules* of *the game* particularly if they are complex, such as in child protection court hearings. On the other hand, some clients are rather more street-wise than professionals, and can readily find out about and use (or misuse) legitimate or illegitimate loopholes that they perceive in order to thwart safeguarding plans. As another example, it is well known that some clients will create a commotion to get their own way, perhaps utilising the media or a sympathetic politician. They know that most organisations and managers have little stomach for a fight and are likely to give in to their demands, even though this almost always means that other clients (normally not so visible, on a waiting list) will receive less or no service (Taylor, 2006b).

CASE STUDY **2.6**

Questions to engage parents when a child is admitted to care

- *Did you read the assessment of your child's needs before it was presented at the review?*

- *Were you satisfied with your level of involvement in your child's care plan?*

- *Were you satisfied with the level of communication with the key worker during the placement?*

Co-operation is often required in order to achieve the goals that you (and your profession and organisation) desire. Negotiation and collaboration are essential in order that each person plays their part. Careful thought may need to be given to the best strategy to *win* the desired outcome, particularly in a safeguarding situation, to the ultimate benefit of the vulnerable client, even if other family members may not be seeking the same solution. Aspects such as building trust and encouraging client motivation through approaches designed to elicit co-operation are an important part of the professional task (Alaszewski *et al.*, 2000). We will return to this theme in Chapter 7 in terms of justifying risk-taking decision making and in Chapter 9 in terms of the goals of care planning. The results of various experiments suggests that generosity and openness pay off best in eliciting co-operative behaviour (Hardman, 2009, p167), confirming basic social work values.

Supporting client decision making

Supporting clients in making choices to achieve increased independence may involve risk-taking in situations where clients, professionals and organisations are aware of exposure to potential loss and have to accept that in the hope of potentially greater gains. Supporting clients and families in these complex decision-making processes requires a person-centred approach to practice (Duffy and Sanderson, 2008; Neill *et al.*, 2008). Clients need information upon which to base their choices and a key role for social workers is to inform clients with reliable information based on sound sources of knowledge. Some people can have distorted views about the causes of harmful outcomes or unrealistic expectations of positive outcomes. Part of the social work role may on occasion be to challenge individual clients to reflect on their own knowledge and values in the light of more objective evidence and the values of the wider society.

Taylor (2006b) suggests that Health and Safety legislation (see Chapter 7) and fear of litigation is pushing professionals to be less willing to take risks in their recommendations. The effect may be lost opportunities to promote client health and well-being. The complex issue of client choice *versus* the responsibility of professionals and organisations if some harm should ensue to someone with whom they have had dealings has led to a welcome publication by the UK Department of Health (DH, 2007) on professionals supporting decision making by adult clients. This provides a helpful framework of common principles to underpin good practice. The starting point is the right of clients to make choices unless they are not capable or this would cause harm to others or would otherwise break the law. *The governing principle behind good approaches to choice and risk is that people have the right to live their lives to the full as long as that does not stop others from doing the same. Fear of supporting people to take reasonable risks in their daily lives can prevent them from doing the things that most people take for granted* (DH, 2007, p3, para 5). A number of key principles are outlined in this UK government document for social workers supporting adult client decision making.

To put this principle into practice, people supporting users of services have to:

- *help people to have choice and control over their lives;*
- *recognise that making a choice can involve some risk;*
- *respect people's rights and those of their family carers;*

- help people understand their responsibilities and the implications of their choices, including any risks;

- acknowledge that there will always be some risk, and that trying to remove it altogether can outweigh the quality of life benefits for the person; and

- continue existing arrangements for safeguarding people.

(DH, 2007, pp12–13, para 1.7)

The Department of Health has made available a supported decision tool (see Appendix 2) as an aid to standardising basic best practice. While this does not go into the complexities that are frequently involved in social work decisions with clients, it does provide a sound starting point in terms of supporting client's decisions as a basic normal approach where possible. The very use of such a structured tool should assist in developing consistent, robust decision making, not least by promoting thorough record keeping on decision processes.

This supported decision tool highlights the role of the professional in providing information to assist in client decision making. Too often this role is not noticed because it is not recorded. The provision of timely appropriate information is a practical way in which social workers empower clients to make decisions.

Confidentiality, values and resilience

There are many challenges to supporting client decision making. Some client values are different from those of society in general, as well as from those of the profession. Much careful discussion is required to ensure a common understanding in decision processes with clients, taking account of varying socio-cultural and ethnic perceptions.

Consider what actions you need to take to safeguard your integrity and that of your profession and organisation within decision-making processes with clients. How will issues of confidentiality be handled? How will you ensure that the copy of the child protection case conference minutes that turns up on a bus or a rubbish dump are identifiable as the copy that was given to the client so that a professional will not be blamed wrongly? Tensions can sometimes arise when there are conflicting imperatives, such as protecting another worker by sharing information about threats of violence versus respecting the client's right to confidentiality. Similarly, dilemmas arise with anonymous allegations or where we are told something *in confidence*. How will you establish and clarify the boundaries of confidentiality? What support from your line manager or professional supervisor do you need in order to justify the contexts (such as violence towards staff and alleged abuse) where protecting another person overrides the right to confidentiality?

As well as not underestimating the powerful emotions with which clients may be contending, it is important also not to underestimate the resilience of many clients in the face of adversity. Strengths-based approaches to practice are a growing interest across all client groups (Graybeal and Konrad, 2008). Judgements about risk-taking decision making may depend on considerations of the resilience of the client and hence their capacity to cope with greater trust or independence (Hackett, 1999).

Envisioning the future

One of the tasks for the social worker may be to help the client and family to *envision the future*. This concept is adapted from more recent approaches to conceptualising decision-making processes known as *image theory*, which is part of a broader framework known as *naturalistic decision making* (Beach and Connolly, 1997). Being able to visualise the consequences (both positive and negative) can be particularly difficult when in a state of crisis or at a critical decision point. The multiple conflicting pressures may make it difficult to hope sufficiently to believe in a positive outcome; earnest aspirations for a life with greater independence may cloud judgement about the real hazards ahead. This might be viewed as a decision-making parallel to solution-focused brief therapy methods of helping clients.

Image theory suggests three key main categories of images that people use to guide their decision making. Each image category is used in turn to provide standards that are used to screen out unacceptable options.

1. **Values image**

   Image theory gives a primary place to the values of the decision maker, reflecting the way that they think things should be and the principles that underpin their own and other's behaviour. The starting point in a decision situation is to consider the basic values, principles, conscience and beliefs of the individual. This may be sufficient to address a dilemma and clarify how the presenting situation fits with the rest of the individual's life and purposes.

2. **Life goals image** (also called 'Trajectory image')

   Decision makers have a vision or goal of the situation they want to be in, the way they want their life to be. This constitutes a vision that shapes the decision-making process. If a person's basic values and principles (as in 1) do not clarify the choice to be made, an exploration of their life goals or vision may clarify the choice between alternatives. This ensures that this decision fits within a broader meaningful framework for the individual.

3. **Tactics image** (also called 'Strategic image')

   Decision makers have operational tactics for engaging in decision-making and problem-solving processes, and ways in which they attempt to forecast the outcomes in turn guide how they behave in making or influencing decisions. If the consideration of fundamental values and life goals (as in 1 and 2) does not resolve the dilemma, this consideration of the approach to engaging in a more detailed decision process may be required.

To illustrate this model in practice, a decision may be made on the basis of your beliefs and values (Stage 1). For example, if you do not agree morally with gambling you will use this first category of images to decide to ignore an invitation to buy a lottery ticket. If you are facing a decision where either option is acceptable in terms of your values, this model suggests that you then decide in terms of life goals (Stage 2). As an example you make a career choice on the basis of the job you would like to be doing in ten years' time, although your present job and the one advertised are both morally acceptable (i.e. both meet the standard of the first values image). If you do not eliminate the options through either the first or second option you may make the decision on the basis of the third category of images, tactics or processes to achieve what you want. For example, you want your children returned home from state care (on the basis of your values, image category 1), you want a family lifestyle that includes the children (on the basis of your life goals, image category 2), so the decision is about the tactics of how to engage with the child protection case conference to which you have been invited. If there is still more than one option remaining after reaching this third category of images, you may find it helpful to consider the decision model of *balancing benefits and harms* which is considered in Chapter 7.

Table 2.1 Supporting the client in envisioning the future
(Adapted from Image Theory of decision making – see Beach and Connolly, 1997)

1. *Values image*

   - *What are the relevant values of the decision maker?*

   - *How do they think things should be?*

   - *What beliefs and principles should underpin their own and other's behaviour?*

   - *What impact do these have on the decision?*

2. *Life goals image*

   IF the Values image in Stage 1 does not resolve the decision dilemma:

   - *What vision does the decision maker have of the situation they want to be in?*

   - *How do they want their life to be?*

   - *What goals are most important?*

   - *Which option fits best within the life goals for the decision maker?*

3. *Tactics image*

   If neither the Values image in Stage 1 nor the Life goals image in Stage 2 fully resolve the decision dilemma:

   - *What are the decision making processes for the individual regarding this issue?*

   - *What options are available for engaging in the problem-solving process?*

   - *What outcomes are likely for each option?*

   - *What tactics are likely to be most effective to achieve the desired goals?*

Chapter summary

- People who come in contact with social workers – whether voluntarily or involuntarily – are often at a point of crisis and facing difficult decisions.

- The decisions of clients and families involve emotions, their values and their understanding of information relevant to the decision such as the likelihood of harm, the options that they have and possible benefits in the alternative courses of action.

- Trust, resilience and confidentiality are often key issues for clients as they face difficult choices.

- *Game theory* can help us to understand the dynamics of decision-making processes with clients and families.

- As a social worker you have a role in supporting reasonable and informed client decisions, in accord with professional guidance, values and standards, and the legal and policy frameworks for your practice.

- The decision model known as *image theory* can help us to conceptualise the professional role in supporting clients in decision making in some circumstances.

FURTHER READING

Brown, K. (ed) (2006) *Vulnerable Adults and Community Care*. Exeter: Learning Matters.

This post-qualifying textbook covers a wide range of areas in relation to social work with adults and is useful for understanding the perspectives of a range of adult clients and their family carers.

Department of Health (2007) *Independence, Choice and Risk: A Guide to Best Practice in Supported Decision Making*. London: Department of Health. **www.dh.gov.uk/en/Publicationsandstatistics/ Publications/PublicationsPolicyAndGuidance/DH_074773**

This best practice guide by the UK Department of Health is for the use of everyone involved in supporting adults using health and social care within any setting, whether community or residential, in the public, independent or voluntary sectors. This is a key text giving principles for supporting client decision making, and recognising that caring for people involves supporting them in reasonable risk-taking.

Shulman, L. (1999) *The Skills of Helping Individuals, Families, Groups and Communities*. Itasca, Illinois: FE Peacock.

This is an excellent text for social work practice skills, which are an essential underpinning for working with individuals and families in decision-making processes.

Thom, B., Sales, R. and Pearce, J.J. (eds) (2007) *Growing Up with Risk*. Bristol: The Policy Press.

This edited volume contains summaries of research regarding children in relation to a wide range of risk issues in growing up, together with a critical commentary. It is useful for helping to understand the world of children and risk.

Chapter 3

Consent, human rights and reasonable decisions in law

CHAPTER OBJECTIVES

This chapter will help you to meet the following National Occupational Standards for Social Work.

- Key role 3, unit 11: Prepare for, and participate in decision-making forums.
- Key role 4, unit 12: Assess and manage risks to individuals, families, carers, groups and communities.
- Key role 4, unit 13: Assess, minimise and manage risk to self and colleagues.
- Key role 5, unit 16: Manage, present and share records and reports.
- Key role 6, unit 19: Work within agreed standards of social work practice and ensure own professional development.
- Key role 6, unit 20: Manage complex ethical issues, dilemmas and conflicts.

This chapter will help you to meet post-qualifying requirements for social work in the UK such as the following.

- Work effectively in a context of risk, uncertainty, conflict and contradiction (The Post-Qualifying Award in Specialist Social Work (Generic Level Requirement vii.), General Social Care Council [England], 2004).
- Competence in working effectively in complex situations (Post-Qualifying Award, Requirement PQ2, *Scotland & Wales (= UK Framework 1990–2007)*).
- Competence in exercising the powers and responsibilities of a professional social worker, including the appropriate use of discretion and the management of risk (Post-Qualifying Award, Requirement PQ3, *Scotland & Wales (= UK Framework 1990–2007)*).
- Ability to make informed decisions (Post-Qualifying Award, Requirement PQ4, *Scotland & Wales (= UK Framework 1990–2007)*).
- Demonstrate consistent and sustained sound judgement and decision making in the context of complexity, risk, uncertainty, conflict and contradiction (Specific Award Requirement 3, Northern Ireland Post-Qualifying Education and Training Partnership, 2007).

Give your decisions, never your reasons; your decisions may be right, your reasons are sure to be wrong.

(Earl of Mansfield (1705–1793) quoted in Peter, 1980, p273)

Introduction

This chapter considers legal aspects of sound judgement and decision making which are common across client groups. We consider the principles underlying consent, capacity and negligence as a benchmark for good decision making in legal and, by extension, in other contexts where decisions are challenged also. We outline in lay terms the principles under-pinning the law relating to the tort of negligence as it relates to the duty of care of professionals, highlighting the need to seek legal advice through organisational arrange-ments as appropriate. The law is viewed as supporting reasoned, reasonable risk-taking as something inherent in the professional task. The case law developments are put in the context of the more recent codification of some relevant principles in the Human Rights Act, 1998 in line with European Union requirements. Our basic approach is to help you to be a competent, confident, caring professional through a fuller appreciation of how the law supports reasonable, reasoned decision making.

This chapter is intended only as an introductory guide to legal aspects of professional decision making. Do not rely upon this book as a substitute for legal advice on any indi-vidual set of circumstances. This chapter aims to inform you about general principles and issues so that you are more able to identify when legal advice needs to be sought, and enable you to better understand and discuss the issues. This book does not purport to address the detailed legal requirements in any particular jurisdiction, but to educate on general principles that are common in democratic countries.

The basis of law

There are various remedies in democratic societies for those who are aggrieved, and for applying sanctions, pressure or penalties to those who make decisions that are not regarded as sufficiently robust. In our society these include Inquiries, serious case reviews, inspections, reports by commissions and actions by politicians and the media to name and shame public bodies and individual employees. The law is a primary mechanism for accountability and that is our focus here, although the principles apply in other contexts where professional decisions are challenged.

There are two main branches to the law: criminal law and civil law. Criminal law relates to conduct deemed so undesirable that it is prohibited and made a criminal offence. Civil law provides a forum for a victim to argue the case for compensation or other civil remedy when he feels wronged by another citizen or an organisation. In the UK there are two main sources of law: legislation and common law.

Legislation may place specified responsibilities on government departments and public bodies that employ social workers, such as local authorities and Health and Social Care Trusts in Northern Ireland (where statutory functions are vested in the Health and Social Care Board which then delegates powers and duties to the Trusts). Such statutory func-tions include both powers and duties. Duties are things that the authority *shall* do; powers are things that it *may* do. An organisation or individual can only exercise powers or duties that are prescribed for that organisation or individual.

Common law is formed by the decisions of courts in decided cases. Through an appeal to a higher court the principles on which a judgement has been made will be clarified and the judgement may be upheld or overturned. A precedent is the judgement in a legal case which will then be used in future by courts in decisions regarding similar cases. Higher court judgements become binding on all lower courts (see for example the case of Diane Pretty in relation to her attempt to seek permission from the courts for her husband to assist her to end her own life, http://en.wikipedia.org/wiki/Diane_Pretty). Case law precedent is the basis for most of our consideration of professional negligence and standards of care, although increasingly the Human Rights Act, 1998 is being used in this context.

The law and reasonable decision making

The main aim of this chapter is to reduce anxiety about legal aspects of decision making so as to support confident, sound professional practice. A key concept is that of *reasonable* decision making. Lord Diplock, summing up the court judgement in *Council of Civil Service Unions v Minister for the Civil Service* [1985] AC 374 identified three grounds of review of administrative decisions (illegality, irrationality and procedural impropriety) and suggested that a fourth ground (proportionality – a European Law concept) might also be adopted in the future.

- Legality involves the appropriate interpretation of statutes for their intended purpose, so decisions must take into account relevant criteria and not take into account irrelevant considerations.

- Rationality means not deliberately evading the purpose of legislation by making an obscure, irrational decision that takes advantage of a loophole. It applies to a decision that is *so unreasonable that no reasonable authority could ever have come to it* in the words of Lord Greene (*Associated Provincial Picture Houses v Wednesbury Corporation* [1948] 1 KB 223).

- Procedural propriety means observing the rules of natural justice and giving a fair hearing to the issues, and also observing statutory requirements.

- Proportionality (as a result of the Human Rights Act, 1998) has become an increasingly important ground of review and means asking whether it is necessary to act in a way which will result in the limitation of an individual right and whether the action is the least necessary to achieve the aim being pursued (*R (Daly) v Home Secretary* [2001] UKHL 26).

Decisions about individual clients cannot be made with disregard to the issue of overall resources for services, and the courts generally recognise this. For the chief officer of a public health and social care organisation there may also be a statutory duty to stay within budget.

Decisions themselves must not only be fair but also the manner in which a decision is made must also be fair. We may create and apply a decision policy along the lines that we discuss in Chapter 6, to promote consistency of decision making across the organisation, which would be sound professional practice. However, case law precedents seem to indicate that organisations can be obliged to make exceptions for situations that otherwise might not seem exceptional in relation to the purpose of the decision policy (see, for example, *Eisai Limited v the National Institute for Health and Clinical Excellence (NICE)* [2007] EWHC 1941 (Admin) QBD (Admin)). This makes the development of policies to promote consistent judgement more difficult. The word *normally* might usefully be included in such decision policies! In exercising discretion, professionals and managers must consider the matter at issue and not just say *no*. The following principles can be used to help you make reasonable decisions.

You should:

* *identify the law correctly;*

* *make sure you know what your powers are and do not go beyond them;*

* *follow any statutory criteria (e.g. in the application of terms used in an Act or in any procedural requirements);*

* *identify the purpose of the law and act in accordance with it (this is to do with the 'spirit' as well as the 'letter' of the law);*

* *take into account relevant considerations and do not take into account irrelevant considerations (including avoiding discrimination);*

* *follow the requirements of natural justice (for example: letting people have their say; not making up rules after the event; hearing 'both sides'; avoiding bias);*

* *reach decisions based on the evidence;*

* *act 'in good faith';*

* *be 'reasonable': there should be some rational line of argument that you can adduce to support your decision;*

* *apply the Human Rights Act 1998 which is now relevant to all decisions of 'public authorities'.*

(White *et al.*, 2007, p101)

Gross negligence in criminal law

Our main focus is on negligence in civil law. We should mention briefly that there is the possibility in the most serious cases of an individual being prosecuted for the crime of gross negligence (see for example *Prentice* [1993] 3WLR927 approved by House of Lords in *Regina Respondent v Adomako Appellant* [1994] 3 WLR 288 and [1995] 1 AC 171). As there is no known case at present of a social worker being convicted of gross negligence manslaughter we will not consider the matter further here and the interested reader is referred to a more detailed text such as Carson and Bain (2008).

Consenting to take risks

It is your responsibility to ensure that your client is capable of giving consent to whatever care or treatment you are proposing. In multi-professional teams it is common to look to specific professions to undertake particular tasks so as to create more co-operative working. However, this is not an excuse for a professional abdicating their responsibility for their own care planning with the client and family. There are now mandatory procedures in England and Wales for ascertaining capacity to make decisions through mental capacity legislation. The same principles of good practice apply generally where there is not a specified process.

- *A person must be assumed to have capacity unless it is established that he lacks capacity.*

- *A person is not to be treated as unable to make a decision unless all practicable steps to help him to do so have been taken without success.*

- *A person is not to be treated as unable to make a decision merely because he makes an unwise decision.*

> (Brown and Barber, 2008, p5 quoting from the Mental Capacity Act 2005
> [England and Wales] Part 1, Section 1 The Principles)

If we disregard for the moment safeguarding decisions and illegal activities by clients, once we have satisfied ourselves that an adult client has capacity to make this care decision we have no right to stop them. If we have concerns about the proposed activity, we must then make a separate decision as to whether we in our profession or organisation are willing to support the care plan. There is an important distinction between people being harmed because of our activities and supporting a person with capacity in a decision-making process where they make an informed decision to take reasonable risks, as a result of which inevitably harm will sometimes ensue for some clients, as for any person.

> *An individual who has the mental capacity to make a decision, and chooses voluntarily to live with a level of risk, is entitled to do so. The law will treat that person as having consented to the risk and so there will be no breach of the duty of care by professional or public authorities. However the local authority remains accountable for the proper use of its public funds, and whilst the individual is entitled to live with a degree of risk, the local authority is not obliged to fund it. In very difficult cases, there will need to be a robust process whereby conflict about the acceptability of risk or otherwise can be properly debated and resolved.*

> (DH, 2007, p22, para 2.26)

Decisional capacity

Professional judgements about consent and capacity to consent can be challenging in practice, and sometimes small acts present more challenge. In what circumstances has a care worker the right to take mouldering food out of a fridge? What happens if an ambulance is called and the person then shouts: *I don't want to go to hospital!*? When does weight loss become neglect or self-neglect? In terms of the law, competence to consent is a question of fact in each case. There is a general presumption of competence, that is, it is generally presumed that an adult is competent unless it is shown otherwise. Except as provided under safeguarding provisions in mental health legislation *there is no power at the moment in law for one person to give consent on behalf of another adult . . .* (Dimond, 1997, p36), except that Section 11(7) of the Mental Capacity Act, 2005 (applying in England and Wales only) allows for limited power of consent by an individual with a lasting power of attorney regarding continuing treatment but not life sustaining treatment (Pattison, 2006, p160). The basic principle remains that the professional must act in the best interests of the client.

CASE STUDY 3.1

Enabling a client to understand the risks

Mr Eaton is a man of 88 years who is a widower living in sheltered accommodation. He has health problems and a history of falls which increases his dependency on his daughter for some daily living tasks. Mr Eaton has been subject to financial and psychological abuse from his daughter who has threatened to withdraw her support. The theft of the money was not pursued by the police due to lack of evidence and the reluctance of Mr Eaton to pursue the matter. Mr Eaton is registered as a vulnerable adult and my role is to engage the relevant professionals to assess the risks and create a protection plan. In discussion with Mr Eaton it became apparent how highly he valued his relationship with his daughter despite the abuse, and living in supported housing rather than a residential home. I focused my energies on ensuring that Mr Eaton understood the risks and was able to weigh up the consequences of his choice.

- At what point does a client's expressed choice become so risky that you decide that an assessment of their capacity to make that decision is required?
- What process do you use to ascertain their capacity to make that decision?

Essentially, the question is whether the individual is unable to make a decision for him or herself in relation to the matter because of an impairment of, or a disturbance in the functioning of, the mind or brain. Key issues are:

- a general understanding of the decision to be made and why;

- an understanding of likely consequences of making or not making this decision;

- an ability to understand, retain, use and weigh up relevant information as part of the decision process; and

- ability to communicate this decision (by any means).

(see Mental Capacity Act, 2005 [England and Wales] and Code of Practice)

An interesting case regarding capacity to consent was that of Re: C (adult: refusal of medical treatment) [1994] 1 All ER 819) where a man suffering from paranoid schizophrenia in a secure hospital refused to have his leg amputated even though the result was expected to be premature death. The court held that he was entitled to make that decision as he was competent, using criteria along the general lines outlined above. If a person lacks the mental capacity to make a decision about a course of action, any decision or action must be made on the basis of what is in the person's best interests. For further consideration of this aspect see Brown and Barber (2008).

Decisions by children

In relation to children the courts have taken the approach that children who have capacity should be able to consent to treatment (*Gillick v West Norfolk and Wisbech Area Health Authority* [1985] 3 All ER 402 (HL); R (on the application of Axon) v Secretary of State for Health (Family Planning Association intervening) [2006] EWHC 37 (Admin)). This is now generally known as *Gillick competence* after the former judgement above or as Fraser Guidelines after Lord Fraser who spoke on the issue in the House of Lords. The Gillick case arose in relation to whether there was a duty on a doctor to tell the parents if he or she was providing contraceptives to a child under the age of consent (16 years), contraception being regarded as a medical treatment. The judgement might be viewed as protecting doctors against prosecution for knowingly supporting sexual activity by a child below the age of consent, rather than intending to provide the child with complete autonomy or to have the effect of snuffing out a parent's rights when a child grows in competence. However, this approach has been applied by professionals dealing with children and young people in other areas where consent is necessary, although the court judgements above refer specifically to matters related to sexual and reproductive health. When it comes to refusing treatment the courts do not seem to have applied this rule; instead they tend to allow parents to override consent. Nonetheless, there are examples where *Gillick competence* seems to be used as a practice principle also in terms of refusing consent such as in the case of Hannah, a terminally ill 13 year old who was interviewed by a child protection social worker as part of a process whereby she persuaded a hospital to withdraw a High Court action that would have forced her to have a risky heart transplant against her will (Grice, 2008). The interested reader is referred to Walters (2008) which gives further references.

Human Rights Act

The Human Rights Act, 1988 (HRA) came into force in the UK in October 2000, requiring all courts to take into account the European Convention on Human Rights (ECHR), an international treaty focusing on identifying and protecting certain fundamental rights and freedoms such as the right to life; the right to a fair trial; freedom of thought, conscience and religion; and freedom of expression.

A key article of the ECHR for social work practice is Article 8, whereby everyone has the right to *respect for his private and family life, home and correspondence*. This right is a qualified right, that is it is subject to restriction clauses that enable a consideration of the balance between the rights of the individual and the public interest. This article states: *There shall be no interference by a public authority with the exercise of this right except such as in accordance with the law and is necessary in a democratic society in the interests of . . . public safety, . . . for the prevention of crime and disorder, for the protection of health or morals, or for the protection of the rights and freedoms of others.*

Articles 2 and 3 of the ECHR are also relevant to practice decisions. The convention rights impose positive obligations to promote and protect, such as responding to alleged abuse (see for example *Osman v UK* (23452/94) [1998] 29 EHRR 245 and *Z v UK* (2002) 34 EHRR 3), as well as negative obligations not to interfere. Article 5 and the Bournewood case (*HL v UK* (2004) 40 EHRR) influenced the development of the Mental Capacity Act, 2005.

Contravention of an ECHR right may be made on the basis of a *legitimate aim*, such as when a social worker acting on behalf of a public body brings a court action to protect a child from abuse. Interference with a Convention right must be proportionate, i.e. the interference must be proportionate to the harm that it is intended to prevent, and must be carried out appropriately (White *et al.*, 2007). For social workers the core practice issue is that where there is a relevant right under the HRA, *interference* with that right must be explicitly justified when undertaking compulsory safeguarding actions both in the decision processes and in the decision outcomes.

The tort of negligence

An individual can take proceedings against another in the civil courts for compensation for loss or personal injury, usually on the basis of negligence or breach of statutory duties. The law in relation to negligence is largely determined by case law rather than by statutes. A liability in tort is conduct (other than in relation to a contract) which gives the victim a right to sue for compensation. Our focus is on the tort of negligence, which might be considered as *failure to take such care as the law requires*.

An individual may sue an organisation that employs a social worker, as well as the individual social worker, because they deem the social worker to have acted negligently. They are able to sue an employer as the employer may be liable for the acts of an employee. This is known as vicarious liability. However, if you are deemed to have acted outside of the scope of your authority then the employer will not be liable for the acts of the employee. In this situation only the employee, that is the social worker, will be liable for the payment of compensation. In the tort of negligence the plaintiff must prove that:

- the defendant owed the plaintiff a legal duty of care;
- the legal duty of care was breached; and
- damage was suffered as a consequence.

This suggests five key questions for a professional defending a claim for negligence.

- Was there a duty of care?
- Did I breach the (relevant) standard of care?
- Did my breach of the standards of care cause the losses?
- Are those losses recognised by the law for compensation purposes?
- Were those losses reasonably foreseeable?

(Marsh and Soulsby, 1994; Carson and Bain, 2008; White, 2008)

We will consider these five questions in turn.

Who has a duty of care?

In *Pippin and Wife v Sheppard* [1822] 147 Eng. Rep. 512 the court found that *a medical practitioner has a duty to exercise reasonable skill and care*. This judgement would apply in principle to other professions.

The first question is whether social work is a profession, which was addressed in 1994. *Those who engage professionally in social work bring to their task skill and expertise, the product partly of training and partly of experience, which ordinary, uninstructed members of the public are bound to lack. I have no doubt that they should be regarded as members of a skilled profession* (Sir Thomas Bingham in *M (Minor) v Newham London Borough Council; X v Bedfordshire County Council* [1994] WLR 554). Since that time, social work in the UK has become a profession recognised across the European Union as it now meets the requirements of having a protected title, a register of those permitted to practice, and a requirement of three years of relevant study in higher education to qualify to practice.

One question that courts consider is: *Is it fair, just and reasonable to impose a duty of care on professionals carrying out a public service role* (cf. Carson and Bain, 2008)? Would imposing a duty of care deter or prevent social workers from carrying out essential public functions effectively? This is akin to the debates about the level of criminal activity (for example drug-taking) which a professional, such as a social worker, nurse or youth worker, should be obliged to disclose to the police in order to avoid committing an offence themselves. Would imposing a duty of care make the professional task of trying to help people in these situations impossible or ineffective?

In the case mentioned above there was also consideration of to whom the duty of care is owed. The court concluded that a social worker, like a doctor, owed a certain duty of care to the person in his care, but in the advice given to the employing statutory authority by the social worker [in relation to recommendations to the court about child welfare], the general professional duty was to the employer, rather than to the client. In that particular case the judiciary decided by a majority that the social workers (for whom the authority were liable) owed no legal duty to care to those children who had been on their caseload (*M (Minor) v Newham London Borough Council; X v Bedfordshire County Council* [1994] WLR 554 see also in [1995] 2 AC 633 and [1995] 3 WLR 152 and [1995] 3 All ER 353). Generally, the courts are reluctant to impose a duty of care on public servants. The House of Lords has imposed a duty of care on professionals in relation to a child who had been in statutory care from a few months' old about matters arising while in care (*Barrett v Enfield London Borough Council* [2001] 2 AC 550, [1999] 3 All ER 193). It is generally considered unlikely that courts would impose a duty of care in relation to child protection work (Carson and Bain, 2008) and other areas of field social work as it might render various social work tasks and roles impossible.

The basic message is that the scope of a duty **to** care depends on your personal beliefs and professional values, whereas a legal duty **of** care is a more precise concept defining who might be sued when a plaintiff alleges negligence.

Standards of care

The next question is whether the standard of care is acceptable. It is a defence that the professional acted in a way that would be considered reasonable by a responsible body of professional opinion. A medical doctor is *not guilty of negligence if he has acted in accordance with a practice accepted as proper by a responsible body of medical men skilled in that particular art* (Mr. Justice McNair in *Bolam v Friern Hospital Management Committee* 1957 2 All ER 118, [1957] 1 WLR 582). This judgement in relation to standards of care is now widely known as the Bolam test. The standard of care required is not the best possible practice, or what the majority recommend or what most practitioners do. The question is whether a responsible body of co-professional opinion would have supported the decision, at the date of the event and in the circumstances of the case. In other words, pioneering treatments and changes in care services and practices are not prevented, but there must be a level of professional support for the approach taken. Looked at the other way . . . *a doctor is not negligent, if he is acting in accordance with such a practice, merely because there is a body of opinion that takes a contrary view* (Mr. Justice McNair in *Bolam v Friern Hospital Management Committee* 1957 2 All ER 118, [1957] 1 WLR 582). In Scotland the equivalent test is that a practitioner *has been proved to be guilty of such failure as no practitioner of ordinary skill would be guilty of if acting with ordinary care* (*Hunter v Hanley* [1955], s.200).

The courts will seek to ascertain, as a matter of fact, professional standards of practice at the time of the event. It is normally a decision of the appropriate professional body to set standards of care for practice. However, the courts retain the right to be the final arbiter of a professional standard. Examples of a court overruling a professional standard as being too low are extremely rare. There is a crucial role for professional bodies in stating explicitly standards of practice.

CASE STUDY 3.2

Standards of care and reasonable risk taking

Aquila is 58 years with learning disability. She has epilepsy, is deaf, and has no speech. She was discharged four years ago to a small (24 bed) residential unit from a long-stay hospital. Staff were keen that she developed self-care skills and an agreed care plan was developed. They knew that she enjoyed baths. Over time she developed skills to take baths on her own, eventually locking others out. For three years there was no problem. Then one day staff had to break open the bathroom door. She had experienced an epileptic fit, slipped down in the bath and drowned. The case was referred to the coroner.

- *What do you need to know to judge whether this was a sound care plan?*

- *What standards of care might apply in this situation?*

- *What might be done to ensure that the care plan was perceived as sound even if a tragedy or harm ensued?*

- *Who took what risks?*

- *Did the staff have legal power to stop Aquila bathing on her own?*

- *Is it relevant that the organisation had adopted a 'normalisation' policy?*

    (See also R v HM Coroner for Reading ex parte West Berkshire Housing Consortium Ltd
                                                                (1995) CO/2994/94.)

The Bolam test must now be viewed in the light of the judgement in *Bolitho v City & Hackney Health Authority* [1998] *House of Lords* AC232. This case, involving a paediatrician in a hospital, concluded that professionals must be able to give a rationale such as research evidence or a theoretical basis for their views that an approach was justifiable in the circumstances (Foster, 1998). This judgement emphasises the essential place of *evidence-based practice* – using the best available evidence to inform decisions. We discuss this further in Chapter 5.

Causation

If it is shown that a professional with a duty of care has breached his or her duty of care, then the plaintiff must show that the breach has caused injury. The injury might be deterioration in their condition, an adverse outcome, or treatment that they would not have undergone had the duty of care not been breached. The client has to prove that but for the negligence he or she would have been in a better position. The aim of compensation for negligence is to put the victim back into that position. Clearly, victims cannot turn back the clock. Financial compensation is based on the level of losses incurred in the past (whether physical or emotional) and those that may arise in the future as a consequence. The question at this point becomes: *would the harms or losses have been experienced even if the standard of care had not been breached?*

Recognised losses

The nature of the loss must be recognised by the courts for compensation purposes. This is one reason for the development of psychiatric diagnoses such as Post-traumatic Stress Disorder (PTSD). This makes them an identifiable and recognisable condition for compensation purposes.

ACTIVITY 3.1

Traumatic stress as a recognised loss

You were watching the FA Cup Semi-final between Liverpool and Nottingham Forest at Hillsborough Stadium in Sheffield on television on 15 April 1989 when you saw the human crush that led to the match being called off after six minutes. You needed treatment and time off work because you saw your loved ones among the 96 football fans who perished in the tragedy.

- *Could you sue to seek recompense for your lost earnings or medical, mental health or social care?*

(http://en.wikipedia.org/wiki/Hillsborough_Disaster)

There are three main areas of loss that might be considered for the purpose of establishing a negligence claim: physical injury or loss of functional ability; financial loss; and emotional loss or shock. This latter category has been recognised increasingly in recent years, including in relation to the abuse of children. A basic criterion is that the shock must have been experienced or observed directly.

Foreseeability and acceptance of losses

The issue of foreseeability of harm can raise major issues in relation to supporting clients to take reasonable risks in accordance with government policy and sound professional values and standards. There needs to be clarity about who is taking the risk. Is the client, informed and with capacity and freedom to choose, deciding to take the risk? If risks are taken (as they must be in life, by everyone) then sometimes, unfortunately, harm ensues. If professionals know that harm is possible they need to discuss it with clients so that they can make an informed decision. The key question is whether serious negative consequences should have been foreseen and were not. The sort of *risk-taking* inherent in any independence programme (for example, learning road traffic skills or to use public transport for a person with a learning disability) requires a *reasonable and reasoned approach* to the level of harm that may ensue and its likelihood. Losses can only be recovered if they are foreseeable, that is they are not too remote. A competent adult who acknowledges and accepts a foreseeable risk would not be successful in suing for negligence. Client consent is a full defence to a claim in negligence, hence the importance of ensuring that this is evidenced in records in any risk-taking situation.

ACTIVITY 3.2

Claudia's walk

Claudia was a 17-year-old autistic child living in a residential unit who was taken for a walk by a care worker. Claudia became agitated when she saw Mrs Partington walking towards her and lashed out at her before the care worker could stop her. Mrs Partington sued for damages on the grounds of negligence on the part of the local authority that ran the residential unit regarding their lack of care and control of Claudia.

- *Do you think that the authority or the worker is liable for damages?*

- *What do you want to know about the incident in reaching a judgement?*

- *What do you want to know about standards of practice at the time?*

- *What law or mandatory regulations are relevant if this situation arose now?*

- *How would you decide whether the policies and procedures in the unit were reasonable at the time?*

- *Is it relevant that Mrs Partington has a red and white stick to indicate her visual and hearing impairment and taps this on the pavement as she walks?*

- *In what circumstances would the care worker or the organisation have a right to prevent Claudia from taking a walk? (For a consideration of trespass to the person see Dimond, 1997).*

In this case the court held that the local authority was not liable as Mrs Partington had not shown that Claudia was improperly supervised. *What the duty [of care] involved varied from person to person and, perhaps, from day to day, depending on the handicapped person's mood. . . . The problem was to balance what was best for the handicapped* person with the interests of the rest of the world. (*Partington v London Borough of Wandsworth* [1990] Fam Law 468, reported in the *Independent*, 8 Nov 1989.)

Liability for risk-taking decisions

A key issue is the consent of the individual with capacity to take risks. *An individual who has the mental capacity to make a decision, and chooses voluntarily to live with a level of risk, is entitled to do so. The law will treat that person as having consented to the risk and so there will be no breach of the duty of care by professionals or public authorities* (DH, 2007, p22, para 2.26). However, as discussed in Chapter 2, statutory authorities remain accountable for the use of their funds, which must not be used for inappropriate purposes.

ACTIVITY **3.3**

Consent to take risks

- *Identify a recent case where you felt uneasy about possible conflict.*

- *What is the most likely threat to your judgement?*

- *At what level of concern did you discuss your judgement with your professional supervisor or line manager?*

- *What recording did you make of the decision process?*

Duty to inform

Giving advice to clients is part of a social worker's task.

CASE STUDY **3.3**

Mr Coles had a crushed finger and went to a cottage hospital where he received first aid. No anti-tetanus injection was given; he was told to go immediately to another hospital for further examination and treatment. Mr Coles went home and was seen later by his GP. He subsequently died of tetanus. The court held that the hospital was negligent in failing to explain why he needed to go to the other hospital and to have the anti-tetanus injection. Proper communication was that which was reasonably necessary for safeguarding a patient's interests and sufficient to enable the client to be safe if followed. It was held that the GP was negligent for failing to ensure that the patient received the anti-tetanus injection.

(Coles v Reading and District Hospital Management Committee and Another 1963 107 S.J. 115)

- *What information do you provide to clients where possible harm might ensue if the care plan is not followed?*

- *What do you do to ensure that the information is understood?*

In *Sidaway v Governors of Bethlem Royal Hospital and the Maudsley Hospital* [1985] 1 All ER 643, the House of Lords confirmed that a doctor was under a duty to disclose any substantial risk involving grave adverse consequences. The test was the same as in any other case of alleged professional negligence, i.e. the Bolam test. The lesson is clear: efficient and effective communication is vital. In contentious or high risk cases, consider agreeing what is adequate written advice with your line manager or professional supervisor, and consider what should be evidenced in contemporaneous records in case of any subsequent challenge.

ACTIVITY 3.4

Duty to communicate with carers

As part of an adult placement service, a statutory authority placed a 19 year old with a history of abusing young children with a host family who had young children without informing them of his past. He then seriously abused their two children. (Vale of Glamorgan Council, 2009)

- *What is the responsibility of the authority towards the host family?*
- *What is the responsibility of the authority towards the young man?*
- *What is a reasonable professional decision in such a situation?*
- *What communication would be good professional practice with the parties?*

Despite our general professional value of respecting confidentiality, there are situations where we face a dilemma when we know information *confidentially* which might protect someone from harm. To whom do we have the greater duty? Which harm is the greater? You should be aware that you may have a duty of care to over-ride confidentiality to inform identifiable third parties of a specific risk of violence (*Tarasoff v Regents of the University of California* (1976) 551 P 2d 334 [USA]; *W v Edgell* [1990] All ER 835; Monahan, 1993). This is a complex area and legal advice should be sought.

Conflict, confidence and being sued

This chapter has aimed to provide some clarity in lay language on legal aspects of decision making. Uncertainty about rights and responsibilities in relation to the law can inhibit sound approaches to supporting choice and managing risks (Department of Health, 2007, Executive Summary, para 11). There is, of course, nothing to stop someone commencing an action for negligence against any individual, including a professional. The claim itself may be without merit, but answering such a claim can be stressful. Thankfully it is rare that a social worker is sued, and extremely rare that a social worker is sued successfully! However, you might have to fight a case, which can create much anxiety. A particular aspect that may cause stress is that the loser of the action may have to pay the legal costs of both parties as well as damages. Even though a case against a social worker may be successfully defended, despite 'winning' you may be responsible for some or all of your own costs. Therefore it is essential that you have professional indemnity insurance, such as is available through a professional body such as the British Association of Social Workers.

Chapter summary

- As social workers we are accountable to society, through the law, in the judgements and decisions we make.

- You must ensure that a client has the capacity to consent to whatever care or treatment you are proposing, including risk-taking steps towards rehabilitation, independence or better quality of life.

- The law supports reasoned, reasonable risk-taking decision making as something inherent in the professional task.

- The law of tort provides underpinning principles that help you to articulate reasoned, reasonable decision-making in the face of challenges such as from inquiries, complaints or politicians.

- Seek timely legal advice, through the arrangements in your employing organisation, when you are facing high risk or very contentious decisions.

- If a court is judging reasonableness, a key point is whether your practice is likely to be judged reasonable by some other social workers respected in that field.

- Ensure good communication about decisions and record evidence of decision-making processes in sufficient detail in case of challenge.

FURTHER READING

Brown, R. and Barber, P. (2008) *The Social Worker's Guide to the Mental Capacity Act 2005.* Exeter: Learning Matters.

This text in the Post-Qualifying Social Work series provides a detailed guide to professional practice in undertaking responsibilities under the Mental Capacity Act in England and Wales.

Carson, D. and Bain, A. (2008) *Professional Risk and Working with People: Decision-Making in Health, Social Care and Criminal Justice.* London: Jessica Kingsley.

This is an excellent book on the legal aspects of risk and decision making, particularly the tort of negligence and 'duty of care', and drawing out the way that the law supports as well as challenges decision making by professionals.

Dimond, B. (1997) *Legal Aspects of Care in the Community.* London: Macmillan.

This readable textbook is well structured, clearly written and very accessible to the social worker wanting a detailed grounding in general legal aspects of practice in Great Britain and Northern Ireland, including negligence, trespass to the person and entering locked premises.

White, C. (2008) *Northern Ireland Social Work Law.* West Sussex and Dublin: Tottel.

This is an excellent textbook for social workers on relevant aspects of the law in Northern Ireland.

White, R., Broadbent, G. and Brown, K. (2007) *Law and the Social Work Practitioner.* Exeter: Learning Matters.

This text in the Post-Qualifying Social Work series gives an overview of legal aspects of practice in the main areas of social welfare statutes (child care, mental health, etc.) and some excellent chapters on the legal framework for decision making and the Human Rights Act.

The British and Irish Legal Information Institute website **www.bailii.org** provides access to freely available British and Irish legal information.

Chapter 4
Collaborative and contested decisions

Give every man thine ear, but few thy voice;

Take each man's censure, but reserve thy judgement . . .

. . . This above all: to thine own self be true,

And it must follow, as the night the day,

Thou canst not then be false to any man.

Lord Polonius, *Hamlet* Act I, Scene 3, William Shakespeare (1564–1616)

Introduction

We considered in Chapter 2 the task of engaging and supporting clients and families in decision processes. In this chapter we take the issue of collaboration in decision making further by considering the engagement of colleagues from other professions and organisations, and contested decisions. We discuss inter-professional working in relation to decision-making processes and communicating about probabilities of harm or success. The chapter discusses risk management and legal issues in decision making in groups such as case conferences. We consider rights and conflict, where decisions are contested, and making an argument for a professional opinion particularly in court.

Collaborative decision making

The role of the social worker is often to co-ordinate specialist contributions to decision making into a holistic, person-centred picture and to identify key issues to be addressed in a co-ordinated decision process. This demands knowledge of the roles of other professions and organisations, and skills in managing the decision process. Social workers may have a specialist assessment role in addition to their co-ordinating role, which we consider further in Chapter 8 when we look at the place of assessment tools in decision making. Key tasks in engaging stakeholders in decisions include:

- taking account of relevant values, principles and protocols;
- ensuring appropriate people are engaged at the appropriate stage in the process;
- managing an effective decision-making process if you have a co-ordinating role;
- clarifying with stakeholders (client, family, professionals and organisations) what is expected of them and what they expect of you, for what purpose and within what timescale;
- giving all parties an opportunity (and sometimes support) to make effective, timely contributions, sharing facts and expressing their opinions appropriately;
- ensuring that you are clear on your role and the powers and duties of your organisation, and that these are communicated clearly to others;
- clarifying how the decision will be implemented;
- informing parties of the decision outcome.

The importance of engaging appropriate professionals on the problem-solving task which lies at the heart of much of our decision making should not be underestimated. The range of perspectives brings a breadth of knowledge and skills to bear and provides checks and balances. A joint decision process will normally increase ownership of the decision. Consensus processes help to anticipate possible consequences of the decision and reduce conflicts that might occur later.

ACTIVITY 4.1

Contributors to decisions

- *Recall a recent reasonably complex case.*
- *Who was involved in making the decision?*
- *Who else should have been involved, ideally?*
- *What was your contribution to the decision?*
- *What was the contribution of other key stakeholders?*
- *How might the various contributions have been more effective?*
- *What structure was used for the decision-making process?*
- *How was the decision process managed and by whom?*
- *How did you influence this?*
- *What knowledge underpinned your approach?*

Multi-professional decision making

Different professions and organisations have distinct roles, statutory or otherwise, in relation to the decision. There may be a statutory or policy requirement for partnership in specific areas of practice (Taylor, 1999). A key practice skill in inter-professional working is to respect the various roles and not to demean any.

Inquiry findings

> Inquiries show that too narrow a medical view of mental illness offers an inadequate framework for assessing and managing risk, while an over-reliance on social factors without sufficient attention to medical treatment and medication is potentially as unsafe.
>
> (Reith, 1998, p180)

> It appears essential that a psychiatric patient with a severe psychiatric illness whose recent history is not known should be assessed by a social worker . . . Given the psychosocial nature of the impact of schizophrenia and other severe psychiatric illnesses on the patient, relatives and carers, it is important to ensure that a multidisciplinary and multi-agency approach is always adopted . . .
>
> (Wood et al., 1966, Recommendation 1)

The benefits of inter-professional collaboration in decision making must not blind us to the challenges that can occur in reconciling competing objectives. We may need to challenge opinions on occasion as well as seeking compromises. *The training of social workers must equip them with the confidence to question the opinion of professionals in other agencies when conducting their own assessment of the needs of the child* (Laming, 2003, Recommendation 37). There may also be tensions about issues such as a duty to inform other professionals about evidence of possible violence conflicting with a duty of confidentiality towards a client. You can develop multi-professional decision making by:

- being clear about your professional role and confident about your contribution within that role;

- seeking to understand the tasks of other professionals and organisations and respecting their roles;

- seeking to develop trust through timely, open and honest communication, fulfilling promises and acting with integrity;

- clarifying processes of decision making: options, perspectives and context;

- using social work skills appropriately such as empathy (for example, regarding the uncertainties of making a decision), clarifying (for example, options) and challenging (for example, values and stereotypes of clients and other professionals).

Decision making in groups

Collaborative decisions are often made in group meetings. Our focus here is on multi-professional groups meeting for such purposes as a child protection case conference, a strategy meeting or a panel to allocate publicly funded resources such as home care or admission to institutional care.

There may be value in bringing people together for a decision process, such as being able to see a fuller picture as information is shared face-to-face; creating a new synthesis or understanding as problems and issues are discussed; dealing with any conflict of facts or opinions; co-ordinating activities; getting commitment to an agreed, integrated action plan; and laying a foundation for future collaboration where communication may be less direct through telephone or email. Be aware though that convening a group has a cost in terms of time and often travel. Pressures of work mean that professionals will want to be clear about the value of coming to a meeting rather than communicating by form, letter, telephone or email.

CASE STUDY 4.1

Collaborative decision making

Miss Fulton is a 75-year-old woman with schizophrenia who lives alone. She also has Chronic Obstructive Pulmonary Disease (COPD), which makes her short of breath and prone to chest infections. She was admitted to hospital after a fall. My role was to support her in planning her future living arrangements. The stakeholders in the decision making included Miss Fulton and her family, various professionals in the community rehabilitation team and the manager of the home care workers. I liaised with each of these and sought a consensus for a care plan. However, with hindsight, a formal meeting of key parties would have ensured clarity for all concerned; this is a model that I would use in future similar situations.

- *In what circumstances is it particularly desirable to convene a meeting of stakeholders regarding care decisions?*

- *What challenges might need to be addressed in convening such a meeting?*

The decision about who to invite to a meeting may raise the issue of inclusivity versus the need for a small enough group of appropriate people for constructive interaction and achieving a decision within the necessary timescale. By definition, participants are there to influence each other but with respect for other participants. This is a particular application of social work listening skills! There are many parallels between social group work as taught on social work training and the skills required to lead a group of professionals. Leading a decision-making group involves the following tasks.

- Clarify forms of address.
- Clarify purpose of the meeting and, as necessary, roles and responsibilities.
- Emphasise mutual gain from collaborating in the decision process.
- Create a suitable agenda and keep the discussion focused without unduly stifling discussion.
- Legitimise the sharing of facts and opinions, building a culture of mutual respect for participants with their distinct roles, knowledge and skills.
- Address particular obstacles to the group's decision task.
- Enable all to participate, including supporting those less able to do so.
- Build on the strengths of groups for decision making such as generating a range of ideas and alternatives and gaining ownership of decisions made.
- Ensure that the individual meeting fits within the overall decision process (e.g. timing of court hearings, roles of and reporting by sub-committees).
- Clarify issues, agreements, disagreements and confidentiality.
- Allow time for appropriate reflection and consultation.
- Work towards constructive discussion of conflicts.
- Manage the process and the time.
- Ensure that the group makes decisions that it is charged with making.
- Ensure that the group does not make decisions beyond its remit.
- Ensure that disagreements are clarified and recorded.

What decision does a group make by comparison with the decisions that the individuals would make by themselves in isolation? Will the group judgement be different if the individuals discuss the decision by comparison with the average judgement if the members consider identical information without discussion? As people interact in a group they may behave differently and may make different judgements. Janis (1982) highlighted various mechanisms that might lead to *groupthink*.

- A view of the group as invulnerable and as holding the moral high ground, which leads to excessive *risk taking*.
- Closed-mindedness that stereotypes some members (perhaps other professions) or discounts their views for some reason (such as not being present).
- Pressures to conform to the majority view, whether expressed or only felt by individuals fearing criticism if they voice a counter view.

RESEARCH SUMMARY *4.1*

Variation in professional judgements

A study compared the judgements of case managers (social workers) with a multi-professional panel comprising medicine, social work and nursing. Generally, the case managers estimated the risk of the older person requiring institutional care during the coming months higher than did the panel members. There was low level of agreement amongst panel members, but more than there was between the panel and case managers. Interestingly, the social workers on the panel agreed more with other panel members than with the case managers even though these were social workers. The authors concluded that the low reliability of decisions underscored the complexity of the decision situation. The variation might also be due to factors such as case managers knowing detail about the clients and their families that is not conveyed in the written materials; panel members having an appreciation of wider issues due to their role; organisational pressures being greater on panel members; or case managers having to go back to clients to convey in person the rejection of their request for services. (Austin and Seidl, 1981.)

Early research and theory suggested that the effect of a group may be to make a decision that is more risky than the average of the decisions that would be made by the same individuals acting alone without group discussion. This became known as *risky shift*. It was speculated that this increased risk-taking effect may be because:

- the group members became more familiar with the decision topic and became more comfortable with taking greater risk (familiarisation theory); or

- the sort of charismatic personality willing to take risks is also more likely to be the sort of personality to get others to go along with his or her way of thinking in the group (leadership theory); or

- individuals feel less responsibility for the outcome in a group (crowd effect); or

- risk is valued as a positive social norm, so that individuals tend to move in this direction under the influence of the group (risk as value theory) (Stoner, 1968).

More recent research suggests that the effect may be due to the social norm of riskiness attached to a particular option. In other words, some types of decisions may produce a *cautious shift* (the group decision is less risky than the average of the individual judgements) while others produce a *risky shift*. These findings led to the general demise of the first three theories above, while the *risk as value* theory adapted itself to become a *risk or caution as value*. While risk-taking might be given social value in some contexts (e.g. bravery in battle), caution might be valued in others where risk-taking might be viewed as reckless (e.g. doing something for a dare) and hence might lead to a *cautious shift*. The direction of the *choice shift* may be towards the social norm rather than necessarily towards greater risk-taking.

There is little research on group decisions involving social workers. The work by Farmer and Owen (1995) on child protection case conferences illustrated how the process of *assessing risk* in such groups can sometimes lead to *accumulating concerns* (p145) and a disproportionate sense of impending harm, and thus to more *risk averse* group decisions than the judgements of individuals acting alone. This perhaps reflects the views of wider society which might choose less risky options than professionals. Their research high-lighted how pressure can be experienced to conform to the majority view in the meeting. However, there is some evidence that child protection case conferences assume a more extreme position than the average of the members individually, whether more *risk taking* or more *risk averse* (Kelly and Milner, 1996), perhaps because of the need to make a clear decision with an explicit justification.

Liability for decisions in teams and groups

Engaging the appropriate range of professionals in making a decision may be viewed (in addition to any other possible benefits or responsibilities) as good risk management. If something goes wrong the blame may be shared by the group. Also one would hope that the group would be less likely to make a poor decision about the care of the client than any professional or profession acting alone.

It should be noted that case law suggests that courts do not recognise legal liability of a team, unless it is constituted as a *legal person* in its own right (*Wilsher v Essex Area Health Authority* [1986] 3 all ER 801 (CA)). A useful working principle might be to regard each pro-fession as accountable for the decisions that fall within its domain of competence. Similarly, each organisation is responsible for decisions that lie within its purpose, powers and duties. You and your supervisor are responsible for your actions, not other professions or organisa-tions. You must take into account the facts available and opinions of others in forming your own judgement, and must inform others of the decisions of your profession or organisation. And you must not, of course, sabotage the decisions of others to the deliberate detriment of the client. Each profession must make those decisions that are within its own competence and each organisation those decisions that are within its mandate or statutory function. The group may have some formally defined powers of its own, for example, in relation to child protection, deciding that a child requires a formal safeguarding plan or ceasing one, but these group decisions are generally very limited for the above reason. However, this is not to dampen enthusiasm for multi-professional decision making, which remains one of the best risk management defences against the culture of blame in which we work!

Communicating information for decisions

Professional communication is a central theme of Inquiries into homicides and suicides by people with mental illness (Boyd, 1996) and child protection Inquiries (Munro, 2008). Effective communication involves consideration of the language that we use for conveying messages to others.

> *The Department of Health must establish a 'common language' for use across all agencies to help those agencies to identify who they are concerned about, why they are concerned, who is best placed to respond to those concerns, and what outcome is being sought from any planned response.*

> (Laming, 2003, Recommendation 13)

In all fields of social work we need precise language so as to enable effective decisions. Effective communication involves consideration of such aspects as:

- who – role clarity;

- when – timeliness;

- what – level of detail to provide;

- why – clarity of issue and expectation of response by recipient, urgency;

- how – in person, telephone, email, letter, fax, group discussion;

- recording – who, when, what, why and how.

PRACTICE EXAMPLE 4.1

Comments in an assessment report
Does 'Mrs Smith has disturbed sleep . . .' mean:

- *Mrs Smith calls out occasionally in the night, waking her daughter?*

- *Mrs Smith gets up usually once a night to go to the toilet but manages this safely on her own?*

- *Mrs Smith frequently gets up in the night and wanders downstairs and tries to open the outer door?*

Communicating about likelihoods

It is not easy to communicate accurately about uncertainty and likelihoods, especially about the possibility of harm. If people are asked whether they would like a surgical operation where there is 90 per cent chance of success, more will say 'yes' than if the same information is presented as 10 per cent chance of failure! Vivid information presented to a decision maker is likely to have greater impact than the same information presented in a dull manner. This may be understood in terms of concepts of bias considered in Chapter 5.

The presentation of information may be a particular issue in formal decision situations such as courts. Words may be easily misunderstood by different listeners, but on the other hand numbers can sometimes have an unjustified air of authority about them. There is little exploration in social work of communicating about probabilities with more visual means such as graphs or charts. One approach is to use both words and numbers, perhaps along the lines of: *Your honour, I would describe the likelihood as '. . . . .', meaning about x% based on relevant research and the evidence available in this case . . .* (cf. Carson and Bain, 2008, p167). There are various initiatives to create a useful correspondence between numbers and words, and one example is given here. We would emphasise, however, that any numbers used to convey probability need to be justified by sound research evidence, and that any words used to convey probability may need some explanation to avoid misunderstanding.

> **RESEARCH SUMMARY 4.2**
>
> *Terms to express likelihood in sexual abuse cases*
>
> - < 5%   *Very unlikely*
> - 5–20%   *Unlikely*
> - 20–40%   *Somewhat unlikely*
> - 40–60%   *Undetermined*
> - 60–80%   *Somewhat more likely than not*
> - 80–95%   *Likely*
> - > 95%   *Very likely*
>
> *(suggested by Wood, 1996)*

Rights, partnership and contested decisions

Social workers may be engaged in *contested decision making*. These decisions are required where there are conflicts between rights, responsibilities and interests, such as where statutory safeguarding powers are being exercised. There are particular issues where information is given anonymously or *in confidence*. Courts are a key mechanism in society to resolve such conflicts and have increasingly clear and stringent expectations of social work judgements. *Expressions of opinion must be supported by detailed evidence and articulated reasoning* (Munby J in Re M (Care Proceedings: Judicial Review) (2003) 2FLR 171 p183).

Safeguarding roles present many challenges for professionals in striving to engage clients and families in decision making and partnership working that will enable therapeutic change in relationships. It is important to be clear that such collaborative partnership working is not an end in itself. Rather, the aim is the protection of the child or vulnerable adult from abuse, neglect or self-harm, or the protection of others from crimes that might be committed by this individual. In such partnerships we should strive towards such goals as *fairness* and *openness*, recognising that as professionals with safeguarding responsibilities we have been given powers and duties by society in order to protect the most vulnerable (Morrison, 1998). The Department of Health (DH,1995) outlines four levels of partnership working that focus particularly on decision making in child protection, but can be applied in other areas of social work.

- Providing information.
- Passive involvement (for example attending a case conference).
- Participating actively, contributing to decision making.
- Joint decision making based on mutual trust, listening and openness.

Roles in court decisions and other formal settings

The most strongly contested decision-making processes are normally conducted in a court. Despite the most ardent efforts to achieve collaborative decisions it is sometimes essential to initiate legal proceedings to achieve a safeguarding decision. As a social worker you may be in court on behalf of an organisation that is a party to the proceedings (such as a statutory authority bringing an action to protect children from abuse) or you may be in court as an expert witness (for example providing a report in a private law dispute between separated parents about custody and access to their children). However, as you are appearing in your professional capacity even in the former case, the courts will generally treat you as an expert in relation to areas within your competence. It is essential to engage your line management, professional supervisor and legal advisor appropriately.

> You may find it surprising, in view of the emphasis on collaborative and inter-discipli-nary working, that in court you are not giving evidence as a member of a team, but as an individual. As an employee, you obviously have to follow the instructions of your managers; if, for example, it is decided in a case conference to recommend the initia-tion of care proceedings and you are instructed to take this forward, then you must do this. However once in court your primary duty is to the court, which requires you to give evidence of your personal knowledge and opinions, not those of anyone else . . . If the court wishes to hear from your team or service manager, or anyone else, then they can be called as a witness, and indeed should be if their views and decisions are important to the case.
>
> (Seymour and Seymour, 2007, p101)

Evidence in a court may include facts about the client, family and context. As a profes-sional you are expected to be knowledgeable in relevant areas, such as (in child care proceedings) attachment and bonding, child development and parenting that inform your judgement. You have to articulate the context, issues, facts, opinions, concerns and strate-gies. Quite apart from moral considerations, as an expert witness you are required by the court to provide a balanced overview of relevant research or theory, not a partisan selec-tion of favourable studies. In such formal decision situations you may be challenged on the facts of the case, on your credibility and on your competence.

It is important to be clear on limits to your competence and to respect the competence areas of other professions. Social workers may be regarded as experts in some child pro-tection issues (*F v Suffolk County Council* (1981) 2 FLR 208) (although it is open to the court to seek additional expert witnesses), but not in the diagnosis of sexual abuse (Re N (Child Abuse: Evidence) [1996] 2 FLR 214). It is often helpful to include in your report to the court or other formal decision forum a clear description of people involved and their relationship to the person at the focus of the decision, and a clear chronology of main events.

> The fullest possible information must be given to the court. The evidence in support of the application for such an order must be full, detailed, precise and compelling.

Unparticularised generalities will not suffice. The sources of hearsay evidence must be identified. Expressions of opinion must be supported by detailed evidence and articulated reasoning.

(Re M (Care Proceedings: Judicial Review) (2003) 2 FLR 171, 183)

The court wants to hear your opinion in order to help the judge or jury to reach a decision. The court needs to know how you formed your opinion so that it can fairly weigh up the arguments. Ensure that your opinions can be backed up by evidence.

A professional opinion expressed in a report should always be based on analysis of material contained in that report. Everyone who reads it should be clear on what facts your opinion is based and to what extent you have personal knowledge of those facts. You should always give the source of any facts of which you do not have personal knowledge, such as case records made before you took over the case.

(Seymour and Seymour, 2007, p73)

Making an ethical argument

Such contested decision making requires us to have logical processes for arguing a case. *Effective clinical reasoning requires skill in developing arguments, establishing the relevance of information to an argument, and evaluating the plausibility of assertions or claims* (Osmo and Landau, 2001, p489). Various frameworks might be used for the decision argument, depending on the context.

The work of Stephen Toulmin and his colleagues (1958) on ethical decision making offers a structured approach to constructing an argument. Explicit ethical argument prompts

---

PRACTICE EXAMPLE *4.2*

Establishing links in the decision argument

- *This was my starting point. I am aware of other potential starting points and I have borne these in mind as the assessment has proceeded.*

- *These were the actions I took to ensure that the child was safe while I gathered all the relevant information. I endeavoured to avoid actions that would prejudice future decisions.*

- *I formed the judgement that the issues causing concern in the case included these elements, and my view on the available evidence was that in these circumstances there could be harm to this degree.*

- *I therefore developed the following strategy to intervene, manage and reduce the risks in the case. These were the outcomes of the strategies.*

- *I can therefore now say that concerns identified have changed in the following ways and the level of risk to the child is now as follows.*

(Hollows, 2008, p58)

clearer engagement with values, knowledge, assumptions, feelings and experiences in arriving at the rationale for pursuing or refraining from a course of action. This model can be seen as a way to assist in guarding against arbitrariness and inflexibility in decision making when balancing the rights of the various individuals involved.

Table 4.1 Steps in explicit ethical argument
(Adapted from Toulmin (1958), Osmo and Landau (2001) and Duffy *et al.* (2006))

1. Make a **claim** about a particular matter or issue (for example, that care proceedings are the best option for a particular child).

2. Provide **grounds**, data or evidence for this claim (the particulars of this situation).

3. **Warrant** the relationship between the evidence and the claim (for example, making explicit reference to research, empirical evidence and theory in warranting and supporting the claim for care proceedings).

4. **Qualify** your claim by expressing degrees of confidence and likelihood that are associated with it (for example, the degree to which care proceedings will advance the welfare of the child based on the evidence presented).

5. Highlight the **limitations** of the claim and situations in which the claim might be weakened (for example, highlight the reasons why a Care Order is not ideal even though that is your conclusion).

6. **Justify** the warrant at stage 3 with further evidence (for example, additional research evidence, practice knowledge and theory to support the reasons for making the claim for care proceedings) to address the limitations.

Table 4.2 Some prompts for arguing your case
(Includes some ideas from Seymour and Seymour, 2007)

Attitude

- Be absolutely sincere and honest in arguing your case
- Aim to be the 'honest expert' on the issues within your competence
- Think of 'we' (i.e. including your employer) rather than 'I' as you speak

Content

- Know the detailed facts about your client, family and context.
- Take reasonable steps to ascertain the views of the client and family, treating them with respect even where you disagree.
- Outline the decision-making processes undertaken, including engaging the client, family and other stakeholders.
- Be able to explain what your profession and organisation has done, with what authority and why.

- Outline what support services your agency and others have offered and what help these have (or have not) been.

- Differentiate between fact, hearsay and opinion.

- Do not say anything that you cannot back up with evidence.

- Explain honestly and clearly the concerns of your agency, what changes are sought and how achievement towards goals will be assessed.

- Acknowledge weak points in the argument and address them before the opposition does.

Verbal aspects

- Don't repeat yourself except very sparingly.

- Keep it simple and to the point; avoid unnecessary detail.

- If you ramble, stop, apologise, say something along the lines of 'let me start again' and say what you want to say in a more focused way.

- You can 'suggest' rather than 'tell', using words such as 'indicated that'.

Non-verbal aspects

- Observe normal dress code to avoid distracting from the decision process.

- Consider the use of possible visual aids.

- Make eye contact as appropriate (and keep eye contact with the judge or magistrate when providing answers, not the barrister for the other party).

- Use short pauses to good effect.

- Gain the empathy of the decision maker(s).

- Vary pace and tone.

Chapter summary

- Decision making in social work in more complex situations often involves collaborating with colleagues from other professions and organisations, requiring good communication skills.

- Although multi-professional collaboration is very much to be encouraged, the responsibility of each profession and organisation needs to be clear.

- Communication about complex and contentious issues needs to be timely and clear, with empathy for the perspective of someone from a different profession or organisation.

- Some decisions are made in contentious arenas, such as child care court hearings. Steps are outlined to assist in reflecting on the quality of your argument for a professional opinion, particularly in the context of recommendations to a court.

**FURTHER
READING**

Carson, D. and Bain, A. (2008) *Professional Risk and Working with People: Decision-Making in Health, Social Care and Criminal Justice.* London: Jessica Kingsley.

This is an excellent book on the legal aspects of risk and decision making, particularly the tort of negligence and 'duty of care', and drawing out the way that the law supports as well as challenges decision making by professionals.

O'Sullivan, T. (1999) *Decision Making in Social Work.* London: Macmillan.

This is a useful book looking at engaging clients and other stakeholders such as professionals in decision-making processes.

Seymour, C. and Seymour, R. (2007) *Courtroom Skills for Social Workers.* Exeter: Learning Matters.

This is an excellent book on the interface between social work and the courts as an arena where we undertake contentious decision making.

Chapter 5

Professional judgement, bias and using knowledge

Good judgement comes from experience, and experience – well, that comes from poor judgement.

(Anonymous, quoted in Robertson (ed) 1996, p10) The Wordsworth Dictionary of Quotations Ware, Hertfordshire: Wordsworth Editions no. 212 p10

Introduction

Having set the scene in the earlier chapters on aspects such as client focus, emotions, the law and collaboration with others, Chapter 5 focuses on the process and challenges for the individual professional in making a judgement or reaching an opinion recommending a particular course of action. We consider the framing of decisions and the role of heuristics (short-cuts) and types of bias in professional judgement. The uses of professional knowledge in making judgements about individual situations are discussed. Reflective practice and use of professional supervision are illustrated as essential ways to minimise the effect of individual bias and ensure high standards of decision making in uncertainty.

Reflective practice and learning from experience

This chapter focuses on your individual cognitive processes in forming a judgement prior to or during engaging in decision processes with your client and organisation. How do we form an opinion about a situation? What basis of knowledge and principles come into play in our thinking processes? As social workers we are decidedly not infallible or all-knowing; we learn by using professional knowledge, concepts, theories and models to aid us in reflecting on our practice. As knowledge and skills become increasingly internalised with experience, decisions may become less conscious and might be described as more intuitive (Reynolds, 1965; Benner, 1984). We need to understand the processes of forming a judgement so that we can most effectively learn from experience, build on the best practice of ourselves and others, and teach those newer to the profession. We need to be able to become conscious of the application of our knowledge base – including such as law, psychology, sociology, human growth and development, mental health, illness, disability, criminology and social policy – so that we can minimise bias in the way that we apply it to the unique features of a particular decision and can explain our judgement process to those to whom we are accountable and those who might be learning from us.

An important part of professional skill is to recognise patterns and meanings in the complex information we receive about clients, families and their context. We have to consider these in relation to the professional roles that we carry, including responsibilities for safeguarding, gate-keeping scarce public or charitable resources, and co-ordinating the contributions of diverse professions and organisations into an integrated care process. We might use a model known as *recognition primed decision making* (Klein, 1996) in this facet of our decision making. Because of pressures such as time, rapidly changing circumstances and the need to get a quick overview to identify priority issues, a decision maker may *intuitively* look for similarities with problems tackled previously (Klein, 1996), which might be more efficient for this purpose than a detailed analytic approach, which time may not permit. By contrast, a more analytic approach would be used if the decision is more unusual or more contested and therefore requiring a clearer rationale and justification. Recognising a place for intuitive judgements is not an excuse to avoid the hard work of analysis that may be required to reach a sound, justifiable conclusion in complex cases. Judgements using knowledge and skills at the intuitive end of the spectrum are appropriate in certain contexts and may be the fruit of learning from sound training and years of reflective experience where theory and personal practice have been integrated to generate internalised wisdom.

One way of understanding the multiple factors that have to be taken into account in a professional judgement is through Egon Brunswick's *lens model* (Cooksey, 1996), which illustrates the decision maker using multiple cues for a decision as a parallel to the human eye taking in rays of light from various parts of the scene in view to form an internal image. The decision maker creates an internal representation of the relevant factors as a step in the tasks of seeing patterns and making sense of the data as part of *decision analysis*. It is interesting that research suggests that experts do not use more cues than novices, but rather that they are better at identifying factors that are most relevant to the decision (Gilovich *et al.*, 2002).

Context, role and framing judgements

A primary concept in professional practice is to clarify our role in relation to each situation. In relation to decision making a consideration of role alerts us to seeing ourselves as one player within what is often a complex situation, but nonetheless a useful contributor with a particular range of knowledge and skills. Among professions, social workers tend to have a holistic perspective on situations. The factors that we take into account in order to make sense of a complex, changing mosaic of information may be described as *framing the decision.* These factors include:

- the problem and who is facing what decision;
- your role and the aim of the social work intervention;
- needs, issues and strengths;
- past events, present situation, prospects;
- family, friends, neighbours, community and supportive groups;
- law, regulations, policies, procedures;
- function of your organisation and services available;
- relevant functions and services of other organisations;
- response to and effectiveness of previous services used;
- values, standards, principles;
- knowledge, research, theory and skills;
- potential bias from using this frame of reference.

Eileen Munro (1996, 1999) has studied how errors of reasoning can influence child protection judgements. One of her key conclusions is that the most common problem is that social workers are reluctant to change their minds in the light of new information.

In practice this means that social workers get a 'frame' on a case too quickly, and seek out information that will confirm that view. . . . A clear awareness of the inherent weaknesses in both practice and the systems of the organisations in which social workers operate could go a long way to reducing the problems.

(Hollows, 2008, p53)

ACTIVITY 5.1

Framing a decision
Recall a recent reasonably (but not exceptionally) complex case.

- *What frame of reference are you using for this decision?*

- *What effect might this have on the decision process and outcome?*

- *Reflect on the mental process that you went through in reaching a judgement.*

- *What were the most important factors considered and why?*

- *How did you process or bring together different aspects of the issue?*

Consistency of judgements

Research illustrates the inconsistencies in professional judgements in many areas of professional decision making (Beach and Connolly, 1997; Gilovich *et al.*, 2002), including various aspects of health and social care such as medical diagnoses of physical and mental illnesses (Eddy, 1996, Chapter 29), eligibility and safeguarding decisions in child protection (Spratt, 2001) and decisions about the long-term care of older people (Austin and Seidl, 1981). *Between the macro level of governmental risk management initiatives and the micro level of professional communication with an individual service user, there is a less explored domain of how health and social services professionals make sense of such complex issues in reaching a judgement about appropriate care* (Taylor, 2006b, p1413),

Heuristics and biases in judgements

The cognitive processes that might lead to bias may also be essential shortcuts or *heuristics* that aid us as human beings in making complex decisions in everyday life. Such heuristics are invaluable in simplifying decisions. It is neither possible nor efficient to go through life undertaking a detailed analysis for every decision. Such a journey would take us towards *analysis paralysis* or mental illness! The development of such heuristics can also be seen as part of the learning process by which we generalise from previous knowledge of similar decisions (Reynolds, 1965). We build on our decisions by creating internalised rules to help us to achieve the same result more efficiently in similar situations. The subsequent judgement is more efficient and possibly effective because of our previous experience, but also it may be biased by previous experience. A variety of ingenious experiments have been conducted in this field (Greeno, 1978; Kahnemann *et al.*, 1982; Kahnemann and Tversky, 2000). Most of the research tends to focus on these heuristics in terms of the way that they might distort our decision making from what might be a more objective outcome.

Table 5.1 Heuristics and biases

(Compiled from various sources including Baron (2008), Chapman and Elstein (2000), Hardman (2009), Kahneman and Tversky (2000), Luft (1969), Macdonald and Sheldon (1998), Munro (1996), Taylor (2006b), Thompson (2002) and Tversky and Kahnemann (2003))

• **Anchoring bias**	We often judge new situations in relation to some known 'related' point (for example, regarding normal child development or ageing) but this may be biased by an inappropriate judgement of what is normal.
• **Adjustment bias**	Judgements may be unduly influenced by initial information that shapes our gathering and perspective on subsequent information. New information is selectively processed to support judgements already made.
• **Compression bias**	We have a tendency to overestimate unlikely undesirable events (risks) and underestimate likely undesirable events.
• **Credibility bias**	We may be more likely to reject something if we have a bias against the person, organisation, or group to which the person belongs. We may be more inclined to accept a statement by someone we like.
• **Illusion of control**	Humans tend to underestimate future uncertainty because we tend to believe we have more control over events than we really do.
• **Optimism bias**	We tend to want to see things in a positive light and for them to turn out happily for all concerned.
• **Over confidence**	We have a tendency to be over confident about the extent and accuracy of our personal knowledge.
• **Prejudice**	Bias from conscious or unconscious stereotyping.
• **Recall bias**	(similar to availability bias and recency effect) Recent and dramatic cases or incidents in the team or the media can have an undue effect. Humans have a tendency to overestimate the likelihood of types of events that are familiar from their experience or where an event of this type becomes well known through conversation or the media.
• **Repetition bias**	A willingness to believe what we have been told most often and by the greatest number of different of sources.
• **Wariness of lurking conflict**	Staff may be anxious in case they are assaulted, subject of complaints, sued, censured, criticised by Inquiries, the media or politicians, etc.

Does it make a difference to your recommendation if you are the one who will go back to the client to tell him or her about the decision? How does resource availability fit into the decision-making process? How do the needs of other patients and clients affect your judgement (for example, problems of delayed discharge from hospital and the tendency to ignore the unseen clients on the waiting list)? Does it make a difference knowing that this client is related to a local politician, or has threatened to go to the press if he or she does not get what is demanded? Are such influences on the decision outcome legally permissible and ethically right?

CASE STUDY 5.1

Avoiding potential bias

Terence aged 15 is on Probation for stealing a car. My role is to advise, assist and befriend him with a view to reducing the likelihood of him reoffending, and also to assess the risk that he presents to others so as to protect society. In seeking to help Terence I am aware that I need to understand his world. My own upbringing was very different from his; he had no father or father-figure, he is living on a housing estate with a high crime rate, he is under pressure to conform and has received threats from peers and adult criminals. At each point where I am seeking to help him to take positive steps forward I have to consciously avoid the bias of my own upbringing.

- *What expectations do you have from your own upbringing and life in terms of such aspects as how to bring up children, how to respond to social pressures or threats or bullying, how to manage money, etc.?*

- *How can you tune-in most effectively to the circumstances of your clients, while also holding out for them hope for growth and change?*

On the other hand, errors may occur because of a lack of anchoring a judgement. For example, risk factors indicating a higher probability of abuse may be insufficiently understood or used, theories may be used that are untested, and theory and research may be used unsystematically (Munro, 1996). As humans we need categories and labels (which we relate to known *anchors* of knowledge) to make sense of the world; as professionals we need them to determine need for and eligibility for services. The very mechanisms that enable us to learn and to take complex decisions are also the same mechanisms by which we may be open to bias.

ACTIVITY 5.2

Avoiding bias

- *What benchmarks (anchors) am I using in judging client behaviour?*
- *Is my practice influenced by previous experiences: (a) growing up; (b) at work; (c) adult life outside work?*
- *What strengths and dangers are there for professional decisions in anchoring decisions in your own previous experience?*
- *Am I unduly influenced by recent or dramatic events?*
- *What ways are there to moderate against inappropriate bias?*
- *How do you learn from life and work experience yet avoid bias?*
- *On what am I basing my estimate of the probability of harm (or success)?*
- *Am I giving due weight to the various sources of information?*
- *Am I ensuring that I do not discriminate on such grounds as sex, ethnic origin or political persuasion?*
- *Am I unduly confident or over-optimistic?*
- *What would it take to change my mind since the last assessment point?*

Using professional knowledge to inform judgements

Although experience is a valuable source of knowledge, social workers who rely solely on personal experiences to inform their practice run the risk of bias (Darragh and Taylor, 2009, p149). We need to use sound professional knowledge in our judgement so as to be transparent and fair in our decision processes, and so as to achieve the best outcomes for clients. This has come to be known in recent decades as *evidence based practice,* although the essential principles are not new. The origins of social work in western democracies might be viewed as rooted in efforts to apply the question *what works?* to the endeavours of Christian and socialist charitable activities in the 19th century. The essence of *evidence based practice* is not that professional expertise will be rejected in favour of some mechanistic method. Rather, *evidence based practice* is about consciously identifying, understanding and using the best available relevant knowledge to inform practice decisions. It involves having skills such as being able to appraise the quality of research rather than treating something as completely authoritative when it lacks rigour, being able to consciously apply research and theory to practice, and for social workers in appropriate roles to contribute to the development of the profession's knowledge base through well-designed research on priority topics. Professional knowledge is important in decision making for the following reasons.

- *Well-informed decisions by social workers are vital to the immediate life opportunities and outcomes for clients and their families.*

- *Well-informed decisions may be regarded as a right for clients whose long-term well-being depends in part on social care decisions which can have a substantial impact over time.*

- *Where compulsory powers are exercised, requiring best evidence provides safeguards in the decision-making process.*

(Marsh *et al.*, 2005, pp3–4)

A growing number of organisations seek to distil and disseminate *best evidence* into a digestible format for busy practitioners and policy makers, utilising a variety of approaches (Walter *et al.*, 2004). In the United Kingdom, the Social Care Institute for Excellence (SCIE) promotes *better knowledge for better practice* in social care. When considering the usefulness of knowledge to inform our practice, there are two key questions.

- How robust, rigorous or good is the knowledge in its own right?

- How relevant is the knowledge to this client situation?

As a researcher, the challenge may be to design and carry out studies that will have the greatest credibility in informing practice within available resources. As a practitioner, we often have to rely on *good enough* studies, and accept that ideal studies are not available and perhaps not achievable within legal, ethical and resource constraints. A key issue is to understand the limitations of the knowledge that informs our decisions.

CASE STUDY 5.2

Using knowledge to inform a judgement

Benjamin is 12 years old and recently moved from primary to secondary school. His parents separated just prior to his change of school and his grandfather, to whom he was close, died shortly afterwards. His school attendance presented no problems at primary school, but his attendance at secondary school has been unsatisfactory and he has been referred by the school to the Education Welfare Service. Studies show that limited school attendance is a factor in mental health problems and social isolation, and also increased involvement in crime. Lengthy absence from school makes reintegration progressively harder. One conclusion of the assessment was that Benjamin's development had been arrested by the shock of his parents' separation and his grandfather's death. Benjamin's need to behave like a much younger child playing with cuddly toys was understood in terms of Bowlby's theory of attachment. A care plan was created to build self-esteem and confidence through a series of small successes using a task-centred approach.

- *What types of decisions most require a clear knowledge base?*
- *How can you access the knowledge that you require?*

RESEARCH SUMMARY 5.1

Difficulties in identifying risk factors for child abuse

- *Loose definitions of severity of abuse (e.g. combining mild bruising and multiple fractures as one category).*
- *Whether to study only court-confirmed cases, substantiated cases or also at-risk cases.*
- *Whether abuse reports are accepted at face value or judged by the researcher.*
- *Selection of cases for study (often based on centres with special expertise rather than typical child care teams or facilities).*

(Jones, 1998)

Using knowledge of the effectiveness of interventions

A crucial area where research could provide less biased knowledge than individual experience is on the effectiveness of interventions. We want to know whether clients in similar situations achieve better outcomes with one intervention rather than another. *To rule out other factors that might influence the outcome (such as family factors, age, and changes in society more generally), the best approach is to assign participants randomly to two groups, one (the 'experimental' group) that receives the intervention being studied and one (the 'control' group) that does not. This basic design is known as a randomised controlled study* (Darragh and Taylor, 2007, pp149–50). There are ethical as well as practical challenges in undertaking experimental studies in social work, and much research to be done if we are to make the substantial progress that is necessary to inform practice most effectively.

Decisions about types of interventions should be based on robust knowledge of *what works*. We might well question the value of a single research study, particularly as evidence in highly contested decisions such as in court. There is steadily increasing recognition that a *systematic review* of research (Dempster, 2003; Petticrew and Roberts, 2006) is of more value than any one individual study. A *systematic review* embraces:

- an explicit process of searching databases to retrieve all relevant research on the topic (Taylor, 2003; Taylor *et al.*, 2003);

- an explicit process of deciding which studies to include in terms of content and quality (Taylor *et al.*, 2007); and

- an explicit process for combining (synthesising) the studies to produce a unified message to inform practice (Fisher *et al.*, 2006).

CASE STUDY 5.3

Using research on effectiveness of interventions

As a Guardian-ad-Litem I am responsible for a case where Paul (aged 8 years) has been cared for by his mother who has an addiction problem. Paul was recently admitted to care on a voluntary basis as his mother knew that she was not coping well with him but Mrs Roberts has now requested that Paul be returned home. However, the child care social work department responsible for safeguarding children is concerned that she is not yet fit to resume custody of Paul. The legal advisor for Mrs Roberts is arguing that she no longer has an addiction problem having been to a well-known treatment programme.

- *What do you need to know about theories and research on addiction?*

- *What studies are there of the effectiveness of treatments for addiction?*

- *What do they tell us about recovery times and patterns?*

Using knowledge of the application of interventions

While it is important to know what types of interventions are most effective in particular sorts of situations, it is also important to understand helping processes in making a judgement on what intervention is appropriate. The views of clients can help to sensitise us to crucial issues. Some of the knowledge that is useful but less tangible and less amenable to generalisable research might include:

- perceptions of key stakeholders about *this problem* and possible ways forward;

- knowledge of resources to implement the proposed care plan or helping process;

- knowing what is needed to help the client to engage with the helping process (transport? child care? emotional challenges?).

We need to know what works and we need to know what is required to make it work in this particular situation. You need to know what works well for you as well as challenging yourself to extend your repertoire of skills. Personal experience is perhaps better in helping to adjust a method to the immediate situation than in judging what works generally.

Professional knowledge and reflective practice

A primary mechanism for professional development is reflecting on your practice in relation to professional knowledge and on your knowledge base in relation to practice experiences. Having the self-awareness to relate judgements to law, regulations, policies and procedures and professional knowledge is a safeguard against bias. Such professional knowledge may be drawn from theory and research on such issues as risk factors, causes of problems, and the effectiveness and processes of interventions. Donald Schon (1983) describes *reflection-in-action* as thinking on one's feet, involving looking to personal experiences, connecting with personal feelings, and attending to theories in use; while *reflection-on-action* entails building new understandings that inform individual actions in the situations that unfold, with the new understandings emerging after the encounter.

ACTIVITY 5.3

Prompts to aid reflection on your professional judgements
- *What was my role?*
- *What was the goal of the decision and intervention?*
- *What was the issue on which I had to form a judgement?*
- *What information about the client, family and situation was most significant in shaping my judgement?*
- *In what way did this information influence my judgement?*
- *What professional knowledge informed my judgement?*
- *What research or theory underpinned this knowledge?*
- *What particular challenges were there in this decision situation?*
- *What skills did I use?*
- *How could my judgement have been improved?*
- *What additional information or knowledge would I have liked to have had?*
- *What learning from this might inform my judgements in future?*

Chapter summary

- In making judgements about situations you may be influenced by your own childhood and by recent or dramatic life and professional experiences. If unrecognised, such influences can bias our judgements.

- The frame of reference that you use for a decision should be an explicit sound structure for a decision process and avoid inappropriate influences.

- Various types of bias that affect human decisions are considered, and also the place of these same characteristics as heuristics, or shortcuts, that we use in everyday judgements.

- There is a challenge for the profession in creating, locating, appraising, synthesising and using the best available evidence to inform practice.

- Reflective practice, professional supervision and robust, supportive systems in organisations are emphasised as tools to minimise the effect of individual bias and ensure highest standards of decision making.

FURTHER READING

Benner, P. (1984) *From Novice to Expert: Excellence and Power in Clinical Nursing Practice*. Menlo Park, CA: Addison-Wesley.

This book captures something of the journey from being a novice within a profession to having a more internalised knowledge base and greater ability to identify and respond to subtle cues that might be missed by those less experienced.

Campbell Collaboration (C2) **www.campbellcollaboration.org** – an international, non-profit and independent organisation dedicated to making available up-to-date, accurate information on the effectiveness of social, behavioural, educational and criminal justice interventions.

Cochrane Collaboration (CC) **www.cochrane.org** – an international, non-profit and independent organisation, dedicated to making available up-to-date, accurate information on the effectiveness of health and social care interventions.

Darragh, E. and Taylor, B.J. (2008) Research and Reflective Practice (Chapter 11, pages 148–60), in Higham, P. (ed) *Post Qualifying Social Work – From Competence to Expertise*. London: Sage.

This chapter in a textbook on post-qualifying social work focuses on the use of research within the learning processes of reflective practice for the skilled practitioner.

Gilovich, T., Griffin, D. and Kahneman, D. (2002) *Heuristics and Biases: The Psychology of Intuitive Judgement*. New York: Cambridge University Press.

This is a classic, comprehensive text summarising the best research describing how individuals make real-world judgements.

Hardman, D. (2009) *Judgement and Decision Making*. Oxford: Oxford University Press.

This is a well-written, detailed textbook for psychology students outlining the main theories and models of decision making and giving references to underpinning research.

Newman, T., Moseley, A., Tierney, S. and Ellis, A. (2005) *Evidence Based Social Work: A Guide for the Perplexed*. Lyme Regis: Russell House.

This is a very readable textbook outlining key stages for a practitioner in basing practice on best evidence, including skills in defining the practice evidence question, searching for relevant materials and appraising research.

Social Care Institute for Excellence (SCIE) **www.scie.org.uk** produces resources that summarise key messages for good practice. SCIE hosts the UK social work database: SocialCareOnline.

Thompson, C. and Dowding, D. (eds) (2002) *Clinical Decision Making and Judgement in Nursing.* Edinburgh: Churchill Livingstone.

This is an edited volume where contributors outline key elements that contribute to judgement and decision making in a profession with similarities to social work.

Chapter 6

Safeguarding judgements and predicting harm

CHAPTER OBJECTIVES

This chapter will help you to meet the following National Occupational Standards for Social Work.

- Key role 1, unit 3: Assess needs and options to recommend a course of action.
- Key role 3, unit 11: Prepare for, and participate in decision-making forums.
- Key role 4, unit 12: Assess and manage risks to individuals, families, carers, groups and communities.
- Key role 4, unit 13: Assess, minimise and manage risk to self and colleagues.
- Key role 6, unit 18: Research, analyse, evaluate, and use current knowledge of best social work practice.

This chapter will help you to meet post-qualifying requirements for social work in the UK such as the following.

- Work effectively in a context of risk, uncertainty, conflict and contradiction (The Post-Qualifying Award in Specialist Social Work (Generic Level Requirement vii.), General Social Care Council [England], 2004).
- Competence in working effectively in complex situations (Post-Qualifying Award, Requirement PQ2, *Scotland & Wales* (= *UK Framework 1990–2007*)).
- Competence in exercising the powers and responsibilities of a professional social worker, including the appropriate use of discretion and the management of risk (Post-Qualifying Award, Requirement PQ3, *Scotland & Wales* (= *UK Framework 1990–2007*)).
- Ability to make informed decisions (Post-Qualifying Award, Requirement PQ4, *Scotland & Wales* (= *UK Framework 1990–2007*)).
- Demonstrate consistent and sustained sound judgement and decision making in the context of complexity, risk, uncertainty, conflict and contradiction (Specific Award Requirement 3, Northern Ireland Post-Qualifying Education and Training Partnership, 2007).

Ideally [professionals] should protect all children who are at risk of abuse while not disrupting any family providing adequate care. Abused children should return only to families who have changed and no longer pose a threat to their offspring. These ideals however are impossible to achieve.

(Munro, 1996, p793)

Introduction

Chapter 6 focuses on the crucial issue of attempting to predict harm as an aspect of professional decision making, spurred by feelings of blame in our *risk society*. This is related to diverse practice issues from protecting child to supporting independence steps by people with a disability, as well as attempts to predict homicide, suicide and re-offending. We consider in particular the extent to which we can predict harm as seems to be expected by some media and politicians. This chapter highlights the issues involved in any assessment process where we are attempting to make a *yes-no* decision, as there will always be some people incorrectly identified as *at risk* and some incorrectly identified as *not at risk*. Actuarial and clinical prediction methods are explained and discussed in terms of their application in social work. We consider the social work role in relation to clarifying the mandate for intervening compulsorily in family life, and making a *criterion-based judgement* in relation to threshold criteria for statutory measures to protect an individual.

Risk, blame and predicting harm

A major challenge in social work practice is the apparent expectation of some media and politicians that social workers and other professionals should be able to predict precisely harm that may be caused to a human being, normally by another (violence, abuse) or by themselves (self-harm, self-neglect, avoidable accidents). This chapter explores how risk factors may be used to inform professional judgements and decisions and the limitations to human ability to predict harm (or anything else). Assessing the likelihood of harm is a particular focus in safeguarding decisions, where society provides statutory mandates for safeguarding measures to *protect this individual and others* (Taylor, 2006b; Tooth, 2009) from serious harm. We consider organisational responsibilities in relation to the *blame culture* in Chapter 10.

CASE STUDY 6.1

'They should have detected that he was a real danger to himself and others,' said Mrs Linda Abram regarding her son Michael Abram, later diagnosed paranoid schizophrenic, who broke into George Harrison's home on 30 December 1999 and stabbed him several times [quoted by Nigel Bunyan (2001) 'Doctors "let off hook" in report over ex-Beatle's attacker' Daily Telegraph 24 October]. Oxford Crown Court jury in 2000 accepted that he was insane at the time and ordered indefinite detention.

- *Who are 'they'?*

- *What is their responsibility?*

- *Could they have detected that he was a real danger?*

- *To what extent can such assaults be anticipated?*

The classic text by Brearley (1982) might be viewed as opening up the concept of *risk* in social work. Although social work has many ideas relevant to risk and its assessment and management, it was not until the 1980s and 1990s that it was conceptualised as such (DH, 1993). Since then, there has been an increasing focus on *risk* in social work as a way of thinking about our work. Increasing areas of social work are now being conceptualised in terms of assessing and managing *risk* of future harm rather than exclusively on meeting appropriate presenting needs. The focus on the likelihood of possible harm is most prominent in the areas of child protection (abuse), mental health (in relation to both homicide and suicide) and criminal justice (preventing re-offending), although protection of vulnerable adults from abuse and intra-familial ('domestic') violence are receiving increasing attention. The justification for providing services is increasingly conceptualised in terms of *risk* rather than *need*. However, what must be clearly understood is that there will always be a degree of error in any prediction about the future well-being of a client or family. *Since risk assessment is, by definition, making judgements under conditions of uncertainty, there is an unavoidable chance of error. It is impossible to identify infallibly those children [or other clients] who are in serious danger of abuse [or other harm]. Professionals can only make fallible judgements of the probability of [the undesirable event occurring]* (Munro, 2008, p40).

Predicting from professional experience

How will we as professionals predict harm? The starting point might be to look first to form a judgement based on intuition. Inevitably, this will be based on life experiences (both as a child and as an adult) that are often subconscious. With professional training we might more consciously draw on a knowledge base that includes such areas as human growth and development, psychology, law and sociology, as discussed above. With practice experience we can draw increasingly on our experience of similar cases, transferring knowledge to new situations by analogy. We may also draw on colleagues, utilising whatever knowledge and experience they have and can articulate with us. This type of process of forming an opinion based on a wide-ranging, useful but ill-defined body of practice knowledge and experience is known in the literature as a *clinical* approach to prediction.

There are several challenges in attempting to predict some undesirable event (for example, violence or abuse) using such a *clinical* approach.

- Judgements are often over-reliant on self-report of the person being assessed.

- Professionals may be exposed to a non-representative range of clients.

- Professional perceptions may be subject to bias such as more recent or more dramatic events having undue impact.

- Professionals may be subject to bias from economic considerations, political pressure and personal and societal prejudice.

- Professionals often get limited feedback on the outcomes of their interventions.

Psychiatrists and psychologists are accurate in no more than one out of three predictions of violent behaviour over a several-year period among institutionalised populations that have both committed violence in the past (and thus had high base rates for it) and who were diagnosed as mentally ill (Monahan, 1981, p48). We discuss below the significance of the frequency with which an event occurs (*base rate*) for the accuracy of prediction. I would not suggest that social workers are any more accurate than other professions at attempting to predict harm!

Can we improve on such intuitive approaches by developing more thorough methods? A key avenue for exploration is obviously to look at how often in the past a similar event has occurred. If we could understand past events better perhaps we could improve our predictive ability. We might ask what factors correlate with harm occurring. If we knew that, we might look out for such factors in future situations. This is called an *actuarial* approach. We aim to calculate the probability of harm to or by this individual on the basis of the frequency with which this event has occurred in the past.

Risk factors

The factors that are found to correlate with a specific undesirable outcome are generally known as *risk factors*. In order to use *risk factors* that correlate with some particular harm (such as abuse or neglect) occurring we can learn from approaches in the insurance industry. Actuaries calculate the likelihood of a ship being lost to storms or pirates and the value of a ship and its cargo to calculate the insurance premium accordingly. For example, if one ship in a thousand were lost then the insurance premium would need to be one thousandth of the average value of a ship and its cargo in order for the insurance company to break even (not counting operating costs).

Table 6.1 Risk factors for child abuse
(From Bridge, 1995; Dalgleish & Drew, 1989; Hagell, 1998; Macdonald, 2001)

Risk Factors (1) Parents

- *Parental expectations of child*
- *Parent's self-esteem*
- *Locus of control (impulse control)*
- *Child management skills*
- *Conflict resolution skills*
- *Mental illness*
- *Substance misuse*
- *Employment*

Risk Factors (2) Child

- *Premature birth*
- *Developmental history*

- *Learning disability*
- *Physical disability*
- *Temperament*
- *Behaviour*

Risk Factors (3) Family

- *Attachment*
- *Discord between parents*
- *Family history*
- *Domestic violence*
- *Family size*
- *Poverty*
- *Housing*

Risk Factors (4) Environment

- *Social isolation*
- *Social and educational resources*
- *Cultural and social values*
- *Social systems for identifying and managing abuse*
- *Legislation*

Clinical and actuarial approaches to predicting harm

Similarly, there are *actuarial* approaches in health and social care that seek to identify factors that correlate with particular (usually undesirable) outcomes (Munro, 1999; Kemshall, 2008). The same statistical approaches can in principle be applied to identifying the factors that correlate with any *social ill-health* or *social dis-ease*. The best developed actuarial approaches in social welfare work are in the prediction of re-offending (e.g. Hood and Shute, 2000; Maung and Hammond, 2000; Raynor *et al.*, 2000), homicide and violence by people with mental illness (e.g. Monahan *et al.*, 2001), suicide (e.g. Gunnell, 1994) and to a more limited extent, child abuse (e.g. Macdonald, 2001). This knowledge can be used to inform professional practice, for example through the design of assessment tools (McCormack *et al.*, 2008a and see Chapter 8). From such research we can identify factors that increase or reduce the probability of the outcome we are trying to avoid.

RESEARCH SUMMARY **6.1**

There are many studies of the risk factors for admission of older people to institutional care, using a wide variety of research methods. The main findings can be grouped as:

- *client needs*
  - o *cognitive functioning;*
  - o *physical functioning;*
  - o *medical condition;*
  - o *presentation of needs;*
- *demographic factors;*
- *services currently received;*
- *client choices;*
- *family support;*
- *capacity of family to cope.*

(Taylor and Donnelly, 2006b)

In our field of work we can start with a wide population base, and narrow down to more precise estimates of the likelihood of harm occurring. For example, if there are approximately 80 child homicides a year in England and Wales (Creighton, 2004a&b) in a population of approximately 12 million children (OPSI, 2009, estimating that approximately 90 per cent of children in the UK live in England and Wales), then a first estimate of the probability of any particular child in England and Wales being deliberately killed by another person this coming year is 80 in 12 million or 1 in 150,000. If we have more precise data about sub groups of children we can make more accurate estimates. For example, if we knew that urban children were three times as likely to be killed as children living in rural areas (I know of no evidence for this, it is purely an example) and there were equal numbers of children living in rural and urban areas, then the likelihood of homicide for a child living in a rural area would be 20 in 6 million (1 in 300,000) and for a child living in an urban area it would be 60 in 6 million (1 in 100,000). If we were to calculate the effect of identified risk factors such as those in Table 6.1 we could make a more precise estimate.

It is possible to express the probability in terms of the increased likelihood of harm to, or by, this individual. Table 6.2 illustrates *risk factors* for suicide, which have been calculated in terms of how much more likely it is that an individual will commit suicide if he or she is described by that factor. For example, a person who is unemployed, a farmer or a doctor in England and Wales, is twice as likely to commit suicide in any particular year as the average person in the whole population.

Table 6.2 Suicide risk factors (England and Wales) (Gunnell, 1994)

• First 4 weeks after discharge from psychiatric hospital – male	*200
• First 4 weeks after discharge from psychiatric hospital – female	*100
• History of parasuicide	*10–*30
• Alcohol abuse	*20
• Drug misuse	*20
• Samaritan client	*20
• Current or ex-psychiatric patient	*10
• Prisoner	*5
• Doctor	*2
• Farmer	*2
• Unemployed	*2

* For a person with the characteristic indicated in the left hand column, multiply the average suicide rate for the population by the factor given in the right hand column.

Types of risk factors: clusters, static and dynamic factors

Researchers often focus on particular clusters of risk factors, because the issues have to be made manageable conceptually and so as to complete studies with limited resources. *Risk factors* may be considered in categories such as:

• *historical or developmental factors;*

• *dispositional or personal factors;*

• *symptom (presenting issue) factors; and*

• *contextual or situational factors* (Righthand et al., 2003, p35).

What is important for practice is to identify the risk factors that present the greatest threat (Jones, 1998) and that are amenable to influence, and to indicate how these will be addressed in the care (or safeguarding or risk) plan. Although the relative importance of risk factors has been explored for predicting certain types of reoffending and for homicide and suicide by people with mental health problems, the work on risk factors in child abuse and many other areas of social work is less well researched (Taylor and Zeller, 2007). Studies often identify *static* risk factors such as age, gender and past events which are not amenable to intervention. What is of more interest to us is *dynamic* risk factors such as anger, impulsivity and thought patterns which might be a target for helping a client to change and hence reduce the likelihood of harm.

Another form of analysis with less precise risk factors is to create categories. For example, Agathanos-Georgopolou and Browne (1997) create three categories – high, medium and low probability of the undesirable event – in relation to predicting physical abuse of children. Risk factors may be incorporated into professional assessment tools, which we discuss further in Chapter 8.

Statistical prediction in practice

The majority of studies show that *actuarial prediction* is more accurate than *clinical prediction* (Meehl, 1954; Dawes *et al.*, 1989; Plous, 1993), despite measures by professionals to avoid bias. It is rare to find a study showing *clinical prediction* as more accurate than *actuarial*. There are a number of reasons why this is common sense. Firstly, factors that are studied and refined for actuarial prediction are those identified by clinicians (i.e. professionals, including social workers) as being the most worthy of study. As further factors are identified by professionals they are defined more closely and studied so as to determine whether or not this factor really does influence the outcome. They thus become *risk factors* amenable to an *actuarial* approach. Secondly, human beings are sometimes inconsistent with their own *decision rules* due to stress, tiredness or emotion. Some actuarial tools modelled precisely on an individual decision maker's own rules can predict more consistently than the individual on whom it is based. We need to strengthen professional practice with actuarial (statistical prediction) approaches to overcome the inherent bias of each professional relying on their own individual experience only, while also recognising the limitations of actuarial tools.

RESEARCH SUMMARY **6.2**

Grove and Meehl (1996) appraised 136 studies comparing clinical with actuarial prediction in medicine and psychology. Of the 136 studies, 64 showed that actuarial prediction was more accurate; eight showed clinical prediction as more accurate; and in the other 64 studies there was no significant difference between actuarial and clinical prediction.

Having argued that actuarial methods of prediction based on the measured frequency of past events is superior to unaided professional judgement we now outline the major difficulties facing any attempt to predict future events in relation to a particular individual. We focus on the prediction of possible harm, but the same argument applies to the prediction of the possible benefits of decision outcomes as discussed in Chapter 7.

Generally, major foreseeable harm that may befall individuals is addressed in terms of insurance for people or organisations that are facing the same type of undesirable outcome (car accident, home fire, burglary, travel disruption, etc.). Such situations require us to predict the likelihood (and costs) of undesirable consequences across a range of similar situations. For example, in car insurance the likelihood of harm is now calculated in relation to sub-sets of drivers. Young drivers are sometimes charged higher car insurance premiums because studies have shown that young drivers are more likely to have accidents. In this context it is sufficient to predict that this group of drivers is more likely to have accidents and to charge higher premiums to those that fit the criteria.

Health and social care professionals seem on occasions to be expected by some of the media to predict harm by or to an identified individual, which mathematically is totally different from predicting the general level of harm to a population (Littlechild and Reid, 2007). This apparent expectation is equivalent to expecting an insurance company to predict which *particular* young drivers will have an accident! As another example, on a population level we may be able to do an experiment to show that a certain type of advertising of washing powder produces a measurable increase in sales. That is quite different from trying to predict whether an identified Mrs Smith will alter her purchasing behaviour in response to a particular advertising campaign! Our professional task is intrinsically about predicting individual human behaviour. Human beings have free will to choose, and the outcomes of their decisions are not always rational or predictable.

False positives and false negatives

Trying to predict rare events such as abuse among a large and diverse population presents particular problems, as can be illustrated. Imagine that we have an assessment tool that we are proposing to use to predict some particular undesirable harm. There are four possible outcomes, in that the assessment tool will:

- correctly predict the harm (called a *true positive* because the tool correctly identified the thing that we want to predict); or

- indicate that harm will not occur, but it does (called a *false negative*); or

- correctly predict that harm will not occur (called a *true negative*); or

- indicate that harm will occur, but it does not (called a *false positive*).

ACTIVITY 6.1

Using an assessment tool to predict harm
Assume that you have a test that is 90 per cent accurate at predicting harm and in predicting that harm will not occur. The task is to predict a rare event (such as abuse, violence or suicide) that occurs 1 in 10,000 people per year in the population served by your team, assumed for this activity to be a population of 100,000 people. In the table below, the first column represents situations where the tool predicts that harm will occur, and the second column that it will not. The upper row is where harm does in reality occur, and the lower row where it does not. The task is to identify issues in using the tool by calculating how many are correctly and incorrectly identified by completing the four angle brackets <1>, <2>, <3> and <4>.

TOOL: REALITY:	Yes harm	No harm
Yes harm	<1> *True positive*	<2> *False negative*
No harm	<4> *False positive*	<3> *True negative*

No prediction tool will be 100 per cent accurate. For our purposes we will describe a 90 per cent accurate tool as one that is 90 per cent accurate in predicting harm and 90 per cent accurate in predicting that harm will not occur. When you undertake the Activity you will have a graphic illustration of the challenge in using an assessment tool to predict harm. Table 6.3 illustrates the application to trying to predict suicide (as an example of an undesirable harmful outcome) using real data.

Table 6.3 Using a 90 per cent accurate tool to predict suicide
The suicide rate for Northern Ireland in 2006 was 227 male and 64 female (Northern Ireland Statistics and Research Agency, 2007). For our purpose we will treat this as approximately 300 suicides in a population of about 1.5 million, i.e. 2 in 10,000 people in the year. Could we use a screening (assessment) tool incorporating risk factors to identify these people so as to target services?

- Approximately 300 people commit suicide, so approximately 1,499,700 do not.

- With a 90 per cent accurate tool, we will correctly identify 270 (90%) of the 300 suicides that actually occur (true positives) and will fail to identify 30 (10%) of the suicides (false negatives).

- We will correctly identify 1,349,730 (90% of 1,499,700) situations where no suicide occurs (true negatives) and will incorrectly identify 149,970 (10%) individuals as being likely to commit suicide when they do not (false positives).

TOOL: REALITY:	Yes harm	No harm	Total
Yes harm	270	30	300
No harm	149,970	1,349,730	1,499,700
Total	150,240	1,349,760	1,500,000

As you can see, the crucial issue is not so much the *false negatives*, the situations that we unfortunately miss because of the limitations of our tool. The real issue is the many non-risky situations that are identified as being *risky* with consequences for rights of individuals and for workloads of professions, teams and organisations. In this case, about 150,000 people would be wrongly identified as being at risk of suicide. Trying to predict rare events such as abuse, violence or suicide in a large population presents particular problems.

> *False negatives are extremely easy to spot with the benefit of hindsight. False positives on the other hand often can't be spotted even after the event because we can never be sure what would have happened. . . . But the fact is that false positives can also be a disaster for a child. A false positive might mean a family broken up, a child separated from parents in order to avoid a perceived danger, which in fact would never actually have come to pass.*

(Beckett, 2008, p46)

Base rates and other challenges in prediction

A key challenge to the use of prediction data in health and social services assessment is that statistical prediction is less useful in predicting the likelihood of events (such as abuse, violence or self-harm) that occur only rarely (Gigerenzer, 2002; Munro, 2008). This problem leads to many fallacies in reasoning, even in some Inquiries into child abuse tragedies (Parton *et al.*, 1997). The sensitivity of the assessment tool in correctly identifying situations where the harm will occur, and the specificity in correctly identifying the situations where harm will not occur, have to be related to the incidence of the harm within a particular population of people during a stated time interval.

> *One of the key findings in the literature pertaining to human aggression and inter-personal violence is that violence is very difficult to predict . . . violence is a rare event, and rare events are inherently difficult to predict because of what is known as the base rate problem. Put simply, if an event occurs one time in one hundred thousand . . . it is exceptionally difficult to predict the one time in one hundred thousand that it will occur.*

> (Righthand *et al.*, 2003, pp33–4)

Of course, to make a calculated prediction from among those referred to a social work team (provided the numbers analysed are sufficiently large) should be more accurate as the incidence of the undesirable harm is likely to be higher in that group of people than in the whole population. Similarly, predicting re-abuse (on which there is very little research) may give scope for greater accuracy than predicting abuse among the general population.

Predicting harm – achievements, challenges and prospects

Predicting serious re-offending by known serious offenders is probably the best researched area of prediction studies relevant to social work. The best statistical (actuarial) tools in this area are achieving overall accuracy rates of 70–80 per cent (Beaumont, 1999). This is useful to underpin a professional judgement, and such risk factors built into an assessment tool will support staff in focusing their minds on key issues. However, even at this level of accuracy we must be conscious of its limited use in practice in terms of prediction. *Trying to predict serious offending (even amongst known serious offenders) is the researcher's equivalent of hunting a needle in a haystack* (Beaumont, 1999, p84). The tools available for predicting harm in other areas of social work such as abuse, suicide and neglect are more limited.

ACTIVITY **6.2**

Repeat Activity 6.1 above, using a prediction tool with 70 per cent accuracy.

Consider the implications for practice of the false positives.

The problems of false positives as well as false negatives are a greater problem with a less accurate tool. But in case you are tempted to retreat from this statistical endeavour, recall that professional (clinical) judgements alone almost always achieve less accurate prediction when compared! Although these alternatives have been contrasted here, in practice social workers make use of assessment tools that embody both tested (actuarial) factors and those that are less thoroughly researched but based on professional consensus. Professional (clinical) factors (i.e. knowledge of child and family perspectives, professional knowledge of nuances of family and cultural context, etc.) come into their own in the care planning stage of intervention, and we discuss this more fully in Chapter 9.

Criterion-based judgements and decision policies

Every day social workers ask themselves questions along these lines.

- Is this family safe for this child or can it be made safe?
- Does the possibility of harm to this child require removal from the family?
- Is this parent's recovery from addiction, etc sufficient for this child to return home?
- How safe is this person with a disability living with this level of independence?
- What harm might this person with mental illness do to himself or herself?
- What risk (probability and seriousness) of harm does this person pose to others?
- To what extent does this older person understand the risks they are taking?

We recognise that safeguarding measures by their nature often require client choice to be over-ridden in the interests of another person or the individual themselves. *There is a delicate balance between empowerment and safeguarding, choice and risk. It is important for practitioners to consider when the need for protection would override the decision to promote choice and empowerment* (DH, 2007, p30, para 2.50).

In these types of decisions the task is to draw a line between dangerous and safe situations, situations requiring safeguarding or not. Such thresholds (criteria) are common in social work – for example, thresholds of significant harm, criteria for Approved Social Workers regarding compulsory admission of patients to psychiatric hospital and eligibility criteria for social care services. The implication of policy guidance is often that there is a threshold. The task is to identify whether the *risk* puts the child or vulnerable (using the term very broadly) adult above or below the threshold so that the vulnerable individual (in this document a child) *is provided with immediate protection in situations where their life is at risk or there is a likelihood of sustaining a serious injury if this action is not taken* (Department of Health Social Services Inspectorate, 1993, para 14).

Although major thresholds are outlined in statutes, regulations and organisational policies, we also use decision policies and thresholds created by professional standards. Examples might be where a judgement has to be made about parenting ability, or the safety of a person who is elderly or disabled living alone. Sometimes, such thresholds are incorporated into tested assessment tools, which we discuss further in Chapter 8.

> *The basic problem addressed by practice policies is that most health [and social work] decisions are too complicated to be made on a one-by-one, day-to-day basis. . . . If every practitioner attempted to do this [making the entire decision from scratch] for every decision, the result would be either mental paralysis or chaos. Practice policies have been used for centuries to help solve this problem by enabling practitioners and researchers to analyse decisions before the fact, cast the conclusions as policies, and apply the policies to simplify future decisions. While many decisions can be addressed only on an individual basis, others recur frequently in similar forms. It is these 'generic' decisions that are the targets of practice policies.*

(Eddy, 1996, p18)

The essential judgement and decision task in such situations might be considered as a *criterion-based judgement.* In other words, the task is to decide whether this situation is above or below the *line,* using a *decision policy* to give consistency. A *decision policy* is a set of rules for making a decision in a defined range of situations, created and adopted by an individual, group or organisation in order to simplify decision processes or to standardise decision outcomes. Such decision policies may come from legislation, regulations and guidance of government; aims, principles, strategies, policies and procedures of organisations; personal and professional values; theoretical models and research; and understanding and interpretation of patterns from experience of similar situations. Such decision policies enable organisations and individuals to be more consistent in their decisions, and thereby have greater credibility (Taylor, 1999). Such decision policies may use thresholds used to define eligibility for services, as in the example for publically funded child care services below.

1. *Base Population*

2. *Children with Additional Needs*

3. *Children in Need*

4. *Children with Complex or Acute Needs*

(DCSF, 2009)

We might view *standards* and *regulations* as inflexible decision policies, mandating what must always be done. By contrast, *guidelines* serve as recommendations or reference points that should be followed generally but an argument can be made for adapting them to individual circumstances. Despite efforts to clarify thresholds for decisions, there is still scope for professional discretion to take account of individual circumstances of the client or family in safeguarding or service eligibility decisions. If there is no mandatory decision policy, or you are still undecided after applying all external relevant decision policies, then you might consider using your own professional decision policy. If the application of relevant decision policies still leaves much scope, an individual approach to the decision (or these factors of the decision) may be more appropriate, *balancing benefits and harms* as discussed in Chapter 7.

Practice issues in predicting harm and safeguarding decisions

The capacity of any person to predict a particular harmful event through either experiential (clinical) or statistical (actuarial) methods is limited.

> *Research therefore cautions us that [in mental health] as in other fields such as medicine and child protection there is no such thing as a 'risk free' assessment . . . There are NO criteria which enable us to place individuals into sharply defined, once-and-for all categories of 'dangerous' or 'not dangerous' [or at risk of a particular harm, etc.]. Rather there is a continuum of statistical risk with uncomfortably limited predictive capacity.*

(Perry and Sheldon, 1995, p18)

Rather than seeking to define an individual as a *risk* or not, it is often more productive to consider *relevant environmental and personal variables, and their inter-relationships both now and historically* (Jones, 1998, p91). Some factors will carry greater weight in seeking to predict harm. Statistical methods of looking at the interaction effects between risk

---

CASE STUDY 6.2

Thresholds and creativity for a safeguarding intervention

I am a social worker in a community mental health team for older people. Mr Gardner is an 81-year-old man with Alzheimer's dementia. Mr Gardner has consistently refused to allow care workers or family to light his fire, even in the coldest weather. There is no other heating in the home. The manager of the home care worker has recently informed me of the increased risk due to lack of heating. Mr Gardner's insight into the risks was impaired, and the family advised that he was always very adamant when he had made up his mind. Mr Gardner absolutely refused to consider moving elsewhere; he had lived 40 years in this house and said that he sensed his wife's spirit in the home even though she had died years earlier. In discussions with other professionals it was agreed that there was a substantial risk of serious physical harm to Mr Gardner.

The possibility of needing to initiate a compulsory removal under mental health legislation for his well-being prompted consideration of alternative solutions to manage the risk. On the basis of an assessment of capacity it was clear that Mr Gardner was unable to make a competent decision regarding this issue. The consultant psychiatrist suggested that an electrical safety heater might be placed behind a table at the far end of the living room without Mr Gardner knowing. This could safely raise the temperature of the room to a level that would reduce risk, and thereby avert the need for a distressing removal from his home. This was regarded as being in his best interests.

- *Think of a recent situation where you have faced an ethical conflict because a client is putting themselves in danger through not recognising a serious threat to their health and well-being?*

- *What are the main issues in resolving such dilemmas?*

85

factors will undoubtedly increase the accuracy of our predictions beyond an intuitive approach in time. However, the development of methods for combining risk factors within a practice tool is still in its infancy in social work.

As a competent professional you should be knowledgeable on risk factors for the safeguarding areas of your practice. No less might be expected by a court or an educated member of the public. However, you also need to be able to explain why such *prediction* is limited in its usefulness in relation to individuals. We are not just assessing the situation now, but are concerned about what harms might occur in the future in the light of changing circumstances and possible professional interventions (Hollows, 2001). We also need to be aware of the emotion that may arise. A false positive in a medical test may elicit an emotional response of *phew* when you discover subsequently that you do not have the illness after all; in social work a false positive may be a child taken into care inappropriately and a family wrongly disrupted.

Risk factors work well for strategic planning of services. You can estimate relatively accurately across a large population how many homicides, suicides and abuse cases are likely to occur each year and use this information in planning services and setting budgets. The much greater challenge – perhaps impossibility – is in predicting harm to a particular individual. Use risk factors whenever available to assist in forming a judgement, but beware of their limitations. *Lists of risk factors, therefore, can do no more at the present time than suggest to practitioners that they might look again at their established or settled perceptions of risk* (Perry and Sheldon, 1995, p19). In practice we more often use *fuzzy* approaches to considering the relative strength of risks and the interplay between them, as discussed more fully in the next chapter.

CASE STUDY **6.3**

Resilience

Jack and Ruby Harris are in their late twenties and have two children aged 3 years and 5 years. Social work involvement began two years ago due to Ruby's mental health problems and alcohol misuse. There are concerns about the children's welfare when in the care of their mother. Resilience and protective factors in this situation are that both Jack and Ruby are engaging with services to get help, the children present as happy in the family home, and Jack is supportive to his wife and can recognise when her mood is deteriorating.

Use of risk factors may raise ethical issues of stigma and bias. For example, poverty is a risk factor for child abuse (i.e. a child living in poverty is more likely to be abused than one who is not) (Macdonald, 2001). However, it remains a fact that most children living in poverty are not abused. We must be wary of false positives (as above) as well as false negatives. As reports predicting possible harm containing statistics (such as might be derived from prediction based tools) can have an air of authority about them it is important that we give a warning about the limitations of such figures, while at the same time demonstrating how they have informed our professional judgements and actions.

One of the dangers is that our attempts to put language to the complex and inter-related concepts involved in judgement and decision making itself steers our thinking in ways that we have not anticipated. In particular, we need to be wary that once we start talking about *risk* we do not become trapped in a situation where neither professionals nor organisations are prepared to describe a situation as *low risk* for fear of consequences if something goes wrong. The use of alternative terms such as *concerns* may help in developing a deeper understanding of behaviour in its context (Morrison and Henniker, 1999).

Chapter summary

- The focus of social work has moved over the past few decades from improving people's welfare when they present for help to trying to manage the possibility of harm in the future. Some media and politicians seem to expect social workers to be able to predict all future harm.

- Risk factors give an estimate of how much more likely this individual is to come to harm than an average member of the population. Risk factors that have been tested through thorough research are the best tools we have to inform decisions about the likelihood of harm. Where available, risk factors can inform judgements in relation to diverse practice issues from child protection to independence steps by people with a disability, as well as attempting to predict homicide, suicide and re-offending.

- In any assessment process where we are attempting to make a yes-no prediction about individual behaviour there will always be some incorrectly identified as at risk of harm and some incorrectly identified as not at risk, as well as those correctly identified.

- Where the social work role involves compulsory intervention in family life it is important to clarify the mandate for action. A *criterion-based judgement* is often required in relation to threshold criteria for statutory measures to protect an individual.

FURTHER READING

Beaumont, B. (1999) Risk Assessment and Prediction Research, in Parsloe P (ed) *Risk Assessment in Social Care and Social Work.* London: Jessica Kingsley.

This is a useful chapter on the possibilities and pitfalls of prediction as an aspect of risk assessment in social work.

Calder, M.C. (ed) (2008) *Contemporary Risk Assessment in Safeguarding Children.* Lyme Regis: Russell House.

This volume contains some excellent chapters on current issues and technical developments in safeguarding children, which might be generalised to other contexts.

Gigerenzer, G. (2002) *Reckoning with Risk: Learning to Live with Uncertainty.* London: Allen Lane The Penguin Press.

This is a popular book highlighting the dilemmas and common misunderstandings about probability, for example regarding the likelihood of success or undesirable side effects.

Monahan, J., Steadman, H.J., Silver, E., Appelbaum, P.S., Robbins, P.C., Mulvey, E.P., Roth, L.H., Grisso, T. and Banks, S. (2001) *Rethinking Risk Assessment: The MacArthur Study of Mental Disorder and Violence.* Oxford: Oxford University Press.

This is a detailed book outlining improved approaches to predicting harmful events, in this case in relation to violence by people with a mental disorder.

Munro, E. (2008) *Effective Child Protection.* 2nd ed. London: Sage.

This is a valuable book focusing on decision making in child protection and child welfare work, and exploring useful concepts to develop professional knowledge and skills.

Chapter 7
Taking risks: values, gains and hazards

CHAPTER OBJECTIVES

This chapter will help you to meet the following National Occupational Standards for Social Work.

- Key role 1, unit 3: Assess needs and options to recommend a course of action.

- Key role 2, unit 9: Address behaviour which presents a risk to individuals, families, carers, groups and communities.

- Key role 4, unit 12: Assess and manage risks to individuals, families, carers, groups and communities.

- Key role 6, unit 18: Research, analyse, evaluate, and use current knowledge of best social work practice.

This chapter will help you to meet post-qualifying requirements for social work in the UK such as the following.

- Work effectively in a context of risk, uncertainty, conflict and contradiction (The Post-Qualifying Award in Specialist Social Work (Generic Level Requirement vii.), General Social Care Council [England], 2004).

- Competence in working effectively in complex situations (Post-Qualifying Award, Requirement PQ2, *Scotland & Wales (= UK Framework 1990–2007)*).

- Competence in exercising the powers and responsibilities of a professional social worker, including the appropriate use of discretion and the management of risk (Post-Qualifying Award, Requirement PQ3, *Scotland & Wales (= UK Framework 1990–2007)*).

- Ability to make informed decisions (Post-Qualifying Award, Requirement PQ4, *Scotland & Wales (= UK Framework 1990–2007)*).

- Demonstrate consistent and sustained sound judgement and decision making in the context of complexity, risk, uncertainty, conflict and contradiction (Specific Award Requirement 3, Northern Ireland Post-Qualifying Education and Training Partnership, 2007).

Sarayu laughed. 'I am here Mack. There are times when it is safe to touch, and times when precautions must be taken. That is the wonder and adventure of exploration, a piece of what you call science – to discern and discover what we have hidden for you to find.'

'So why did you hide it?' Mack inquired.

Why do children love to hide and seek? Ask any person who has a passion to explore and discover and create. The choice to hide so many wonders from you is an act of love that is a gift inside the process of life.

(Young, 2008, p132)

Introduction

We begin Chapter 7 by considering the way we value health and social well-being, and the motivation to reduce harm and dis-ease in society. We discuss the tensions between the principles of Health and Safety at Work legislation to take *reasonable steps to protect others from harm*, and the professional role and responsibility to take reasonable risks and to support clients in taking reasonable risks to further care plan goals such as greater independence, motivation, quality of life and re-uniting families. We consider briefly the personal safety of staff. This chapter then focuses on the social worker making judgements involving *balancing benefits and harms* and supporting clients in doing the same, drawn from the well-established Expected Utility models of decision making. *Vulnerabilities*, *triggers* and *strengths* are considered as a non-statistical approach to weighing evidence to form a judgement.

Risk, health and social well-being

Risk is essentially about uncertainty and as such pervades all of life and occupies much of our social discourse and public policy debates. Is it ever appropriate to *take risks* or should we, morally or legally, always seek to *avoid risks*? How can we justify risk-taking in decisions, for example, a business making a *risky* investment decision or a health and social care authority supporting a *risky* patient or client care plan? It has been argued that we live in a *risk society* (Beck, 1992) because risk has a different significance than in previous historical eras (Gigerenzer, 2002). One of the side effects of technological and social advances means that we sometimes need specialised expertise to identify and assess the dangers we face.

ACTIVITY 7.1

Risk taking in everyday life

- *What risks do you consciously take in your everyday life?*

- *Now that you are reflecting on these issues afresh, what other risks do you take on a daily basis in living at home, going to work and undertaking recreational activities?*

- *How do you justify to yourself taking these risks?*

- *Do some risks change from being conscious at one stage and then becoming less conscious when they are a regular part of your life?*

Health and safety at work

As societies have evolved they have developed increasingly sophisticated mechanisms to protect the health and well-being of their citizens. From simple beginnings, legislation about health and safety at work has now become a major feature in many countries. Such legislation was a response to the increasing number of deaths and accidents during the Industrial Revolution, perhaps caused by such aspects as the higher concentration of people into larger workplaces and the greater use of machinery.

The current underpinning statute in Great Britain is the Health and Safety at Work Act, 1974, and in Northern Ireland the Health and Safety at Work (NI) Order, 1978. The Health and Safety Executives established by this statute aim to *prevent death, injury and ill health in workplaces* (HSE, 2009a).

Table 7.1 Health and safety law: what you need to know

What employers must do for you

1   *Decide what could harm you in your job and the precautions to stop it. This is part of risk assessment.*

2   *In a way you can understand, explain how risks will be controlled and tell you who is responsible for this.*

4   *Free of charge, give you the health and safety training you need to do your job.*

5   *Free of charge, provide you with any equipment and protective clothing you need, and ensure it is properly looked after.*

10   *Work with any other employers or contractors sharing the workplace or providing employees (such as agency workers), so that everyone's health and safety is protected.*

What you must do

1   *Follow the training you have received when using any work items your employer has given you.*

2   *Take reasonable care of your own and other people's health and safety.*

3   *Co-operate with your employer on health and safety.*

4   *Tell someone (your employer, supervisor, or health and safety representative) if you think the work or inadequate precautions are putting anyone's health and safety at serious risk.*

(Health and Safety Executive, 2009b, extract)

The general approach is that employers and those who create risk are responsible for managing it, and that employees have a right to protection but also a duty to care for themselves and others. In our context *others* might include staff in your own or other organisations, and visitors to work premises including users of services. As the focus of the legislation is workplace health and safety, what is less clear is the definition of *a place of work* for those such as a home care worker or foster parent, and the implications of extending legislation designed for factories, mines and offices into people's homes (Taylor and Donnelly, 2006a).

Look at the website of the Health and Safety Executive and identify publications relevant to your work such as those relating to:

Stress: **www.hse.gov.uk/pubns/stresspk.htm**

Slips and trips resulting in falls: **www.hse.gov.uk/pubns/hsis2.pdf**

Violence at work: **www.hse.gov.uk/pubns/indg69.pdf**

Working alone in safety: **www.hse.gov.uk/pubns/indg73.pdf**

Minimising situational hazards

The Health and Safety Executive defines a *hazard* as something that may cause harm. Relevant examples might be a slippery mat on the floor in the home of an older person or poor hygiene by someone with a learning disability. A *risk* is considered as the chance that somebody could be harmed by a *hazard* and an indication of how serious that harm could be (HSE, 2009d). The following points help to assess the risks in your workplace.

1. *Identify the hazards.*

2. *Decide who might be harmed and how.*

3. *Evaluate the risks and decide on precaution.*

4. *Record your findings and implement them.*

5. *Review your assessment and update if necessary.*

(HSE, 2009d)

Risks in your work role
- *What does 'risk' mean in your job?*

- *What types of risks are involved in your work?*

- *What are the harms that you are trying to help clients to avoid?*

- *What are the most serious risks?*

- *Do you ever 'take risks' at work and, if so, what sort of risks?*

- *Do you justify taking these work risks in some way and, if so, how?*

- *Are we 'gambling' with clients' lives? Why not?*

- *What degree of risk is reasonable to take, and why?*

RESEARCH SUMMARY **7.1**

Childcare workers are exposed to several health and safety risks in their work environment, the most common being infectious diseases, musculoskeletal injuries, accidents, and occupational stress. Pregnant childcare workers have an additional risk of potential harm to the foetus. (McGrath, 2007)

This approach might be referred to as *minimising situational hazards* (Taylor, 2006b). When there are hazards inherent in an activity, whether for a client or a colleague, it makes sense and is required that we consider how possible harm can be avoided. Such activities may be part of a detailed care plan for an individual or a group activity in, for example, a day centre or residential facility.

Personal safety

Personal safety concerns are an aspect of *health and safety at work*, and add to the complexity of decision making in social work. The number of assaults on social workers, care workers and allied professions is appalling (HSE, 2009c; Newhill, 1996; Varma, 1997). Safeguarding roles frequently bring conflict with abusers and alleged abusers who may already have been violent to others. In addition to assault there are less tangible dimensions that must be taken into account in making judgements, such as threats and verbal aggression. It is beyond the scope of this book to do more than outline some key pointers for personal safety, and point to sources for further knowledge and skills development (Bibby, 1994; Mason and Chandley, 1999; Varma, 1997; Turnbull and Paterson, 1999). Some key aspects of personal safety for front line staff are to:

- understand the context and possible predisposing and trigger factors (see below) for aggression with your client group and setting;

- avoid and manage situations that are likely to be scenes of dangerous conflict, such as when undesirable news must be given;

- manage a safe environment as far as possible, such as being aware of potential weapons, escape routes, available assistance, etc.;

- learn skills in defusing an aggressive situation;

- learn breakaway techniques to escape from being held by an aggressor;

- learn skills and develop team work in control methods if you are in high-risk work (such as a children's home, day centre for people with learning disability or psychiatric ward).

CASE STUDY **7.1**

Personal safety of staff

Fred (aged 51 years) is deaf and partially sighted. He is generally unkempt and unshaven, and sleeps in his clothes unless he is prompted. He is neglected or shunned by his family. Fred requires a home care service to provide support for personal hygiene and dressing as

>
> *well as day care to improve his socialisation and personal care. He is inclined to be per-ceived as invading people's body space which might be attributable to his combined sensory impairments. Because of concerns by staff about such mannerisms, initially two home care workers were allocated to care for him at all times even though this is not required in terms of functional needs.*
>
> *The plan was to reduce this to one worker (in line with his functional needs) after three months. However, the home care workers are not comfortable with reducing to just one worker because they perceive him as a threat and because they feel isolated as mobile phones don't work in the rural locality of his home. The Risk Manager advised that if the staff perceive this situation as threatening then their perceptions must be used to guide the decision and as the social worker managing the case I amended the care plan accordingly.*
>
> - *What options are possible in similar situations that you face?*
>
> - *What ethical issues are raised by one person being allocated additional publicly funded resources in such situations when resources are limited?*

Reasonably practicable steps to protect people from harm

Having identified a hazard, *the law requires you to do everything reasonably practicable to protect people from harm* (HSE, 2009e). While health and safety legislation has been of tremendous value in reducing deaths, injuries and illness there are some conflicts inherent in this approach for the social worker. What is a *reasonably practicable step*? Thus it is usually *reasonable* and *practicable* to move electrical cables to a position that will minimise the likelihood of someone tripping and being injured if we take for granted the decision that the computer will be used on this particular desk. When it comes to personal care tasks in somebody's own home it may not be so obvious what constitutes *reasonably practicable steps*. To what extent do we accept the person's normal lifestyle arrangements as *given* and work around these? To what extent do we insist on change (or withdraw services) if persuasion is not effective (Taylor and Donnelly, 2006a)?

Social work judgements are complex as we often have to operate outside of controlled environments. Sometimes our clients make minor spontaneous decisions which have more serious consequences than expected. Examples might be a young person in residential care being led astray by a friend while on a social activity with peers, or a frail elderly person standing on a chair to change a light bulb rather than asking for help. Risks taken by a client as part of employment, social or recreational activities (for example while a resident in a home, member of a day centre or in receipt of home care or family support services) will often involve an element of possible harm yet would not be considered as unacceptably *risky* by most people in society. The level of the dangers might range from crossing the road to get on a bus to go to work or the cinema through taking the risk of getting mugged while visiting friends or shopping to undertaking something more adventurous (*risky*) such as playing football or mountain walking. Where do individuals in society draw the line? To what extent should our support for clients' choices reflect our own values, our profession's values, society's values or the values of clients' sub-groups within society? Engaging with the challenges of these types of decisions is also part of the social work role, as well as more considered judgements such as safeguarding and long-term care decisions.

Balancing this tension between rights and risk-taking is a core area of knowledge and skill in social work practice. Government policy in the UK is beginning to recognise this and provide some support for pro-active rather than defensive approaches to managing risk through supporting reasoned and reasonable client decision making:

> . . . there will often be some risk, and . . . trying to remove it altogether can outweigh the quality of life benefits for the person.

(DH, 2007, p9)

> The Health and Safety Executive endorses a sensible approach to risk, which seeks to address these concerns. Health and Safety legislation should not block reasonable activity. Through the care planning process risk assessments are undertaken which should also fulfil the requirement under health and safety legislation, providing the risk to both the person using the service and their family carer are considered . . .

(DH, 2007, p26, para 2.35)

Balancing client rights with care worker health and safety

> The assessment of A&B, two young disabled people, identified that they liked and responded positively to swimming and to horse riding, but the application of manual handling regulations meant that they were unable to do either. The court decided that the rights of care staff to a safe working environment had to be balanced against the rights of A&B to undertake activities they enjoyed. This meant that the risks to the health and safety of the staff must be kept to a minimum that was consistent with A&B being enabled to exercise their human rights. Article 8 is not an absolute right, but any interference with it must be justified and proportionate. In the first place it was for the local authority to formulate its manual handling policy and to make the appropriate assessments.

(DH, 2007, p23, extract; see also A and others v East Sussex County Council and another [2003] All ER (D) 233 (Feb))

Can we justify taking risks?

Health and safety legislation focuses on taking reasonable steps to avoid possible harm but everyday life and care decisions inherently involve making choices and taking risks. An everyday example of taking a risk might be deciding whether to cross a road when there is

95

a gap in the traffic, balancing the time saved against that spent waiting, and bearing in mind the possible pain and other consequences of being knocked down. How do we understand or conceptualise such risk-taking decisions?

ACTIVITY 7.4

Risk and allocating blame

- *Is playing a sport a foolhardy risk-taking exercise?*

- *Should people who play sports and get injured be regarded as having self-inflicted injuries?*

- *Does your sense of blame depend on the sport?*

- *How does your view relate to your understanding of the rules of the sport, your perspective on the benefits and your knowledge of the dangers?*

- *What might justify taking the risks inherent in the sport?*

We take the premise that a rational decision is made to achieve some sort of benefit – interpreted broadly to include such things as good health, financial gain and social independence – or to ensure one's own moral integrity. Taking risk is intrinsic to human decision making, and hence to social work practice in advising and supporting clients to make decisions. *'. . . perceived risk [i.e. possibility of harm] must be tested and assessed against the likely benefits of taking an active part in the community, learning new skills and gaining confidence. What needs to be considered is the consequence of an action and the likelihood of any harm from it'* (DH, 2007, p4).

Taking a risk cannot be justified on the basis that no harm in fact occurs after the decision is made. At the time that the decision is taken, the outcome is not known. Sometimes a risk-taking decision will result in an undesirable outcome and sometimes it will not, by the

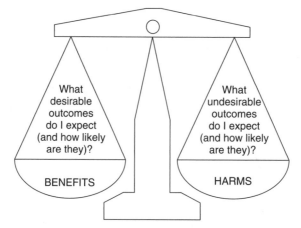

Figure 7.1 Balancing potential benefits and possible harm

very nature of the fact that we are talking about decisions in uncertain situations. The justification for taking the risk must be established at the time the decision is taken and can only be based on what is known at that time. Drawing on everyday life, the justification is generally in terms of the potential desirable outcome of the decision. We cannot know the outcome for certain, but we make a judgement as to whether the potential gain is worth the possible loss. This is regarded as a basis for a good, informed decision or sound professional advice (Carson and Bain, 2008).

Child development and risk taking

Amid increasing concerns about the dangers to children from such as drugs, abuse and violence on television and computer games (Porter, 1986), the state intervenes increasingly in decisions that were once made entirely by families, for example in areas such as health, well-being, safety and education (Schaffer, 1990). A side-effect of some of the well-intentioned policies and services to improve the life chances of families (Social Exclusion Task Force, 2008) may be to limit the exposure of children to the challenges and judgement calls essential for growth into responsible adulthood. *During the past decade the list of 'don'ts' applied to children has, according to media reports, proliferated to include a rash of . . . activities from snowballs and conkers to football during school breaks and more besides* (Ball, 2007, p58). It is not clear whether this rapidly developing aversion to taking risks is really in the best interests of children, or even whether the number of accidents has decreased. The unintended consequences of such decisions as driving children to school rather than letting them walk or use public transport – such as loss of independence, exercise and opportunities to socialise – are a negative side-effect of the laudable desire to ensure that certain foreseeable harms – such as encounters with

---

CASE STUDY 7.2

Balancing benefits and harms

Karim is 19 years of age and has a moderate learning disability. He is due to go on a respite holiday where the provider has facilities for outdoor activities including a rope traverse across a river. Karim has heard about rope traversing from his (non-disabled) brother and is very keen to do this.

- *Will you recommend that Karim be allowed to do this activity?*
- *If so, how would you justify this judgement?*
- *What safeguards against possible harm would you want to see in place?*
- *Does the suitability of the activity for other young people with similar physical ability but no learning disability have any relevance?*
- *What possible benefits are there for Karim in undertaking this activity?*
- *Would you weigh up the possible benefits against the possible harm in some way, and if so, how?*
- *What would you want to do to ensure that the decision was seen as sound if an accident did occur?*

paedophiles – are avoided. Accidents are increasingly regarded as preventable, with implications for many social work judgements when we must make justifiable recommendations about diverse matters including child-rearing practices.

The paradox is that we need to take risks to progress as individuals and as a society, but we seem to be becoming more risk-averse, or at least fearful of being blamed if an undesirable outcome ensues.

> *The Health and Safety Executive has become concerned at the possibility of over protection of children and their lack of risk experience. A degree of managed risk is necessary for children's development . . . Sensible risk management is NOT about stopping well managed recreation and learning.*

(HSE, 2009f)

Table 7.2 Myths about health and safety regulation

Myth:	*Children need to be wrapped in cotton wool to keep them safe, November 2008*
Reality:	*Health and safety law is often used as an excuse to stop children taking part in exciting activities, but well-managed risk is good for them. It engages their imagination, helps them learn and even teaches them to manage risks for themselves in the future. They won't understand about risk if they're wrapped in cotton wool. Risk itself won't damage children, but ill-managed and overprotective actions could.* (HSE, 2008)
Myth:	*Health and safety rules take the adventure out of playgrounds, March 2009*
	We're all for playgrounds being exciting and challenging places. Children should have fun in them, get fit, develop social skills and learn how to handle risks. What's important is to strike the right balance – protecting children from harm while allowing them the freedom to develop independence and risk awareness. Exciting and challenging playgrounds do this, poorly maintained or badly designed ones don't. Health and safety laws don't stop children having fun but ill-considered and overprotective actions do. (HSE, 2009g)

Potential benefits of risk-taking decisions

To support social workers in these complex risk-taking decisions, the Department of Health *acknowledge[s] that there will often be some risk, and that trying to remove it altogether can outweigh the quality of life benefits for the person* (DH, 2007, p9). The task is not simply judging how much of the likelihood or consequences of possible harm should be removed. Rather, the decision may be essentially about justifying the possibility of harm by evaluating the possible benefits of the course of action. *By taking account of the benefits in terms of independence, well-being and choice, it should be possible for a person to have a support plan which enables them to manage identified risks* (DH, 2007, p10).

CASE STUDY 7.3

Discussing benefits and harms with clients and families

Mrs Heaney is a 79-year-old woman living alone. She has had increasing memory problems during the past few years and there have been concerns about her ability to continue living at home. Mrs Heaney visits neighbours in an agitated state and has been found wandering the streets at night unable to find her home. I had a discussion with Mrs Heaney and her son and daughter about the possible benefits and risks in staying at home versus entering residential care.

After discussion the perceived benefits of staying at home were: a fuller family life; Mrs Heaney's right to choice and to live in her own environment; the enjoyment of the companionship of friends and neighbours of long acquaintance; the opportunity to remain active and engage in activities that she enjoys; and Mrs Heaney would remain independent with family and community support. The perceived risks of staying at home were: Mrs Heaney's lack of co-operation with home help support; probability of inadequate nourishment due to missed meals; limited compliance with medication; risks associated with fire lighting; risk of agitation and distress due to loneliness; and risk of wandering out on her own when distressed.

In the family discussion the perceived benefits of Mrs Heaney being admitted to residential care were: Mrs Heaney's needs would be met in a safe environment; she would have adequate warmth, nourishment and medication; her mental state and wandering could be monitored; there would be companionship of other residents; and there would be supervised access to activities and outings of her choice. The perceived risks of admission to residential care were: possibility of greater depression due to confinement; loss of independence and freedom; risk of falls in an unknown environment; risk of infections; and the possibility of increased confusion.

The consideration of each option in terms of potential benefits and possible harm was a helpful way to structure the discussion with the client and family. The key issues were clearly identified and discussed.

This process of *balancing benefits and harms* entails verbalising with clients, and recording potential gains from the decision as well as possible harms that might ensue. A critical issue will be helping the client to clarify the relative value that they place on a particular benefit or harm. This is making explicit what is often considered implicitly in making a judgement about whether or not to *take the risk*. Potential gains for clients in risk-taking decisions include:

- rehabilitation;
- skills development;
- self-esteem;
- self-control;
- independence;

- quality of life;

- motivation;

- co-operation in treatment and care;

- supportive relationships;

- satisfying relationships;

- participation in society.

CASE STUDY 7.4

Potential benefits in a care plan

Grace is 37 years old and has been a patient in a psychiatric hospital for six months. She has been expressing suicidal thoughts throughout her stay, having been admitted when she intended to commit suicide. The decision is whether to permit a period of home leave. I found it helpful to articulate some of the benefits of a period of home leave or a day pass, to bear in mind alongside the more frequent consideration of the possibility of Grace harming herself.

- *Reduce the growing dependency on the hospital staff and environment.*

- *Reduce detachment from her home community.*

- *Promote Grace's own coping skills and independence.*

- *Develop support in the community from her father.*

- *Taking a step forward, in discussion with Grace, that begins to move more responsibility back to her when she is ready.*

- *Begin the process of Grace using community rather than hospital supports to grieve, with support from her family and a counselling service.*

Values and decisions

Our clients come to us as members of the same society as ourselves, with their own needs, tensions, perspectives and values in terms of risk-taking and decision making (Scott-Jones and Raisborough, 2007). There has been some exploration of how clients and carers conceptualise *risk* (Manthorpe and Alaszewski, 2000), including children (Thom *et al.*, 2007), older people (Moriarty *et al.*, 2007), those with dementia (Buri and Dawson, 2000) and people with learning disability (Manthorpe *et al.*,1997). Clients may have different perceptions of what actually constitutes *risk* (Ryan *et al.*, 2001). Wynne-Harley (1991) explored the concept of *voluntary risk-taking* from the perspective of the rights of the older person. Boeije *et al.* (2004) studied the risk perception and seriousness of wheelchair dependence in people with multiple sclerosis. A key issue is how your clients and their families value the possible outcomes of a decision in which they are engaged with you.

RESEARCH SUMMARY 7.2

Parents' perceptions of risks to children and their management

Freel identified low income, urban African-American families with their two- and three-year-old children as a population at high risk for injuries. Parents created safe environments for their children by changing their household environment to make it safer, by having rules banning hazardous objects, spaces and activities, and by monitoring or watching the child. When rules were transgressed, parents used discipline, usually reasoning along with corporal punishment or commands, to both stop the behaviour and to teach future safe behaviour. Parents said that they were influenced by many factors such as their perceptions of the children's knowledge about danger, how much control they had over the possible injuries, to what extent they could prevent injuries to their children and their beliefs about children needing freedom to play, explore and exercise their growing physical skills. (Freel, 1995)

Sometimes, people's response to taking a risk depends on the degree of voluntariness. Our exposure to possible harm may vary from voluntary situations (for example, choosing to walk on mountains in stormy weather conditions or to visit a nightclub that will involve travelling home at a more dangerous time of day) to involuntary (for example, we have limited control over the spread of epidemic diseases or exposure to the electromagnetic radiation inherent in the use of electrical appliances such as mobile phones and televisions). The *fear factor* may be increased as a result of the danger being unknown, loss of control in the situation, lack of reliable information or a sense of unfairness in who suffers (Calman *et al.*,1999).

CASE STUDY 7.5

Positive and negative indicators

Mrs Rodriguez is 67 years of age and has a problem with alcohol addiction. Her son Alberto lives with her occasionally. One of the areas identified in the assessment was the risk of family breakdown. On the negative side, Alberto is beginning to disengage from caring for his mother because he finds her depressed mood and erratic eating and sleeping increasingly difficult to cope with. On the positive side, family and friends do maintain contact with Mrs Rodriguez at present, and generally have positive feelings towards her.

It is important that a consideration of possible harm or loss is not limited to the particular individual who happens to be your *client* at this moment. Professionals have responsibilities to consider a wide range of risks including possible harm by clients to themselves; harm to other patients and clients, friends, neighbours, co-residents, other tenants; dangers to yourself and colleagues including, for example, foster parents and home care workers; risks to the organisation and to workers in other organisations; and dangers for the general public.

RESEARCH SUMMARY **7.3**

Professional understanding of clients' care-related values

A study involved 39 case managers (mostly social workers) in the USA, of whom approximately half received an intervention designed to make them more responsive to the values of the clients (older people), such as:

- *taking part in workshops to develop a care values assessment form to use with clients;*
- *training in using this care values assessment form;*
- *development of a large print brochure for clients; and*
- *case conferences to apply the process to individuals.*

The group comprising the other half of the case managers received no intervention, but were 'tested' at the same times as the experimental group as a control. The intervention was found to improve the awareness of client values, but a key finding was that case managers were generally inaccurate in predicting how their clients would state their care-related values three months after referral. In general professionals greatly underestimated the importance of religious activity to clients, underestimated their desire to be protected, overestimated their desire to take risks and underestimated their willingness to forgo help in order to maintain privacy in financial affairs. (Kane et al.,1999)

Balancing values of benefits and harms

When faced with two or more alternatives we might well start by listing (at least mentally) the desirable and undesirable aspects of each option. For an everyday example consider the choice you face regarding going on holiday or buying a car where the positive and negative points of each option are compared. In relation to care decisions, the same model might be used although the issues are likely to be of greater importance for the individual's future well-being. The outcomes in everyday decisions might be evaluated in terms of the gain or loss of money or pleasure as well as more basic needs of life such as health and security. In care decisions the priority is more often about benefits to health and social well-being, and possible harm whether from other people or accidents, so the terms *benefit* and *harm* are used here. This model of *balancing benefits and harms* is adapted from a well-established judgement model known as *expected utility* (Baron, 2008; Hardman, 2009). This approach is based on the premise that the decision maker maximises the expected value of the outcome of the decision. That is to say, you choose the option which seems to offer, on balance, the greatest beneficial outcome when you weigh up the benefits (potential desirable outcomes) against the harms (possible undesirable outcomes).

The distinction between considering only possible harms when we make a decision, and weighing possible harms against possible gains is in certain respects a parallel in modern *risk language* to the traditional ethical debate between *non-maleficence* (i.e. first, do no harm) and *beneficence* (i.e. the duty to do good) (Payne, 1996). Concerns about health and safety legislation and fear of litigation seems to be influencing professionals to focus more on avoiding harm and thus to avoid some more positive approaches to promoting health and social well-being that involve greater inherent danger. This balancing of benefits and harms might be undertaken quite simply by listing factors in two columns. *In particular in cases involving, as they so often do, the weighing of risks against benefits, the judge before accepting a body of opinion as being responsible, reasonable or respectable, will need to be satisfied that, in forming their views, the experts have directed their minds to the question of comparative risks and benefits and have reached a defensible conclusion on the matter* (Lord Browne-Wilkinson, in *Bolitho v City & Hackney Health Authority*, 1988, p1159).

Balancing potential benefits and possible harms

ACTIVITY 7.5

Identifying potential benefits and possible harms
Identify potential gains and possible losses in these situations.

- *A toddler walking along a low garden wall when mum is not watching.*
- *A teenager sneaking out of the window to go to a nightclub when Dad has said 'no'.*
- *An older person hospitalised after a stroke walking across the ward for the first time.*
- *A person with a disability moving to greater independence in supported housing.*
- *Charles Blondin walking across the Niagara Falls on a tightrope (this 55-year-old French acrobat performed this feat and then repeated the stunt blindfolded pushing a wheelbarrow a few days later. The Chicago Tribune, 4 July 1859, **www.discovergreeneville. com/andrewjohnson/articles.php?r=4**).*
- *A recent situation on your caseload.*

It is important to be clear that balancing benefits and harms is not *gambling*. Decisions about health and social care are important matters to patients and clients. *Gambling* would imply that the decision process itself is undertaken for enjoyment rather than because the outcome is important. We support people to achieve *worthwhile*, normally agreed, life goals in accordance with professional values, the purpose of the organisation by which we are employed (i.e. care-related goals in a broad sense) and the legal and policy parameters of our society. This is the answer to any accusation that we are *gambling with clients' lives* by supporting risk-taking.

ACTIVITY 7.6

Weighing up possible benefits and harms
Consider the situation of a young man with moderate learning difficulties. It is identified as part of his care plan that he would like to learn to use public transport independently and that this would be helpful for his future life and his family.

> ## ACTIVITY 7.6 (CONT.)
>
> - *What are the potential benefits of facilitating his request?*
> - *What are the potential hazards in facilitating his request?*
> - *What might be the vulnerabilities and trigger factors?*
> - *What strengths might he have that might improve the success of the plan?*
> - *How would you maximise the potential gains in a care plan?*
> - *How would you minimise the potential for harm in a care plan?*

Likelihoods of benefits and harms

In reality, the potential benefits and the possible harms resulting from our decisions are not certain. For a fuller approach this *balancing benefits and harms* should consider the likelihood of harm occurring and the likelihood of achieving the desired benefits.

> ## ACTIVITY 7.7
>
> ### Patterns, severity and probability of risks
> Consider the pattern of risk in a recent case in terms of:
>
> | Risk identified | Pattern of risk | Severity of risk | Probability of risk |
> |---|---|---|---|
> | Insert here a clear description of the risk identified | 1 Isolated | 1 Mild | 1 Unlikely |
> | | 2 Occasional occurrence | 2 Moderate | 2 Likely (expected) |
> | | 3 Repeated occurrence | 3 Serious | 3 Highly probable |
> | | 4 Established pattern | 4 Fatal | 4 Certain |
>
> - *In what ways does this framework help you to discuss risk issues with your supervisor and colleagues in other professions?*
> - *What are the main strengths of using a tool like this?*
> - *What are the main limitations of using a tool like this?*

The generally accepted formula is that *risk = hazard (severity or value placed on the undesirable outcome) times the likelihood (probability of that outcome)*. In other words, we should multiply the seriousness of the particular outcome by the likelihood of that occurring in our balancing of options. Thus, we would multiply the value that is placed on the beneficial outcome by the probability (likelihood, chance) of achieving that, and would multiply the (negative) value that is placed on an undesirable outcome (consequences) by the likelihood of it occurring. In practice, such formulae cannot be used precisely. A good care plan probably has to address as a priority those areas that are high in severity even if low in likelihood of occurrence, as well as those that rate as high risks overall taking into account both severity and likelihood.

CASE STUDY **7.6**

Weighing likelihood and severity

Mrs Ferguson is aged 79 years and is suffering from dementia. She lives alone but has a son and daughter-in-law living nearby. In assessing Mrs Ferguson I applied the scoring system in my employer's risk assessment which rates frequency (f) as rarely (1), occasionally (2) or frequently (3), and which rates severity (s) as low (1), medium (2) and high (3). I then multiplied these to give a score for the overall degree of risk.

- *Mrs F loses her purse in the house and blames her daughter-in-law.*

  - *severity 1 * frequency 1 = overall risk 1*

- *Neighbours in adjoining flats who are usually very helpful to Mrs F (and help to maintain her at home) are complaining that her visits at strange times are becoming a nuisance.*

  - *severity 2 * frequency 2 = overall risk 4*

- *Mrs F leaves the cooker on inadvertently on occasions, presenting a fire risk.*

  - *severity 3 * frequency 1 = overall risk 3*

- *Mrs F is not bathing herself properly and is refusing to co-operate with home care staff in this, resulting in possibility of sores.*

  - *severity 1 * frequency 3 = overall risk 3*

The scoring system helped me to communicate more clearly about concerns with other professionals. However, I do not think that the overall scores necessarily reflect the priorities for action. The high severity risk (setting fire to the block of flats) must be a high priority despite not having the highest overall score. Similarly, the two areas that scored 3 overall are not equally deserving of priority attention.

Decision trees

Where we have detailed information on the values of appropriate stakeholders in the decision, and the likelihood of each possible outcome, *decision trees* may be used to assist in analysing the alternative outcomes. The essence of a decision tree is to:

- identify the options being considered;

- identify the possible outcomes for each option;

- add the likelihood of each outcome occurring; and

- add the value placed on each of these outcomes.

These latter steps are akin to the model above in judging severity and likelihood of a particular harm. The difference with a decision tree is that it can also show beneficial as well as harmful outcomes (positive values as opposed to negative values ascribed to particular outcomes) and how particular choices depend on other decisions.

Sometimes, professionals struggle emotionally to give an estimate of the likelihood of a particular outcome, perhaps feeling that this in some way diminishes their whole-hearted endeavours to help the client or family. The realism required to recognise that our best efforts will not always achieve complete success is essential to professional helping. Creating and discussing a decision tree may well assist in clarifying options and the likelihood of success; in no way should it be allowed to diminish the efforts to help the client or family.

In practice it is uncommon to have sufficiently detailed data to calculate likelihoods with useful accuracy for social work decisions. If you are supporting a client in making a decision you might consider creating simple categories of value (e.g. very (un)desirable, (un)desirable, don't care) and likelihood (highly likely, may happen, unlikely to happen) to aid the discussion of options. The interested reader is referred to Dowie (1993), Dowding and Thompson (2002) or Munro (2008) for further detail.

Strengths, vulnerability, trigger and mitigating factors

Perhaps because of the caution that is required in using numbers to convey the correct message, qualitative approaches are used more often in practice. If the knowledge about risk factors does not exist in sufficient detail to inform actuarial prediction of harm, we can use *fuzzy* approaches to decision making. We will consider three main aspects.

- Factors that predispose the harm to occur, which we will call here *vulnerabilities.*

- Factors that induce the harm to occur, which we will call here *trigger factors.*

- Mitigating factors or *strengths* that might reduce the harm or its likelihood.

Vulnerabilities are also known as *predisposing factors* (Brearley, 1982), *background hazards* (Kelly, 1996) or *historical determinants. Vulnerabilities* are those factors about the client, family or situation that are identified on the basis of some imprecise knowledge of risk factors as making the situation undesirable. *Trigger factors* are also known as *hazards* (Brearley, 1982) or *situational hazards* (Kelly, 1996) or *situational determinants. Trigger factors* are factors that may trigger or precipitate harm occurring. A *strength* is a factor that mitigates against the undesirable harm occurring. As examples, the age of the child and the parents' inability to manage alcohol may be *vulnerabilitites*. A social event at a pub or the child crying may be a *trigger factor*. In this scenario the *harm* to be avoided is an alcoholic binge resulting in assault on the child, and a *strength* may be a close neighbour who has looked after the child at her house overnight if the parents are out late.

Vulnerabilities may include *dynamic* risk factors where we might work with clients and families on underlying problems to reduce the likelihood or severity of a harmful outcome. *Trigger factors* indicate situations to avoid or manage more carefully so as to reduce harm. If it is not possible to undertake a calculation of the probability of harm it may be helpful in practice to consider these types of factors and the sort of interplay between them that

---

CASE STUDY **7.7**

Vulnerability and trigger factors

Case One

Samuel was involved in a road traffic accident as a child which led to mental and physical impairments. He is now 33 years old and has epileptic fits, weakness down his right side and stumbles on uneven surfaces. He presents a danger to others, particularly females, and is assessed as Level 1 on the Multi-Agency Sex Offender Risk Assessment and Management Procedures. The pre-disposing vulnerabilities include his low self-esteem, social isolation and low motivation. The triggers that might precipitate a problem include how a female is dressed, photographs of females especially if only partly clothed and drinking alcohol.

Case Two

Amelia Williams is aged 48 years and has a learning disability and some physical disability. She lives with her mother, Mrs Williams, who has been diagnosed with dementia. Vulnerabilities were identified as being that Amelia requires supervision and assistance with mobility and relies on others to maintain an awareness of danger; and that Mrs Williams is becoming less aware of dangers and it is anticipated that her mental health will deteriorate with time. Trigger factors were identified as being that there are considerable amounts of time when they are alone without support and that Mrs Williams' other daughter (who has been providing support to them) is under stress and her contribution to the care arrangements is in danger of breaking down.

- *Identify the vulnerability (predisposing) factors in a recent case.*

- *Identify the trigger (precipitating) factors in a recent case.*

- *In what ways is it helpful to consider these separately?*

---

might occur as the client or family situation evolves. Appendix 1 gives some pointers towards designing or completing an assessment using these concepts.

Chapter summary

- The Health and Safety at Work legislation in the European Union has achieved much in reducing harm and disease in our society. As employees we are required to take reasonably practicable steps to avoid death, injury and illness in social care workplaces.

- There are some tensions between the principles of Health and Safety legislation and the professional responsibility to support clients in taking reasonable risks to further care plan goals such as greater independence, rehabilitation, motivation and quality of life.

- Risk-taking decision making is an intrinsic function of the professional role in enabling clients and families to achieve worthwhile care-related life goals.

- We use the model of *balancing benefits and harms* to conceptualise the social worker making these judgements and supporting clients in doing the same.

- Practical concepts and tools to support this aspect of professional decision making include considering vulnerabilities, trigger factors, mitigating factors and decision trees.

FURTHER READING

Baron, J. (2008) *Thinking and Deciding.* Cambridge: Cambridge University Press.

This fairly heavy textbook gives a detailed consideration of the strengths and paradoxes of the well-researched models of decision making generally known as Expected Utility.

Brearley, P. (1982) *Risk in Social Work.* London: Routledge & Kegan Paul.

This classic text was one of the forerunners in exploring the concept of risk as applied to social work. Paul Brearley introduced the concepts (using different terminology) of vulnerability, trigger factors, strengths and mitigating factors in social work decisions.

Health and Safety Executive in England

www.hse.gov.uk/index.htm

Health and Safety Executive in Wales

www.hse.gov.uk/welsh/

Health and Safety Executive in Scotland

www.hse.gov.uk/scotland/

Health and Safety Executive for Northern Ireland

www.hseni.gov.uk/

Health and Safety Executive Bookfinder

www.hsebooks.com/Books/default.asp

The Health and Safety Executives are the enforcing authorities for health and safety in a range of work situations including district councils, government departments, hospitals and nursing homes. The websites provide a wealth of attractive materials including details of legislation and current policy issues in support of their mission *to prevent death, injury and ill health in the workplace.*

Kelly, G. (1996) Competence in Risk Analysis (pp108–23) in O'Hagan, K. (ed) *Competence in Social Work Practice.* London: Jessica Kingsley.

This chapter outlines a practical approach to considering background hazards, situational hazards, strengths and dangers in decisions.

Chapter 8

Assessment tools and decision support systems

C H A P T E R O B J E C T I V E S

This chapter will help you to meet the following National Occupational Standards for Social Work.

- Key role 1, unit 3: Assess needs and options to recommend a course of action.

- Key role 4, unit 12: Assess and manage risks to individuals, families, carers, groups and communities.

- Key role 6, unit 18: Research, analyse, evaluate, and use current knowledge of best social work practice.

This chapter will help you to meet post-qualifying requirements for social work in the UK such as the following.

- Work effectively in a context of risk, uncertainty, conflict and contradiction (The Post-Qualifying Award in Specialist Social Work (Generic Level Requirement vii.), General Social Care Council [England], 2004).

- Competence in working effectively in complex situations (Post-Qualifying Award, Requirement PQ2, *Scotland & Wales (= UK Framework 1990–2007)*).

- Competence in exercising the powers and responsibilities of a professional social worker, including the appropriate use of discretion and the management of risk (Post-Qualifying Award, Requirement PQ3, *Scotland & Wales (= UK Framework 1990–2007)*).

- Ability to make informed decisions (Post-Qualifying Award, Requirement PQ4, *Scotland & Wales (= UK Framework 1990–2007)*).

- Demonstrate consistent and sustained sound judgement and decision making in the context of complexity, risk, uncertainty, conflict and contradiction (Specific Award Requirement 3, Northern Ireland Post-Qualifying Education and Training Partnership, 2007).

'It is not possible' Cai was saying as we entered, 'and even if it were, the risk is terrible.' Arthur smiled and reached across the board to ruffle Cai's red curls. 'Trust Cai to count the risk.' 'God's honour! That is the truth. I do heed the risk . . .' Cai <responded>.

(Lawhead,1989, p120)

Introduction

Chapter 8 focuses on the function of assessment within judgement and decision making, considering the main components as gathering, ordering and analysis of information. Principles of staged and single (unified) assessment processes are considered as a response to the need for proportionate assessment and effective inter-professional decision making. We have highlighted the need for social workers to have knowledge and skills in using appropriate specialist assessment tools as well as the ability to co-ordinate a range of specialist assessments from different professionals. Theories that underpin health and social care assessment are discussed. We consider the potential for decision aids (including assessment tools) to assist in supporting decision making. The need to develop further methods of analysing assessment data is highlighted, with illustrations of recent developments. The potential of the emerging realm of *decision support systems* is highlighted.

Assessment processes and gathering information

Assessment is the basis for good judgement and decision making . . . (Simmonds, 1998, p177). In the context of this book, the aim of assessment is to gather and order information for analysis so as to inform professional judgement and decision processes about care. *Assessment is a tool to aid in the planning of future work, the beginning of helping another person to identify areas for growth and change* (Taylor and Devine, 1993, p7). The terms *care* and *work* here mean the range of possible social work interventions such as care planning (including safeguarding and supporting clients in taking reasonable, reasoned risk-taking decisions), and the wide variety of psychosocial interventions undertaken by social workers with individuals and families (Roberts and Greene, 2002). Some examples of psychosocial interventions undertaken by social workers (some require post-qualifying training) include:

- social care planning including safeguarding and decisions regarding resources such as home care workers, family support workers, family centre services, respite and placement schemes, fostering, adoption, day care and support, supported housing and long-term care;

- crisis intervention;

- task-centred casework and problem-solving counselling;

- behaviour modification interventions;

- non-directive and mediating model counselling;

- cognitive behavioural therapy;

- family work and family therapy;

- youth justice and family group conferencing;

- solution-focused brief therapy;

- transactional analysis;

- motivational interviewing;

- narrative life review including life story work and reminiscence therapy;

- reality orientation.

Assessment is the process of systematically gathering and analysing information about the client, family and context (Taylor and Devine, 1993):

- as the beginning of helping another person or family;

- to aid in the planning of future work together;

- to make sense of the situation for the client and the worker;

- to build up a picture of what happens, probable causes and consequences;

- to relate the decision to law, policy, procedures and standards;

- to understand the situation in relation to a professional knowledge base;

- to identify motivations, strengths and resources that may support change;

- to identify the effect of race, culture and religion on need and service provision;

- to identify areas of concern for learning, growth and change;

- to ascertain the response to and effect of previous interventions;

- to facilitate information sharing between professionals and organisations;

- to inform safeguarding decisions;

- to inform decisions about allocation of public social care services;

- to contribute to decisions about wider health, social care and justice provision;

- to establish a base line against which to measure progress; and

- to provide anonymised, aggregated information for service management and development.

Our focus here is on assessment in terms of gathering, ordering and analysing information to inform a judgement and decision process. The assessment process through which the client and family engage with a social worker and begin to form a trusting working relationship is essential. Tuning-in, scene setting, clarifying your role and reaching below the immediate presenting problem to identify the underlying problems and strengths is an essential social work practice skill (Shulman, 1999) but is not our focus here.

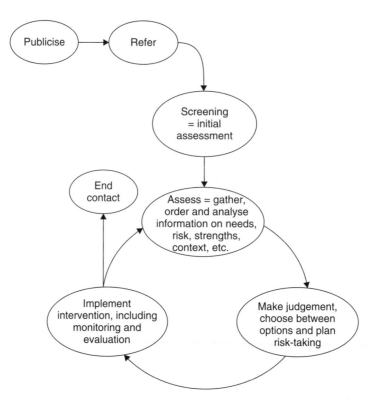

Figure 8.1 Screening and assessment as part of decision making

Some practice pointers on gathering information for decisions:

- Gathering an appropriately wide range of information for the decision.
- Thinking the unthinkable in terms of exploring possible abuse.
- Avoiding irrelevant, impertinent and non-cost effective information gathering.
- Considering the influence of the data gathering process on the accuracy and comprehensiveness of data gathered.
- Using direct observation when appropriate to the decision.
- Appraising the credibility of sources of information.
- Recognising how your potential biases may influence your information gathering.
- Recognising how leading questions may influence answers given.
- Recognising the effects of memory in telescoping dates, remembering more emotional memories more clearly, etc.
- Assessing facts and meaning; the impact of situations as well as contextual facts.
- Recording the source and type of information e.g. fact, hearsay or opinion.
- Recording significant evidence underpinning the decision process.
- Recording the understandings about confidentiality and access to information.

Assessment tools and ordering information

Assessment tools assist in ordering information that is gathered to make a decision. Many assessment tools function as checklists, in effect saying to the practitioner *don't forget to gather information on . . . and consider this aspect*. Examples include tools used for assessing children in need (Department of Health, 2002), mental health (Ryan, 1999; Morgan, 2000) and older people (McCormack *et al.*, 2008a). Some tools contain prompts for interviews, for example in relation to harm to others and harm to self (Alberg *et al.*, 1996, p44 and 54).

CASE STUDY *8.1*

Strength factors in assessment tools

My role is as a social worker in a physical disability team. Franklin (26 years of age) suffers from a brain injury from a car accident. My role is to assist him towards independent living. I am piloting the use of an assessment tool with him to assist in assessing the risks of the options that he faces. During the discussion he commented that I was highlighting every single risk that could possibly occur! This comment made me realise that I must recognise strengths more explicitly. I adapted the interview (and future interviews) to consider more fully his strengths such as income, family support and the quality of neighbourhood. This required me to stretch myself in terms of gathering a more rounded picture of the client's situation. I also reported back to the Senior Practitioner who was leading the development of the tool that I thought that there should be more focus on strengths, and prompts to assist the worker to explore these with the client.

- *What tools do you use to support your assessment of the possibility and severity of harm (risk assessment)?*

- *To what extent does the tool support the assessment of strengths of the client, family, neighbourhood and situation?*

Tested assessment tools are a valuable support for professionals in making rational judgements and decisions. Use of appropriate assessment tools can help to inform and educate newer practitioners and develop practice at a standard based on professional consensus and current best knowledge. Decision processes are becoming increasingly complex and open to challenge (for example, allowing the media into family courts); hence increasingly sophisticated assessment tools are required to support professional judgements.

Appropriate knowledge and interpersonal skills are required to use assessment tools effectively; it is not simply a matter of completing forms. Assessment and care planning is a professional responsibility. Appropriate parts of the assessment and care planning tasks might be delegated to staff such as a foster parent or a day care worker, but accountability for supervising the overall assessment and care planning remains with the appropriate professional. Assessment tools must be *used* by the professional, not the professional used (or abused) by the tool! Assessment tools and other decision aids are a support to professional judgement and cannot replace it. No assessment tool can make a decision; it can only inform.

Table 8.1 Principles of assessment tools to support decision making

Client perspective

- information is gathered once and is appropriate to needs and services;
- proportionate assessment;
- respects the individual;
- client is involved in decision making regarding levels of care and risks;
- client's views and wishes are kept to the fore;
- paints a holistic picture of needs, abilities, strengths, goals and motivation;
- considers effects on quality of life;
- embodies consent to assessment and information sharing;
- if client lacks capacity, facilitates participation and safeguarding of interests.

Family and carer perspective

- captures the role and support of family and carers;
- captures family views and perceptions on the older person's needs;
- acknowledges their right to assessment;
- enriches information gathered.

Professional perspective

- well structured and easily understood;
- realistic and appropriate assessment time;
- facilitates appropriate identification of need;
- standardises principles of best practice;
- reflects a strong evidence base;
- in accord with professional values;
- supports professional judgement;
- simplifies access to information;
- is transferable across services and care processes;
- promotes integrated working and facilitates information sharing;
- guides the collation and analysis of relevant information.

Organisational perspective

- supports the mission, principles and standards;
- in accord with (or adapts) current policies;

- in accord with (or adapts) current service development strategies;

- reduces inappropriate referrals;

- supports effective use of resources;

- promotes integrated ways of working; and

- provides information for managing and developing services.

(adapted from McCormack *et al.*, 2008a,b)

Co-ordinating and communicating about care

A key requirement for integrated health and social care provision across professions, organisations and service areas is communication about the assessment stage of decision making. English and Pecora (1994) found that one of the main strengths of assessment processes was to document decisions and to make information more readily available and thus improve communication (Morrison and Henniker, 1999). The development and use of standard single (or integrated or unified) assessment systems are central to supporting effective communication between professionals.

CASE STUDY **8.2**

Using an assessment tool

My social work career has been entirely in child care work. I have worked in various teams, and with various assessment arrangements. As has been highlighted through some inquiries into children killed by family members, professionals can focus their attention on one aspect of a family situation and neglect other important aspects. I have found that the Common Assessment Framework ensures a rounded, holistic picture of the child, family and circumstances, although you can still give extra attention to aspects that are particularly important.

- *What assessment tool do you use (or contribute to) that provides a holistic picture of the social care needs of the individual (and family or carer as appropriate)?*

- *What are the strengths of this tool, and what are its weaknesses?*

An important aspect of assessment tools is the extent to which they support effective communication with clients. Traditionally, assessment tools were written for professionals to read. Some assessment tools are beginning to word their assessment directly to the client rather than to the professional, even if it is recognised that the assessment will normally be completed jointly with an appropriate professional (McCormack *et al.*, 2008a).

Integrated and proportionate assessment

Staged assessment processes have been developed in order to avoid the situation where clients are subjected to unnecessarily complex assessment, and also to ensure that assessment is sufficiently complex where necessary. This desire for proportionate assessment and also to support co-ordination of care has led to *integrated assessment systems* that incorporate more than one stage in the assessment process. Some clients will use the fullest complexity of the system whereas others will be assessed using only some parts of the system. The aim of an integrated assessment system is to be suitably comprehensive at each stage as well as to aid communication between professionals and co-ordination of care.

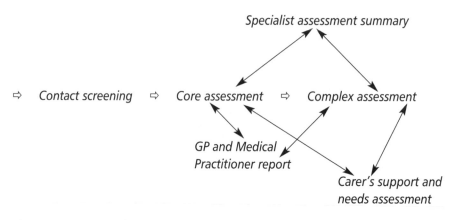

Figure 8.2 Integrated Assessment Systems: The Northern Ireland Single Assessment Tool for the Health and Social Care of Older People (McCormack et al., 2008b)

Specialist assessment tools

Although a particular strength of social work is to bring together specialist assessments into a holistic, person-centred whole for a co-ordinated decision process, there is also a role for social workers in undertaking specialist assessments within their sphere of competence. This is an aspect of social work that is generally under-developed at present. Some specialist assessment tools are linked to particular methods of intervention; for example, systemic family therapy or a behaviour modification intervention. Others might relate to particular problem areas facing a client or family such as attachment, carer support, anxiety, depression, stress, anger management or trauma. Professionals proposing to use a particular specialist tool are often required to undertake a short training course in the use of that particular tool. This should be seen as standard practice in social work, as in other professions. Below is an example of the Graded Care Profile tool.

PRACTICE EXAMPLE 8.1

Usefulness of a specialist assessment tool

I am a Senior Social Worker (team leader) in a Family and Child Care Team. Judging the quality of care received by a child is an essential component of any assessment in a child welfare or child abuse context. The Graded Care Profile (GCP) (Srivastava et al., 2003) is a

PRACTICE EXAMPLE 8.1 (CONT.)

validated tool which offers a standardised framework which allows the component parts of quality of care to be separately assessed against predetermined criteria. The aim of this audit project, undertaken as part of a post-qualifying programme, was to evaluate how well this tool works in assessing child neglect in a busy team. Data was collected from files (to create a profile of recent neglect cases) and from questionnaires completed by social workers in relation to each family where they used the GCP over a three-month period (to gather data on their perceptions of the usefulness of the tool).

Comments on the Graded Care Profile were particularly positive in terms of its practical usefulness, providing an objective measure of parenting, and as a mechanism to facilitate discussion of practicalities with parents where neglect was a concern. The summary of the GCP is readily transferrable to the standard UNOCINI common assessment framework to enable co-ordination with other professionals and other parts of the process.

(McKillop, 2007)

CASE STUDY **8.3**

Using a specialist assessment tool in learning disability

My role is as a social worker within a large hospital for people with learning disabilities. Tariq, a man of 31 years with a minor criminal record, is being considered for discharge. As part of the assessment of John, I completed an Anger Scale and Provocation Inventory (Novaco, 1994) with him. This provided valuable insight into the situations that Tariq found challenging, and added to my professional contribution to the overall assessment that shaped his care plan.

- *What specialist tools do you use to contribute to the holistic assessment of health and social care needs?*

- *In what aspects of your practice might specialist tools be useful?*

Bringing knowledge into practice

Assessment tools are an important way to apply research and theoretical knowledge to practice (Darragh and Taylor, 2008) in a systematic way. Findings from rigorous research develop into theories, concepts and pointers for good practice that can be embodied into the design of assessment tools.

Theories of assessment

A variety of theories can underpin assessment depending on the purpose of the tool. For example, if you are assessing against eligibility criteria for a service then the assessment tool will need to support you in gathering, ordering and analysing information about current functioning and the need for those services. If you are anticipating the possibility of a behaviour modification intervention you will want the assessment to include consideration of antecedents, behaviours and consequences. If you are anticipating the possibility of a family intervention you will want the assessment (diagnostic) stage to include appropriate dimensions of family functioning. We can consider the theoretical underpinnings on a continuum. The point is not that a particular tool is good or bad in terms of these dimensions; what is required is a tool fit for its intended purpose.

Focus on individual ←————————→ focus on family and social context
e.g. person-centred planning   e.g. human becoming and active ageing theory
(Hardy *et al.*, 1999)   (World Health Organisation, 2002)

Focus on past behaviour ←——→ focus on present ←——→ focus on aspirations
e.g. behaviour modification   e.g. selective optimisation and compensation theory
(Gambrill, 1977)   (e.g. Baltes and Baltes, 1990)

Focus on current functioning ←————→ focus on rehabilitation and relationships
e.g. functional assessment   e.g. new senses framework
(Kane *et al.*, 2002)   (e.g. Nolan *et al.*, 2001)

Figure 8.3 Types of theories underpinning approaches to assessment

Quality of assessment tools

Assessment tools increase the consistency and reliability of assessment (Kemshall, 2008) and hence improve the quality of decisions. We can consider the quality of assessment tools in terms of:

- validity – does the tool assess what it purports to assess?

- reliability – would two professionals using the same assessment tool with the same client complete the assessment form the same way and reach the same decision?

- usability – how easy do users (usually professionals) find the tool to use?

- open (qualitative) versus closed (quantitative) questions and scales – to what extent does the tool embody closed questions (supporting ease of judging need and ensuring equity of service provision with other clients) and open questions (supporting gathering the client's perspective on the issues and context)?

- appropriateness – is the tool appropriate and tested for use with this culture or type of clients?

Validity is difficult to demonstrate, because to do this properly one needs to know the outcomes of the assessment. For example, if the tool predicts that a particular child will be abused, is the child in fact abused? Alternative methods include using professional consensus methods (McCormack *et al.*, 2007a). Reliability may be tested by arranging for two professionals to each use the same assessment tool with the same client within a reasonably short space of time to see how similarly they complete the tool. Alternative methods include using asking professionals to use a tool against a vignette (McCormack *et al.*, 2007b) or with actors trained to role play patients and clients (McCormack *et al.*,

RESEARCH SUMMARY *8.1*

Usability of the Strengths and Difficulties Questionnaire

The systematic assessment of psychological and emotional needs of children on the edge of being taken into state care is recommended. Three focus groups of child care social workers and managers were convened to consider their perceptions of the useful- ness of the Strengths and Difficulties Questionnaire (SDQ) (Goodman, 1997) which they had been using for about three months with a sample of children in state care so as to inform their case reviews. The focus groups reported that the use of the SDQ usefully con- firmed some of their intuitions about mental health needs of the children and sometimes highlighted previously unidentified strengths. Perhaps surprisingly for what was perceived as a specialist tool, there was a theme that the tool gave a more holistic picture of mental health needs such as by highlighting problems that only occurred in one setting (e.g. home) but not in another (e.g. school). Social workers thought that they needed time to assimilate the findings of the SDQ assessment into the holistic assessment and care plan process, and the project highlighted the need for further training in interpreting SDQ scores.

(Whyte and Campbell, 2008)

2008d). Usability may be assessed by asking a range of professionals or clients to report on how they find the tool when they use it (McCormack *et al.*, 2008c). Increasingly, tools are being created that address questions directly to the client, even though they are designed to be completed jointly with a professional (McCormack *et al.*, 2008a,b).

Analysis in assessment

Professionals and organisations are increasingly required to provide a rationale for their decisions. The analysis of data gathered as part of assessment needs to become more explicit in informing the decision process. Analysis within assessment often measures such dimensions as functioning level within particular domains, level of complexity, compound- ing factors, mitigating factors and effects on quality of life. Analysis of patterns of harm is required using theory to support reasoned judgement and decisions. This helps to develop a working hypothesis as to what causes or perpetuates the problem and how it plays out in the life of the client, family and significant others so that a judgement can be made about an intervention to offer the client or family.

One of the main weaknesses in assessment tools in current use is the limited support they give for the analysis required to make a judgement, even though there are many tools that are effective at guiding the collation and ordering of information. Some assessment tools explicitly incorporate established risk factors so as to give the best estimate of the proba- bility of some harm (such as homicide or suicide or some particular form of abuse) on the basis of current best knowledge (Doueck and English, 1993). However, even assessment tools that include reference to prediction in their title or purpose often do not include any methodology for estimating the likelihood of a particular outcome.

Perhaps a reason for this lack of support for analysis in assessment tools is the complexity of social work decision making. Multiple factors have to be taken into account in social work judgements. Statistical approaches to analysis commonly use some variant of *linear regression* to analyse the impact of particular factors. In effect, this approach starts from the premise that any factor is equally relevant for any person within the population under consideration. So, taking examples from the risk factors for child abuse, the parent's impulse control and the child's disability and the environmental isolation would be treated as having equal effect on the likelihood of abuse.

An alternative to linear regression is to use a *classification tree,* which has been used in predicting violence by people with a mental disorder (Monahan *et al.,* 2001). In a *classification tree* model, factors are viewed like branches on a tree so that their influence on the event depends on some factors but not others. For example, the likelihood of a person discharged from prison re-offending might be shown to depend on getting a job and having a family network. In an assessment tool constructed using a linear regression model these two factors would be regarded as contributing independently to the likelihood of reoffending. If the tool were constructed using a classification tree analysis then it could recognise that the impact of one of these factors might be less if the other is present. The study of such complex decisions is known as *multi-attribute decision modelling* and there are useful examples of this such as the *analytic hierarchy process* although the application to social work is not yet well developed.

Another development to assist in analysis in decisions is to create scales that are perpendicular rather than linear. For example, there might be a concern continuum and a strength continuum, which are regarded as being at right angles rather than opposites of each other. Thus, if situations are scored as *high* or *low* on each scale there are four options: *high concern and high strength; high concern and low strength; low concern and high strength; and low concern and low strength.* Each quadrant might suggest different types of intervention. The scales of course could be made more precise by having more than just two points on each scale, for example a three-point scale of *high, medium* and *low*.

PRACTICE EXAMPLE *8.2*

Assessment tool supporting analysis

An assessment tool has been developed for young people who sexually abuse others with four domains (Offence, Developmental, Family or Carers, Environment), each with a number of question areas based on research and theory. For example, the Developmental domain includes resilience factors, health issues, experience of abuse or neglect, witnessing domestic violence, quality of early life experiences, history of behaviour problems, sexual development and interests. Two continuums are used to analyse the information: a concern continuum and a strength continuum, each with high, medium and low markers. A two by two table is then used for each combination of high and low strengths and high and low concerns with indicators of likely key issues and possible service responses for that quadrant. This facilitates communication and a shared understanding of the case across professions and agencies. The third stage of the analysis is to identify the five most important strengths, the five most important concerns and the five most important unknowns. (Morrison and Henniker, 2006)

Safeguarding assessments and thresholds

In a safeguarding situation, early stages of assessment are likely to involve making a *holding judgement* regarding safety and stability for the child while developing a common understanding with the client and family as to why the assessment is being undertaken and who is likely to be involved in decision making (Hollows, 2003). Then decisions will need to be made about managing the process of assessment and decision making to engage appropriate people at the appropriate stage.

There are various developments in *risk assessment tools* in areas such as child protection and mental health. In the USA, the focus tends to be on assessment tools that are designed to predict possible harm by being based on the best researched risk factors. These have the benefit of improving consistency of decision making by providing as clear a benchmark as is available on the likelihood of harm. In the UK, the approach is more often to develop assessment tools that will guide the professional in the task of collating and ordering the data. This has the benefit of not giving a false sense of confidence or misuse of risk factors but a weakness in not guiding the use of knowledge to inform analysis. Such assessment tools are based on a professional consensus, incorporating a qualitative professional knowledge base informed by research rather than having a clear relationship to the best measures of likelihood of harm derived from research. For some examples of UK tools for assessing child neglect see Howarth (2007).

Assessment incorporating professional knowledge (primarily based on research) adds rigour to decision making. If the purpose of assessment is to predict the likelihood of harm, then a reliable assessment tool would incorporate actuarial risk factors in its design. It is important to remind ourselves of the limitations in trying to predict harm or any other rare event in relation to a particular individual. Mathematical risk factors can tell us the likelihood of the undesired event more accurately than unaided human judgement, even for those with experience. Thus we may know that an individual has, say, a 20 per cent chance of being abused or of being reconvicted of an offence. However, even the calculated risk factors cannot tell us whether this particular individual is one of the two out of ten who will be abused or reconvicted, or whether he or she is one of the eight out of ten who will not. Some assessment tools explicitly combine actuarial and clinical factors, and incorporate care planning and management within their format (e.g. RAMAS for mental health, Department of Health, 1998). However, we need to recognise that clinical factors have even more limited predictive value than tested actuarial factors, and as a profession we need to seek further research to test and measure such factors for their validity in prediction.

Another aspect of assessment is the effect of the use of language on the users, both clients and professionals. A narrow approach to assessing risk defined in terms of harmful outcomes and matching against eligibility for resources may limit the vision of participants in assessment by comparison with an approach aiming to build on strengths as well as identifying difficulties. These aspects need to be considered in relation to the expectations regarding safeguarding judgements. Social workers sometimes seem to be expected to act as if accurate prediction were possible, such as to ensure that *the child is provided with immediate protection in situations where their life is at risk or there is a likelihood of sustaining a serious injury if this action is not taken . . . In situations where there are child protection concerns but the child is not in a life threatening situation or at risk of serious injury or harm, careful consideration is given to the degree of risk, how best to protect the child . . .* (Social Services Inspectorate, 1993, paras 14–15). Assessment tools can assist the practitioner in collating and ordering appropriate data, in facilitating communication with clients, families and other professionals, and in supporting analysis through embodying research and theory evidence in the tool design.

Decision support systems

Decision support systems aim to provide the best, relevant, up-to-date knowledge for decision makers to use in making the decision and at the same time to standardise best practice and reduce variation due to errors of judgement insofar as our knowledge enables us to address these. We could regard various aspects of our professional world as non-computerised decision supports, such as regulations, policies and procedures and professional guidelines such as those issued by SCIE. But a major development in the past 20 years has been the various types of computerised systems now in use to support practice. This growth opens up many new possibilities for supporting professional decision making.

The most far-reaching development has been information management systems that store and provide an ordered structure for data on individual clients. This aids decision making in terms of:

- improving accuracy of data on which a decision is based;
- having the essential information readily available and retrievable;
- knowing who key stakeholders are and how to contact them;
- facilitating sharing of up-to-date client information;
- providing anonymised data for managing the service and its development; and
- providing anonymised data for research, studying population needs, and service evaluation.

Slightly more sophisticated systems – sometimes called *passive decision support* – provide a flagging system to focus attention on important aspects of a person's care. Systems can flag up such things as the imminent anniversary of a client's bereavement and the dates of care reviews that are due a specified time in advance. Some systems will flag up if a client has been violent or threatening in the past or if there is other crucial information that someone should know before visiting for the first time. This is particularly useful in situations where a locum worker is covering an urgent referral and has to make a decision while the regular social worker is on annual leave or sick leave.

More in their infancy are what are generally called *expert systems* that provide *active decision support*. These systems provide support based on professional knowledge for assessment and decisions in relation to a particular client situation. Such systems can prompt consideration of relevant legislation, policy, research and professional guidelines relevant to the client assessment. The system may provide access to the relevant documents held on computer or the World Wide Web or may extract data from a number of sources to provide a unique analysis.

Expert systems aim to provide information that might aid the making of a particular decision by bringing together a range of relevant professional knowledge and applying it to the recorded information that we have about the client, family and circumstances. There is relatively limited use of *active decision support* in social work but this is likely to become more common as our knowledge base and technical resources increase. An increasing number of *care pathways* are being developed, charting the expected rehabilitation and treatment journey of a client with a long-term condition such as stroke, based on professional consensus utilising current best evidence. At present, these are mostly in hospital and rehabilitation settings, but are being developed into community services and for an increasing number of chronic conditions. In due time, we can expect that these will be computerised and used to inform professional judgement about the care of an individual.

RESEARCH SUMMARY 8.2

Information requirements for decision making

Increasingly, jurisdictions are adopting universal assessment procedures and information technology to aid in healthcare data collection and care planning. Before their potential can be realised, a better understanding is needed of how these systems can best be used to support clinical practice. We investigated the decision-making process and information needs of home-care case managers in Ontario, Canada, prior to the widespread use of universal assessment, with a view of determining how universal assessment and information technology could best support this work. Three focus groups and two individual interviews were conducted; questioning focused on decision making in the post-acute care of individuals recovering from a hip fracture. We found that case managers' decisional process was one of a clinician–broker, combining clinical expertise and information about local services to support patient goals within the context of limited resources. This process represented expert decision making, and the case managers valued their ability to carry out non-standardised interviews and override system directives when they noted that data may be misleading. Clear information needs were found in four areas: services available outside of their regions, patient medical information, patient pre-morbid functional status and partner/spouse health and functional status. (Egan et al., 2009)

Assessment tools could be seen as static, paper versions of expert systems to support decision making. One advantage of a computerised system is that a much wider range of knowledge can be incorporated. A traditional assessment tool has to be based on the most generally applicable knowledge base for the range of clients and families for which it is intended to be used. With a computerised system, only the knowledge relevant to this particular decision need be presented to the professional to inform his or her recommendations. This information can be selected from a large bank of stored data that would be too large for an individual to memorise in detail. Hence the quantity of knowledge that can be incorporated into the system without swamping the human decision maker can be much greater. Such *expert systems* need to be primed with the general knowledge base relevant to the range of decisions being undertaken, and fed with data relating to this particular client, family and context. Expert systems can be built to use the data from client information management systems, but a major challenge is specifying the information to be used to inform the decision. The quality of data going into the decision system is crucial to its effectiveness.

Expert systems could be used to structure an ideal decision process so as to standardise what is currently agreed (through some professional consensus process) to be best practice in that type of decision. Such expert systems can be designed to use various methods to analyse and synthesise the data, whether linear regression or classification trees or some form of 'fuzzy logic' such as neural networks (Garson, 1998) that can give approximate solutions where there are many variables to consider in a decision. There are many issues to be addressed about the complexity and variation of decision situations and the limitations of systems to model these.

PRACTICE EXAMPLE *8.3*

Computerised decision support

In 1998, the National Health Service in England and Wales set up NHS Direct, a round-the-clock advice service. Key elements include a computerised self-help advice system and a nurse-led telephone advice service. The nurses providing advice make use of a computer-based expert system to assist them in assessing the seriousness of the caller's problem, judging the urgency with which a response should be made and giving standardised, agreed professional advice. (NHS Direct, 2009, **www.nhsdirect.nhs.uk***)*

Chapter summary

- Assessment is a central activity in judgement and decision making. We consider the main components as gathering, ordering and analysing information.

- In order to be person-centred, assessment processes have been developed that are integrated (unified) so as to co-ordinate contributions across professions, and staged so that assessment is in some measure proportionate to general level of need.

- Social workers are particularly suited by training and role to co-ordinate multi-professional assessment in complex cases. Social workers also have a role in using appropriate specialist assessment tools.

- Much attention is often focused on the gathering and ordering of data, to the neglect of how it will be analysed to inform a decision. We consider various approaches to analysis in assessment including statistical and *fuzzy* approaches and a model that views strengths as not the polar opposite of vulnerabilities or risks.

- There is an untapped potential for computerised decision aids to support decision making in social work.

FURTHER READING

Calder, M.C. (ed) (2008) *Contemporary Risk Assessment in Safeguarding Children.* Lyme Regis, Russell House.

This is a detailed book for the child protection specialist interested in cutting edge development of models, theory and research in safeguarding children.

Kemshall, H. and Pritchard, J. (eds) (1996) *Good Practice in Risk Assessment* and *Risk Management 1 and 2.* London: Jessica Kingsley.

This is an edited pair of books with a chapter devoted to assessing and managing risk in relation to the main client groups.

Taylor, B.J. and Devine, T. (1993) *Assessing Needs and Planning Care in Social Work.* Hampshire: Ashgate.

This textbook outlines a sound framework for assessment and care planning, and illustrates skills in assessment based on a practical conceptual model.

Chapter 9

Dynamic decision making and care decision pathways

CHAPTER OBJECTIVES

This chapter will help you to meet the following National Occupational Standards for Social Work.

- Key role 2, unit 4: Respond to crisis situations.

- Key role 2, unit 6: Prepare, produce, implement and evaluate plans with individuals, families, carers, groups, communities and professional colleagues.

- Key role 4, unit 12: Assess and manage risks to individuals, families, carers, groups and communities.

- Key role 5, unit 16: Manage, present and share records and reports.

- Key role 5, unit 17: Work within multi-disciplinary and multi-organisational teams, networks and systems.

This chapter will help you to meet post-qualifying requirements for social work in the UK such as the following.

- Work effectively in a context of risk, uncertainty, conflict and contradiction (The Post-Qualifying Award in Specialist Social Work (Generic Level Requirement vii.), General Social Care Council [England], 2004).

- Competence in working effectively in complex situations (Post-Qualifying Award, Requirement PQ2, *Scotland & Wales (= UK Framework 1990–2007)*).

- Competence in exercising the powers and responsibilities of a professional social worker, including the appropriate use of discretion and the management of risk (Post-Qualifying Award, Requirement PQ3, *Scotland & Wales (= UK Framework 1990–2007)*).

- Ability to make informed decisions (Post-Qualifying Award, Requirement PQ4, *Scotland & Wales (=UK Framework 1990–2007)*).

- Demonstrate consistent and sustained sound judgement and decision making in the context of complexity, risk, uncertainty, conflict and contradiction (Specific Award Requirement 3, Northern Ireland Post-Qualifying Education and Training Partnership, 2007)

Although there are well-recognised decision points, such as reviews, for the most part it is difficult to delineate where decision making starts and finishes. Rather than thinking of decision making having a clear beginning and end, it is more appropriate to think in terms of chains of decisions taken over time, each feeding into the next.

(O'Sullivan, 1999, p11)

Introduction

In Chapter 9 we consider the time dimension, including sequences of decisions and implementing decisions through care planning and decision pathways. We discuss urgency and delaying decisions; contingency planning (*what if?*); planning retrievable *risk steps*; systems for monitoring and retrieving a situation; recording; and evaluating the effectiveness of the decision. We consider the place of Bayes' Theorem as a model for taking account of new information to revise a judgement about the likelihood of a particular outcome.

Sequences of decisions

Most decision theory is about choice at a point in time. This is a severe limitation for application in professional decision making where a crucial aspect is about processes of decision making over time (Killick, 2008). We make decisions at various stages of the care process such as referral, initial assessment, complex assessment, specialist assessment and so on. Many decisions are incremental, like pruning a hedge rather than like cutting down a tree. A decision process over time gives the opportunity to learn and to adjust the course of action to suit the needs of the particular client and family as we weave a path between the challenging *brambles*. There are often options to consider such as whether to seek more information by undertaking further interviews or by involving other professions. Decisions may be made with your line manager under pressure in order to avert a crisis by providing some practical response. Over time, several such emergency decisions may be made.

We can view the emphasis on assessment as a continuous process rather than a single event (Department of Health and Department for Education and Employment, 2000) in this context, although assessment is only meaningful as a process to inform a decision and subsequent action. There has been concern that the welfare of children in state care has been allowed to drift because of a lack of coherent longer-term decision making. Sometimes the care process is complex involving a range of professions – for example, in relation to chronic conditions. In many care contexts it is important to have a periodic overview (review) to monitor the direction that the small decisions are leading and compare the direction with overall goals.

In effect, as social workers we operate within processes of decision making that form pathways of actions, care and intervention (Health & Social Care Change Agents Team, 2003). Each decision forms part of a larger picture encompassing many other decisions by clients, families, concerned others, professionals and organisations. Decisions need to take into account the outcome of previous decisions and the response to previous interventions. Key issues arise as to whether we have enough information to make a satisfactory decision. What prompts or requires a decision to be taken now rather than delayed?

Decide now?

An important feature of professional practice is that doing nothing IS a decision! Once a referral is received, making no response is either a decision to do nothing (yet) or an administrative error. Avoiding a decision is not good decision making, although delaying a decision for a clear, justifiable reason may be wise on occasions. *Professional risk-takers cannot escape liability simply by omitting to take decisions. Failing to detain someone with a severe mental illness, who might injure him- or herself is as much a decision, and the taking of a risk, as would be the positive act of detaining a patient* (Carson and Bain, 2008, p97).

A delay in responding to a particular client may of course be due to competing pressure from other clients and the imperative to prioritise scarce time and resources in accordance with professional or organisational priorities. Often, time is required to build a working relationship with a client so that you can clarify your role and identify options, opportunities and objectives with clients. Some time taken and used effectively at an earlier stage may be better for longer-term care (risk and safeguarding) planning and be a more efficient use of your time and agency resources overall.

It may also be useful to delay making a major decision in order to test a hypothesis as part of the problem-solving process with the client. You might try something that should reveal desired information about the problem and a potential way forward, and evaluate what is learnt, such as within some family therapy models. You could consider parallels with your general medical practitioner trying out a medicine on you for the first time and asking you to come back a short while later to see how effective it is and what the side-effects are. Assessing the ability and motivation of a client and family to change in response to a planned intervention requires a time period. *Trying to identify the issues in a case too soon may have the effect of having too little information, while waiting too long may mean that opportunities for effective and swift interventions are missed* (Hollows, 2001, p14). In some situations it is better to recognise explicitly the need for early, shared information from which hypotheses about problems may be formulated. An essential skill is to assess the urgency of making a decision. A more urgent decision may be more likely to require an *intuitive* approach, whereas a decision with serious consequences but where there is more time might need a more *analytic* approach and use more formal decision processes (Hammond, 1996).

What is 'enough' information for the decision?

Questions arise as to how far we go in gathering more information. It is always tempting to keep on *assessing*, perhaps as an avoidance of making the decision and hoping that problems will be resolved. The general principle in professional assessment is that we want to gather suitably comprehensive information in our assessment in order that an informed decision may be made.

There is a cost in terms of time and resources to gathering *comprehensive* information for a decision. Time may be the limiting factor in a crisis situation, and a decision often has to be made with less information that you would like. Gaining fuller information in order to make a *better* decision has a cost (for the client as well as for the professional), which can be weighed against the possibility of an improved decision with the fuller data that might be expected from a particular exercise in gathering further information (Baumol, 2004). These are known as *fast and frugal models* of decision making (Gigerenzer and Goldstein, 1996). A judgement with adequate time might be based on seeking maximum benefit, whereas a judgement under time pressure might be made to satisfy a small number of minimum criteria. When we are under time and resource pressures, we may select the first available option that meets a small number of essential criteria (*satisficing model of decision making*) so as to make a *good enough* decision (Newell and Simon, 1972). Experienced professionals usually learn to see *patterns* in situations and assess the relevance and importance of particular features more quickly than novices who have to think through more slowly the implications of each new piece of information in relation to each other factor.

CASE STUDY 9.1

Crisis and the satisficing model of decision making

I received a telephone call from the police at about 1am regarding a neighbour who was concerned that two children under 8 years of age were unattended in a nearby house. I went to the house with the police officer, called with the neighbour and the children answered the door to us.

The parents were apparently out drinking; the children are not on the child protection register. The children suggest that they would be happy to stay with their grandparents who live nearby. The police have no concerns about the grandparents, and the neighbour also confirmed that the grandparents visit regularly.

You visit the grandparents and on the basis of your interview with them you are satisfied that it will be safe enough to leave the children with them overnight until the matter can be dealt with more fully in the morning.

The decision has had to be made as the best in the circumstances, based on limited information and under time pressure, and using a few key criteria.

Legal aspects of decisions under time pressure

Many social work decisions are made with less information than desired, potentially false information and rather less than *full* information. This is a fact of life; what is important is that you have a rationale for your information gathering, your prioritising and your judgements.

If you are operating under tight time pressure and with limited information this might be considered as an emergency. Clearly one cannot expect the same rigour of decision

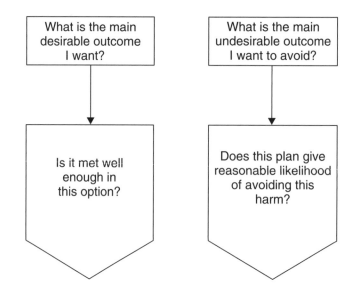

Figure 9.1 Satisficing model of decision making

making, or such assurance of positive outcomes, if decisions are made in an emergency. A dilemma is a decision where there is a lack of harm-free options. Many social work decisions might be framed this way. The law acknowledges emergencies where a lower standard of decision making might be acceptable because of pressures such as time and lack of harm-free options (dilemmas) (Carson, 1988; Rogers, 2006; Carson and Bain, 2008, p320). Dilemmas are not easy emotionally (Lipsky, 1980) but it is important to agonise over some dilemmas and to retain a *healthy scepticism* (Laming, 2003). If a tragedy ensues, what is important is that you record at the time the context of the decision making so that time and resource pressures and the lack of options are clear. In an emergency situation a lower standard of care may be acceptable but you need to think how you would answer the question: *why was this emergency not foreseen?* In recording and report-writing explain the options that are available and the anticipated dangers of each option, bearing in mind how it might look with hindsight.

ACTIVITY 9.1

Recording judgements under time pressure

- *Consider a recent case where you had to make a judgement or recommendation under time pressure, with less than the fuller information that you would have liked and where the option you would have preferred was not available.*

- *How did you record the context of these pressures so that it might be recognised subsequently as an emergency situation or dilemma?*

Care planning and ownership of the decision

Engaging clients in decisions is particularly pertinent in terms of care (risk, safeguarding) planning, in other words, how the decision will be implemented. We have already considered in earlier chapters some issues in engaging clients in the decision process, and consent as a mechanism to manage risk in supporting clients in reasoned, reasonable risk-taking. Where there are multiple challenges facing clients we need to partialise and prioritise in deciding about services and support for change (Doel and Marsh, 1992). Although the main factors to be taken into account in considering the likelihood of harm are those (*actuarial*) factors that are tested through research, the less tangible *clinical* factors take on greater importance in implementing the decision through a care plan. Those less tangible factors about the client, family and their situation need to be considered more fully at this stage so as to:

- seek maximum ownership of the implementation of the decision;

- maximise motivation so as to improve adherence to the plan;

- take into account cultural, religious and ethnic aspects of regular routines of living;

- ensure that the care plan is workable; and

- tailor the plan to the unique needs of this client and family within the framework of an intervention that is proven to be effective in situations that are somewhat similar.

It is important to demonstrate that care planning, like assessment, is based on the best available professional knowledge. However, it must also be recognised within the care planning process flowing from decisions that prediction is always fallible. There will always be inaccuracy in our judgements, and this fact needs to be part of our care planning.

CASE STUDY *9.2*

Creativity in care planning

Mrs Stevenson (68 years) has had mental health problems for many years. She was diagnosed with Motor Neurone Disease and was subsequently admitted to hospital to have a PEG tube inserted. In planning for her discharge it was apparent that she had no family support to assist with practical tasks such as medication administration via the PEG tube. Mrs Stevenson was advised that the district nurses and home care workers were unable to administer medication. I enabled Mrs Stevenson to make a private arrangement for this part of her care needs.

- *What aspects of care planning in your role require particular creativity?*

- *How would you advise a new social worker to go about this?*

A key question in safeguarding decisions may be regarding the prospects of the parents or other family members changing their behaviour sufficiently and sufficiently quickly to avoid the need to take protective measures. It is important that we draw on the best available evidence about the effectiveness of interventions and typical recovery journeys. The decision process can involve setting targets and reviewing progress within an overall safeguarding plan. There are particular issues in agreeing to work on protection without allocating blame, such as issues of exaggerating the dangers and setting the standard too high. A high level of professional interpersonal skills is required for negotiating interventions in high risk situations. Increasingly, standardised documentation is being used for care planning to:

- give structure to the implementation of decisions;
- help to ensure clarity about goals, roles, tasks and timescales; and
- assist in planning the review of decisions.

There are dilemmas in designing care planning documentation if one wishes to have standard documentation that covers a wide variety of types of intervention. Sometimes it is easier to have a care planning tool that relates to a particular service or type of intervention. One question is how flexible or loose the care planning document should be in terms of linking to an equivalent assessment tool. Greater structure does more to standardise best practice in implementing decisions. However, care planning tools need to ensure that they provide sufficient flexibility to accommodate the variation in client needs, strengths and contexts, and the variation in provision of services, systems, roles, etc.

ACTIVITY **9.2**

Values and care plan decisions
Consider a decision-making situation on your caseload.

- *How well do you understand the care-related values of the client?*
- *How well do you understand the care-related values of the family or other informal carers?*
- *How well do you understand the values of other professionals or organisations in relation to the proposed care plan for this client and family?*

Care plan objectives and decision outcomes

A challenge facing us as social workers is being creative in care planning so as to use our skills effectively to engage the strengths of the client and family. One consideration in deciding on an intervention is the extent to which particular problems are likely to be responsive to intervention. This may depend on client capacity to learn, client motivation and resources for learning and growth, your own skills and the public or voluntary resources that you can harness for this client.

It is important to have clear objectives to implement the decision and as far as possible ones that motivate the client. The goals of the care (risk, safeguarding) plan are the justification for taking risk; they need careful thought and justification through such as a mutually understood agreement with the client and a basis in sound research or professionally acceptable theory. In protection decisions the safeguarding mandate needs to be clear. Clarity of care plan objectives to implement the decision is an essential and integral part of reasonable, reasoned risk-taking decision making as part of our professional role. An acronym to assist in thinking about care planning objectives is SMART.

- **Specific** – clarity about the facts and the expectations of the client, carer and professionals in plain language in relation to the care plan and its inherent risk steps.

- **Measurable** – specifying care plan outcomes that can be measured so that you will (all) know when it has been achieved so as to minimise misunderstanding.

- **Achievable** – the care plan goals and risk-steps agreed (if possible) are designed to be successful and to build confidence amongst all parties.

- **Realistic** – the care plan goals and risk-steps are designed to relate to the key issues or problems facing the client and the reason for social work involvement.

- **Time-bounded** – any estimates of risk are put in a time frame, and the care plan goals and risk-steps are clearly specified in terms of time scale.

Contingency planning

In situations where the likelihood of harm is relatively high, contingency plans should be prepared in advance. In other words, consider *what if?* Having a *plan B* helps to relieve some of the pressure that the professional may feel for *plan A* to succeed.

CASE STUDY 9.3

Planning for contingencies

Alfie Giddens is aged 12 years and has severe learning and physical disabilities. There are concerns about his parents' ability to meet his needs. Mr Giddens has periods of very low mood. The recent review of his care plan concluded that an increase in the respite care arrangement would be very beneficial in relieving pressure on the parents and on Alfie. However, due to demands on the service, this need could not be met. In order to manage the level of risk without this service in place it was agreed that I as the field social worker should visit more often.

- *Identify a recent case where a lack of resources has necessitated a change of care plan.*

- *How was this unmet need recorded and used to contribute to service planning?*

Monitoring decision implementation

Monitoring is part of implementing and reviewing decisions. Monitoring means that someone with appropriate knowledge and skills gathers information about the situation at a time after the decision has been taken and acts appropriately so that this information is used to inform a review of the care plan. The person gathering the information directly may or may not be a professional; it might be, for example, a foster parent or home care worker. What is important is that the person gathering the information knows what it is they are looking out for and the threshold criteria for communicating concern to the appropriate professional. The appropriate professional needs to be clear about their responsibility for setting up the system for monitoring the care of the client, ensuring that it is workable and acting on information received. The 5 WH of monitoring are:

- *Why* monitor? Are the objectives SMART and standards clear?

- *Who* will monitor? – family, neighbours, community, agency?

- *What* will be monitored? – what has been achieved, what helped or hindered, what evidence is there?

- *When* will we monitor? How great are the risk steps? What timescale for review of the decision?

- *Where* will we monitor? Where will it happen and be recorded?

- *How* will we monitor? Who will be looking out for what? Who will do what if the situation crosses what threshold?

- *Cost* of monitoring? What level of detail is required so as to monitor efficiently?

CASE STUDY **9.4**

Monitoring and adapting a care plan

Olivia Robinson (11 years) has special educational needs and is on the child protection register due to neglect and potential emotional abuse. Her mother misuses alcohol. An initial case conference created a safeguarding plan which offered various supports to Mrs Robinson and required her not to misuse alcohol while Olivia was in her care. Unfortunately, about four weeks later another incident of Mrs Robinson misusing alcohol while caring for Olivia occurred and the child had to be taken into care.

- *Identify a recent case where you had to adapt a care plan due to changing circumstances.*

- *How do you define thresholds for making a decision that such a change is required?*

Any definition of risk has to include a timescale, and the time periods between monitoring can be thought of as *risk-steps*. What could go wrong between monitoring points i.e.

CASE STUDY **9.5**

Telephone monitoring

Mr Smith has returned home from hospital after a broken femur sustained during a fall. There are general concerns about his well-being but he is adamant that he wants to return home. He has an emergency call alarm system that he can use to alert his daughter who lives nearby. Also someone at the local Good Morning Downpatrick service for vulnerable older people telephones him each day during his recovery period to check on his well-being. If they get no answer then the daughter is called and told of this. If he were to fall and be unable to call his daughter with the emergency call system, the longest period that he would be left lying would be 24 hours before a family member were alerted.

within that risk-step? These *risk-steps* can be thought of as retrievable time intervals for reviewing the decision. Data on critical time periods can inform risk intervals. If, for example, a mother is being required to bring her young child to the health visitor for check-ups because of child protection concerns, how are you deciding on the time intervals between check-ups?

CASE STUDY **9.6**

Child welfare monitoring by a school

A seven-year-old girl, Khyra Ishaq, was kept prisoner and starved to death by her mother and her partner despite them having a (locked) kitchen stocked full of food (Tweedie, 2008; Bennett, 2009).

- *If it were an aim of the school-based social work or education welfare system to monitor such extreme neglect, at what time intervals would a child of this age typically need to be monitored in order to prevent death through starvation?*

- *How might this best be achieved?*

Care pathways, decision options and timescales

As we consider monitoring sequences of decisions and monitoring the implementation of decisions we are gradually building up a picture of a care journey for an individual, now often called a care pathway. Looked at in terms of co-ordinating a number of interventions we might specify normal timescales for assessment and provision of specialist services such as rehabilitation. For more complex situations we may have to consider decision points to choose between different options as well as timescales for this care journey. This then has parallels with *decision trees* but with a time dimension added. There are various examples of care pathways, such as in relation to mental illness in the community (Goldberg and Huxley, 1979) and older people experiencing a crisis, such as falls (Urgent Care Pathway Working Group, DH, 2007). One definition and uses of integrated care pathways (adapted from Bandolier, 2009) are as follows.

- An integrated care pathway (ICP) is a multi-disciplinary outline of anticipated care, placed in an appropriate timeframe, to help a patient or client with a specific condition or set of symptoms move progressively through a treatment or helping experience to positive outcomes.

- Variations from the pathway may occur as professional freedom is exercised to meet the needs of the individual client.

- ICPs are important because they help to reduce unnecessary variations in client care and outcomes. They support the development of care partnerships and empower clients and their families.

- ICPs can also be used as a tool to incorporate local and national guidelines into everyday practice, manage risk and meet the requirements of clinical and social care governance.

Changing your judgement

We began this chapter by considering sequences of decisions as *incremental decision making.* Sometimes, the stage of the case requires a change of decision-making perspective. For example, the early stage of a safeguarding situation may require an approach that might be conceived as *protecting this individual and others.* Once a decision has been made that the child needs to be protected (by whatever statutory means) then the mind-set may have to change to consider *balancing benefits and harms.* In other words, the decision now becomes balancing options rather than considering dangers against threshold criteria.

One aspect of changing a decision that has been studied is known as *sunk costs,* which is when a decision maker continues to invest resources in a previously selected course of action even though it is now perceived not to be the best option (Chapman and Elstein, 2000, p194). It is a common human trait that we are tempted to keep to the status quo and renew our efforts to achieve the option already selected rather than write off the lost effort.

CASE STUDY 9.7

Changing your mind in the light of new evidence

Mrs Wallace is a single mother living with her five-year-old daughter Penny. Mrs Wallace suffers from depression and abuses alcohol. Her care of Penny has given sufficient cause for concern that the child was taken into care. A case conference has been convened to consider the advisability of Penny returning to live with her mother at this time. The factors that would influence my judgement to favour a return home include: whether there is robust evidence Mrs Wallace no longer has an addiction problem; whether Mrs Wallace engages with a member of the community addiction team to address her addictive behaviour; whether there are reliable arrangements that can be put in place whereby family or neighbours will look after Penny when Mrs Wallace is drinking.

A reason why we may change our decision is because of new information. A key issue when we are involved in a volatile or deteriorating situation is to consider what evidence would be required for you to change your mind (for example, about safety in a protection situation or a vulnerable person living alone). As individuals, as well as in our professional roles, we like to hold on to our opinions. A change of opinion can be painful and hard work; it needs to be justified to ourselves if not to others. It is much easier emotionally and in terms of time and effort to go along with the flow. Sometimes we might make an intuitive judgement and then (sub-consciously) focus on information that supports our opinion, tending to discount contradictory evidence.

Bayes' Theorem (Wikipedia, 2009, **en.wikipedia.org/wiki/bayesian_probability**), named after the Rev Thomas Bayes, is a mathematical method for revising an estimate of the probability of an event (for example, a particular harm) in the light of new evidence. Bayes' Theorem allows us to start with an initial estimate of the probability of an event – for example, a person in a particular age group killing someone, based on population figures. If we have an assessment tool with known sensitivity and selectivity then we can combine these figures to give a more accurate revised estimate of the likelihood of harm occurring. The detailed mathematics is beyond the scope of this book; the interested reader is referred to Macdonald (2001, Chapter 14) for a more detailed discussion of the application of Bayes' Theorem in social work. The essential message is that new information needs to be given due weight, irrespective of whether it confirms or contradicts our previous judgement about a situation and the mechanisms at work creating or sustaining the problem. The impact that the new information should have may be greater or lesser than one might think intuitively. Information about increased risk to a low risk case may require a larger revision of judgement than the same increase of risk in a high risk case.

Recording decisions and hindsight error

The ongoing recording of accurate, retrievable information and the summarising of information at intervals are the cornerstones of monitoring the quality of care (Taylor and Devine, 1993, p81). Record keeping is essential to the social work task to improve the effectiveness of service delivery and to enable accountability for standards of practice, use of time and resources. Recording is also vital in decision making in order to:

- record client involvement;
- record the client's understanding of the process;
- record decision processes;
- record options considered and choices made;
- provide an opportunity for reflection and evaluation; and
- provide evidence of factors taken into account in case of subsequent challenge.

The rationale for decisions needs to be retained in client records as well as the option actually chosen. The context, options available, client views, discussion and reasoning about decisions are all an important part of the decision process that should be recorded in contentious cases. When something *goes wrong* people and organisations may want to blame someone (or another organisation). The micro-scale interactions of interviews are rarely captured in written records. What is required is a sufficiently accurate record of critical issues that influence decisions, particularly if you are concerned that there are possible harms with serious consequences, particular contention or interest in the decision from politicians or the media. It is worth paying close attention to how you word your records. How does it sound out of context? What impression might your words convey months or years later if a tragedy occurred?

- *It was a gamble your honour and it went wrong . . .*
- *It is disappointing that it went wrong, your honour, but we had to take a risk . . .*
- *We are sorry about the harm that occurred, your honour, but we were facing a dilemma . . .* (cf. Carson and Bain, 2008).

It has been shown through many experiments that after an event people think that what actually occurred was more obvious before the event than it appeared at the time or to people who do not know the real outcome. Typical experiments in this field present two groups of people with an identical decision scenario (for example, with a harm to be avoided) except that one group is told the *actual outcome* in terms of harm, and the other is not. Almost always the group that knows the *actual outcome* thinks that people should have been able to predict that outcome to a greater extent than does the other group. Recording needs to address the temptation to *hindsight error,* which faces every Inquiry reporting on a tragedy.

> *If you have reason to believe that an event is possible, but unlikely, then you should declare and record that likelihood in an explicit form. Unless it can be shown that your estimate was inappropriate it will prove powerful in discouraging any court or other form of inquiry from utilising hindsight in order to conclude that the harm, which has now occurred, was more likely than it then seemed. The court has to try to avoid hindsight; why not help it?*

(Carson, 1996, p10)

There are many problems with relying on memory for the detail of events, decisions and sequences of these, hence the need for contemporaneous records.

> *The sooner after the event a record is made, the more accurate it is likely to be, which is why your case records are so important. If they are detailed, objective and compiled promptly, there is a good chance that a court will regard them as accurate accounts of the events concerned. In cases with a significant amount of contemporaneous documentary material, courts are likely to accept as accurate evidence which matches the documents.*

(Seymour and Seymour, 2007, p128)

ACTIVITY 9.3

Memory and recall of events

- *Try to remember what you were doing this time last week.*

- *What time did you leave work this day last week?*

- *If you think you know, is that because you remember or because you usually or always leave at that time?*

- *What time did your last journey by car or public transport begin and end?*

- *Where did you last park your car other than at home or work?*

- *Describe the people sitting near you the last time you were on public transport.*

Records assist in evaluating progress with implementing decisions. They also support reflective practice so that you can learn from each situation and transfer learning to other similar situations.

Chapter summary

- Individual decisions are sometimes part of a sequence of decisions that can be viewed as a *care decision pathway*. Unnoticed incremental decisions may result in drift, where the care plan direction is not clear.

- It is always worth considering the degree of urgency that attaches to a decision. Delaying a decision for a sound, rational reason may be wise on some occasions.

- When a decision is being made it is valuable to consider *what if*, and to plan for the most likely or most serious contingencies.

- A series of short, retrievable risk steps may be better than larger steps so that professionals are more likely to be aware and able to respond.

- Bayes' Theorem is a model for conceptualising how we take account of new information to revise a judgement about the likelihood of harm occurring.

- Systems for monitoring (and retrieving) a situation and recording are key elements of decision processes.

- The effectiveness of decisions should be evaluated, but avoid the error of assuming that a good outcome demonstrates a sound decision process or that a harmful outcome demonstrates a poor decision process.

- Inquiries into tragedies often fall prey to this *hindsight bias*. Key implications are that contemporary recording must take account of the range of contextual factors, and that the quality of decisions must be judged on the quality of decision processes, not outcomes.

FURTHER READING

Carson, D. and Bain, A. (2008) *Professional Risk and Working with People: Decision-Making in Health, Social Care and Criminal Justice.* London: Jessica Kingsley.

This excellent book contains much useful material on legal aspects of decision making including dilemmas, emergencies and making decisions with less than the full information that you would like to have.

De Luc, K. (2000) *Developing Care Pathways: The Handbook Vol. 2: The Toolkit.* London: Radcliffe Publishing for National Pathways Association.

A handbook giving valuable practical guidance on developing integrated (multi-professional) care pathways to support improvements in care where clarity about timescales and decision points is helpful.

French, S. (1989) *Readings in Decision Analysis: Chapman & Hall Statistics Text Series.* London: Chapman & Hall/CRC.

This book contains a section on the application of Bayes' Theorem to decision making for the enthusiast who wishes to know more.

Middleton, S., Barnett, J. and Reeves, D. (2001) What is an integrated care pathway? *Evidence Based Medicine,* 3(3) 1–8 (www.evidence-based-medicine.co.uk) available at **www.medicine.ox.ac.uk/bandolier/painres/download/whatis/What_is_an_ICP.pdf**

A clear, well-written article outlining key elements of integrated care pathways in health and social care.

Chapter 10

Managing decisions: support, blame and learning

If a railway company really put the safety of its passengers first, it would run no trains.

> Albanian Proverb – Miles Kingston, The *Independent*, 9 January 2002, p3

Introduction

This chapter considers the effective management of decision making including the demand to *account for resources and priorities*. Tragedies and Inquiries are considered in relation to the lessons of studies of hindsight bias, and the implications for practice including recording. We emphasise the need for managers and senior professionals to provide effective support for reasoned, reasonable decision making by front-line professionals that empowers clients to achieve care (risk, safety) plan goals. This includes the use of supervision in managing decision making. This chapter discusses issues facing organisations in developing decision support systems, policies, training, strategies, and appropriate engagement in inter-organisational working. The management of decisions by the organisation is viewed within the framework of social care governance, creating a learning organisation, and managing effective risk-taking decision making through learning from safeguarding incidents, including near misses as well as tragedies. The responsibility of all professional staff to evaluate decision quality and contribute within their own role to sound decision making as an aspect of social care governance is emphasised.

Accountability to society

It is quite proper in a democratic society that as social workers, just as members of any other profession, we are held to account for our actions. Inquiries, courts, questions by politicians and the activities of the media are all valuable, when used appropriately, in playing their part in providing checks and balances that ensure as far as possible that the activities of professionals and organisations are carried out responsibly, justifiably and fairly. As professionals we have a responsibility to manage decisions:

- in accordance with the values and standards of the profession;
- to the best of our knowledge and skills, within available resources;
- in good faith and in the best interests of the client;
- in partnership with clients, families and other professionals as far as possible;
- utilising sound principles and processes; and
- using robust professional knowledge to inform our decisions.

The challenge for society is to have effective accountability mechanisms in a complex arena of rights, risks, needs, resources, knowledge, skills and values yet also support professionals to carry out an effective job. Many decisions involve a measure of risk-taking, just as in everyday life. This cannot be avoided. Even if it could be avoided, taking risks is essential to both children and adults for growing and learning by tackling new challenges and enjoying the richness of life.

Safeguarding and service prioritisation decisions sometimes take place in a context of conflict. This conflict may be through a challenge to professional and organisational decision making at a case conference or through a judicial process. Aggrieved parties may express their anger through various legitimate and illegitimate means. In a democratic society the rights of citizens are enshrined in law which is enforced through the courts. Decisions by social workers and other professionals are open to challenge by those regarded as having a legitimate right. These mechanisms have a valuable place when used properly. This context of conflict is part of the price we pay for democratic accountability, but can be stressful for those workers and managers who are the unwilling focus of attention. For the practitioner there is a clear message that if you believe that a politician or the media have an interest in a particular case or that a complaint may be forthcoming you should inform your line manager as soon as possible (DHSS, 1998). Politicians and media have a proper role, but their involvement challenging decisions in an individual case can waste valuable public resources when we have to respond to issues raised on the basis of limited and misleading information.

Tragedies and hindsight

When a tragedy occurs – such as a child homicide or homicide by a person with a mental illness or learning disability, or a potentially preventable death of an older person – an inquiry may be held and a detailed report produced. Inquiry reports can be useful learning tools. The narrative (story) approach is accessible; professional readers can empathise with the misfortune of victims and the professionals who might possibly have been able to protect them. *The narrative approach can prove effective for students since it portrays the 'real' world of practice with its resource constraints, movements of personnel, difficulties in communication and general realignment of services, policies and imperatives* (Stanley and Manthorpe, 2004, p10).

There are also limitations to learning from inquiry reports. Professions and organisations need to learn from good decisions and near misses as well as extreme situations of tragedy. Because of the frequent unrealistic expectations about predicting harm, Inquiries can fuel exaggerated allocation of blame. It is difficult after the event to appreciate the challenges that were faced at the time, including limitations of information, time and resources. *Hindsight bias* has been well researched, and occurs when, after the event, decision makers inflate the probability that they would have got the answer correct if they had been making the decision at the time (Chapman and Elstein, 2000). *Some of the more reflective inquiry reports acknowledge the distinction between hindsight vision and the viewpoint available at the time to professionals under scrutiny* (Stanley and Manthorpe, 2004, p3). An inquiry report that avoids hindsight bias more than most is Perry and Sheldon (1995). What seems *obvious* in hindsight often did not seem so obvious to many sensible people at the time! With hindsight, the influence of other important factors at the time, such as the feared reaction of family, politicians and media if a stronger safeguarding intervention were used, fade into the shadows in the light of the knowledge that the outcome is tragic.

If a decision involves risk, then even when one can demonstrate that one has chosen the unarguably optimal course of action, some proportion of the time the outcome will be suboptimal. It follows that a bad outcome in and of itself does not constitute evidence that the decision was mistaken. The hindsight fallacy is to assume it does (Macdonald and Macdonald, 1999, p22). A good decision makes effective use of the available information and of the context of systems, legal, policy and procedural aspects. Even this will not prevent harm from occurring on every occasion given the inherent unpredictability of human behaviour and the limitations of the knowledge we have available. Blame should not ensue if a sound decision-making process has been used, regardless of the outcome. We can only do our best to reduce the likelihood and consequences of citizens harming each other; we will never be able to prevent all harm while respecting basic human rights.

Decision making in social work is inherently complex, and the potential for predicting emotive human behaviour is limited. We must accept that there are limitations to predicting human behaviour, even with the best actuarial tools and the most experienced professional opinion. We need to establish realistic expectations of ourselves as a profession so that we can be confident in the face of adverse publicity that might seek to convey the impression that a social worker should be some sort of fortune-teller.

We have limited control over the situations that we address compared to a hospital or a school environment. It is no more reasonable to blame a Director of Social Services for the homicide of a child by his or her parents than to blame a Chief Constable for failing to prevent all crime or a Chief Education Officer for failing to prevent any child leaving school without a string of academic qualifications! Organisations and professionals can only take reasonable, reasoned decisions based on the information and resources that they have available at the time. Of course, the relevant senior managers of organisations need to be held to account for their particular responsibilities, such as having in place robust systems, policies and procedures, how they have used resources or the way that staff recruitment and retention issues are being addressed. However, that is a far cry from believing that we can predict with precision the behaviour of each individual in society, especially when they are experiencing distress or anger, or struggling with addiction or mental health problems.

The real strength of inquiries is to inform improvements to future decision-making systems and services (Cambridge, 2004). For a valuable summary of reviews of child abuse inquiries see Reder and Duncan (2004) and for useful summaries of inquiries into homicides by people with mental illness see Sheppard (2004). We need to learn from tragedies. But to learn best from inquiries we must not fall into a blame culture where some politicians or some of the media turn their (understandable) distress into anger at social workers or other professionals because of their own inadequate understanding of the limitations to predicting individual human behaviour.

Organisation culture and defensive practice

The experience of a *blame culture* in society and organisations does not promote good practice. We cannot predict accurately, although we could improve our estimates with the use of sound statistical approaches and more rigorous research as discussed earlier. *Social work decisions are often problematic balancing acts, based on incomplete information, within time constraints, under pressure from different sources, with uncertainty as to the likely outcome of the different options, and the constant fear that something will go wrong and the social worker will be blamed* (O'Sullivan, 1999, p3).

ACTIVITY **10.1**

The culture of society and your organisation

- Do you feel that you are working in a 'blame culture'?

- What are the main sources of pressure that you think would influence you to feel 'blamed' if a tragedy ensued after a decision?

- What do you think are appropriate mechanisms for accountability of professional and organisational decision making in your ideal society?

- What might be done by the social work profession to support you more in professional judgements and decision making?

- What might be done by your employer to support you more in judgements and decision making?

- What might you do so that if a tragedy were to ensue your judgements and decision-making processes would still be regarded as sound?

It is estimated that there are approximately 80 child homicides each year in England and Wales (Creighton and Tissier, 2003; see also Creighton, 2004a,b). If there are very approximately 160 local authorities responsible for child protection work in the same geographical area (**www.idea.gov.uk/idk/org/la-data.do**), then they should each expect on average to have one child homicide every two years. Given the variation in risk factors, some authorities can expect to have more than that and some less. This is (sadly) what our society is like at the present time. To suggest that professionals have necessarily failed in their responsibilities because someone in our society kills someone or commits suicide is nonsense. Predicting individual human behaviour using actuarial and clinical risk factors is better than guesswork or tossing a coin, but is a long way from being precise.

Measures of success might realistically be set in terms of reducing the total number of homicides, and similarly for abuse and other undesirable harms. It is estimated that expenditure on child protection in England and Wales is approximately £1 billion per annum (Creighton, 2004) having risen from £735 million per annum a few years earlier (National Commission of Enquiry in the Prevention of Child Abuse, 1996). This includes part of the expenditure on such as health and education services as well as social work, but excludes such as prison and addiction services which may be required for adults as a result of abuse when a child. A first order approximation might be that doubling the expenditure *might* possibly reduce the number of child homicides by, say, a quarter. That is assuming, of course, that whatever interventions are developed are acceptable to society in terms of justice and human rights. Aiming to have 60 rather than 80 child homicides per year in the jurisdiction would be an ambitious enough target even with such a substantial increase in resources. The investment would, of course, have to be over a sustained time period to allow opportunity for professional post-qualifying training, supervised practice experience at a more skilled level and research to underpin the development of professional knowledge and skills. A further doubling of resources might reduce the remaining number by a further quarter of that figure and so on. A similar argument may be made in relation to any other major harm by one person to another that society wishes to reduce. This would at least be a debate rooted in reality rather than empty rhetoric (Pritchard, 1992). The evaluation of decisions and decision processes must focus on understanding the information available to individuals at the time, their knowledge and skills, the goals being pursued (including the influence of law, regulation and policy) and the context of culture, systems and procedures within which the decision is being taken (Woods *et al.*, 1993).

Evaluating decision processes

If a crisis occurs, organisations may be under pressure to blame someone even though practice and decisions may have been sound in the circumstances. A poor outcome does not necessarily mean that a poor decision has been made; conversely, a good outcome does not necessarily mean that a good decision has been made. What professionals and organisations should be held to account for is the quality of the decision process. Overall, better decision processes based on what is learned through integration into practice of research, theory and lessons from near misses and tragedies will result in better outcomes. But even then a safe outcome is *not* guaranteed on every occasion just because the process is reasonably robust (i.e. meeting the minimum standards expected by society through the law and professional standards at the time) or even if it is exemplary. The quality of decisions attempting to predict human behaviour cannot be judged by their outcome; they should be judged on the way they were reached, that is the decision processes.

A decision to take a risk must be justified against likely benefits, recognising that sometimes harm will occur. If the chance of *success* (for example in successfully returning children home or some independence step for people with a disability) is 99 per cent, then on average harm will occur in one in 100 decisions, or ten in 1,000 decisions. Would you never take a decision with a 99 per cent probability of success? How high a probability would you require, given that absolute certainty is not possible? The potential benefits to the client in terms of the opportunities for growth, change and development needs to be one part of the equation in making a decision.

The danger is that the intense blame culture will lead to defensive practice. It is noteworthy that after a public outcry when a child homicide inquiry report is published the rate of admission of children to state care often increases markedly. Organisations need to take a firm stand against such a blame culture in order to support sound professional decision making that balances rights and risks, needs and available resources in a reasoned and reasonable decision process. *If people are entrusted to take difficult decisions regarding risk taking, it must be accepted that they cannot later be blamed if the outcome leads to tragedy* (Norman, 1980, p27).

ACTIVITY **10.2**

Prompts for reflection on judgement and decision processes
- *What are the main aspects of the context that are driving this decision?*
- *What additional information would I like to have?*
- *Is this a crisis and would it help to delay a decision?*

> **ACTIVITY 10.2** *(CONT.)*
>
> - *What legal issues are important including capacity, Human Rights and health and safety?*
> - *How can I most effectively engage with key stakeholders?*
> - *How are the values of the client, family and society (through you and your organisation) influencing the decision making?*
> - *What responsibilities are there for safeguarding, informing and respecting rights of various parties to the decision?*
> - *What knowledge base is informing my judgement and what more could I usefully know?*
> - *What biases might be influencing me, and how can I counter these?*
> - *What assessment tools, guidelines and other decision aids might help?*
> - *Are coherent plans evolving from the decision processes over time?*
> - *Is the decision process being managed effectively?*
> - *What am I learning from this judgement and decision process?*
> - *What can the organisation learn from this decision process?*

Policies for managing decisions

For the organisation, the challenge is to take steps to avoid a blame culture and to provide systems and processes that support sound decision making. A corporate approach will influence the practice of staff. The board or authority with its non-executive representatives of the public, and senior managers, have a key role in establishing a culture that supports professional staff in good decision making. The organisation culture can be changed by establishing sound overarching policies to support professional decision making, which in turn support reasonable risk-taking by clients.

Decision management policies help to give a consistent approach for clients, staff and managers. Policies exist in most organisations that assist in certain aspects of decision making such as:

- health and safety;
- child and adult protection procedures;
- assessment and care planning in complex cases;
- communication and recording;
- administration of medicines;
- lone working; and
- violence at work.

What is required is an overarching approach that supports reasoned and reasonable risk-taking decision making, recognising that this is intrinsic to human life – including that of our clients – and is hence intrinsic to social work. Elements of a comprehensive decision support policy include the following.

- Service mandate, mission and objectives – the legal mandate, mission and objectives of the organisation, including the main clientele and services, what is (not) permitted by law and mentioning the (varying) limitations of resources.

- Service principles and values – principles to support staff that can be made available to the media, including the right of clients to take risks and potentially controversial issues such as criminality, integration in society, sexuality and alcohol.

- Decision support policy and procedures – standards and support for practitioners and managers in making decisions to use to justify decisions if criticised, particularly when there are pressures of time and resources.

- Knowledge base to inform decisions – the provision of a professional knowledge base (for example, through training and computerised library resources) that can be used to inform decision making.

- Risk strategy context – the location of the policy in relation to governance, management support, supervision, communication, integration across the organisation, training, organisation development, monitoring of services and unmet need, recording and accountability.

- Endorsement – by the appropriate professions and commissioning bodies and a statement about protocols for decision making with other organisations.

Such policies need to seek to do justice to the professional task of supporting prudent risk-taking as the essence of decision making with and on behalf of clients. Where there is dispute over appropriate support a conflict resolution mechanism is required, such as referral to senior management or a multi-professional decision-making body.

> We propose that arrangements be put in place to manage more complex situations where there are different views held between the individual, the family carers or the professionals to seek agreed solutions . . . Such arrangements will enable all those involved to explore the issues and set arrangements which go as far as possible in meeting the individual's aspirations whilst balancing the needs and risks to themselves and others.

(DH, 2007, p4, para 7)

ACTIVITY **10.3**

Decision support policies

- *Identify policies in your organisation that contribute to supporting professional decision making where the possibility of harm must be weighed against potential gains for clients and families.*

- *What are the strengths of the decision support policies?*

- *What are the gaps where policies would be helpful?*

Allocating scarce resources

Resources for health and social care are finite; the demand for services is potentially infinite. Decisions about one client may need to be taken in the light of a decision about the needs of another client when resources are scarce. Social workers and their managers have to *account for resources and priorities* (Taylor, 2006b). Scarce resources, whether funded from the public purse or charitable funding, must be allocated between clients in a manner that can be demonstrated to be fair and meet other legal standards.

Decision policies can assist in meeting the challenge of allocating scarce resources by giving greater consistency of decision making. They help to ensure fairness between different clients. The use of decision policies assists individuals and organisations to make decisions efficiently and consistently, and is a valuable defence against challenge, complaint or litigation. A decision maker may reduce anxiety and stress by identifying the features of this decision that are common to previous decisions, including decisions by others, and hence normalise the activity. A decision policy regarding rationing of services would normally include an explicit system for prioritising services, usually by date order of application, and an explicit system for dealing with high priority, urgent cases that jump the date-order queue.

Such decision policies enable organisations and individuals to be more consistent in their decisions, and thereby have greater credibility. External credibility and staff morale can plummet if decision policies are overridden by managers in the face of irrational external pressures. The people who suffer most in this situation are the *hidden clients* who are on the waiting list for services and who have to wait even longer when someone queue-jumps by soliciting external advocates who exert pressure to change the decision on the basis of emotive or political pressure rather than new evidence, logic or justice.

Inter-agency protocols and decision management

Various government documents emphasise the importance of co-ordinated decision making across organisations, sometimes expressed in terms of co-ordinated assessment processes (e.g. Social Exclusion Task Force, 2008). Co-ordinated decision making requires clarity about roles and responsibilities and a common language.

> To change the culture around the provision of services and address the fear of blame among staff, we propose that organisations and their partners consider establishing a joint choice, empowerment and risk policy that promotes more open and transparent practices. It will need to be supported by senior leadership and shared across the organisation and their partners. There need to be clear lines of accountability and support within the professional team and the respective responsibilities of the council, primary care trust, independent and voluntary sector organisations, the member of staff and the individual using services. The policy would best be supported by appropriate working arrangements and systems.

(DH, 2007, p6, para 16)

Where organisations seek to collaborate, each must be clear about its own function. Collaboration provides a valuable opportunity to learn about the roles of other organisations and to clarify language so as to reduce misunderstanding.

Agreements between agencies need to cover the following key areas:

- *Clear procedures and protocols for joint working*

- *Clear roles and responsibilities*

- *A clear management structure for accountability*

- *A commitment to good quality supervision which includes professional development*

- *Agreed policies and procedures for delivering the service which everyone uses, including responses in crisis*

- *Agreed documentation for the needs assessment process, care planning, risk assessment, monitoring and review, and recording*

- *Information sharing policies with partner agencies*

- *Timely process for resolving complex funding issues – panel with senior decision making/budget holder*

- *Processes for managing complex cases*

- *Processes for conflict resolution.*

(DH, 2007, p41, box 3.9)

Governance: risk and quality of decisions

Organisations have governance systems in order to carry out their corporate responsibilities for managing risks and quality improvement. Professionally, we have Clinical and Social Care Governance, which is about *organisations being accountable for continuously improving the quality of their services and safeguarding high standards of care and treatment* (DHSSPS, 2002, p3 section 6; cf. DH, 1996). Social care governance incorporates both risk and quality dimensions as integral components (Flynn, 2002; Alaszewski, 2003; DHSSPS, 2003). Ensuring the quality of decisions is part of the organisation's governance responsibilities. Every individual member of staff has a role in contributing to the governance processes in the organisation; for professionals, supervisors and managers this particularly includes decision management.

Professional supervision and training

A key mechanism for support and accountability of practice decisions is professional supervision. Social workers in all grades and roles need effective supervision so as to:

- have access to a professional relationship that will provide support, challenge practice, enhance learning and demand accountability as appropriate;

- create a *sounding board* for complex professional decisions as a prompt to consider other perspectives and knowledge to inform the decision;

149

- provide effective direction and monitoring of work, with clear accountability for levels of decision making;

- benefit from a wider range of relevant research and theory through the knowledge and experience of the supervisor to challenge bias;

- ensure that practice is in accord with professional and organisational standards;

- enable communication and gate-keeping to supports (such as legal advice) and some aspects of multi-professional and multi-agency working and management decision making;

- improve practice with insights from a broader knowledge of legislation, policies, procedures, systems and work cultures; and

- provide an opportunity for professional growth and learning for supervisee, supervisor and the organisation through the application of professional knowledge to critical practice issues.

It is important to remember that as an employee you are acting on behalf of your employer. You must, therefore, stay within its functions, policies, procedures and direction from line management. You should, of course, express your own opinion and rationale for your judgements and debate these with your professional supervisor and line manager; you are not expected to be a passive dummy! You would normally expect to face disciplinary issues if you refused to follow your line manager's instructions, but it is possible that you could be criticised for failing to challenge the decision of a line manager (British Association of Social Workers, 2008, p5). If there is a difference of opinion, ensure that accurate records are kept.

ACTIVITY **10.4**

Plan your use of supervision

- *Write a list of points to discuss at your next supervision session.*

- *Make arrangements to meet if these are not made by your supervisor.*

- *What will you do if supervision does not happen as planned?*

As you have worked your way through this book you will probably have become aware of the many aspects of professional practice that interface with decision making. Ongoing training for various aspects of decision making is essential for social workers in all types of roles.

ACTIVITY **10.5**

Training and learning needs

- *How does your training and learning plan (for example, as part of re-registration requirements) need to incorporate topics related to decision making?*

- *What in-service and post-qualifying training courses are available in relation to aspects of professional judgement and decision making relevant to your work?*

- *What is the system in your organisation for identifying and analysing training needs, and how do your training needs get fed into this process?*

Communicating about risk and decisions

There are immense societal pressures to address risk issues and, sometimes, impossible expectations. Some politicians and media may pounce on care decisions where a complaint occurs. In this complex arena of conflicting demands and considerations – from the public, the client, the family, the organisation – the professional needs a robust and yet flexible framework to inform practice decisions such as we are developing in this book. Empowerment of patients and clients to make decisions is more effective if professionals are knowledgeable in their field and can communicate effectively about their judgements and their decision-making knowledge, skills and systems. As an individual professional you should abide by the protocols of your organisation regarding public communication for your own protection as well as the need to support your employer in maintaining public confidence so that the organisation can function most effectively in serving society.

In the interests of justice and confidentiality there are proper limitations on the freedom of organisations and professionals to discuss publicly details of individual cases. The more general challenge is to communicate the nature of the professional task with its possibilities and limitations, and the complexity of information that must be *taken into account* in the critical types of decisions that we make. The challenges in predicting harm to individuals are little understood by the public as is the interplay between rights and intervening to safeguard (Kitzinger and Reilly, 1997). Effective public communication and education by employers, government and the profession need concerted attention. Perhaps as a profession we need to be ready to provide *bite-sized* information to the media in a form that the public can readily understand when a relevant issue arises. Many topics – such as the apparent expectation of being able to predict when a parent is going to kill their child – are so recurrent that materials could be ready prepared.

The learning organisation and evaluating decisions

Both individual practitioners and organisations need to create a culture of learning from decisions (Senge, 1990). We need to learn from good outcomes, near misses, staff insights, and regular feedback from the public and other stakeholders, as well as tragedies. Whistleblowing schemes assist employers in their responsibilities for developing safe systems of work. For practitioners, the opportunity to learn from the outcomes of their interventions is often neglected. Evaluating the decision process and the decision outcomes may be called *review* in relation to individual clients and families. Schon (1996, p26) describes reflective practice as *thoughtfully considering one's own experiences in applying knowledge to practice while being coached by professionals in the discipline.*

Table 10.1 Criteria for evaluating and reflecting on decisions

- What helped and what hindered the decision making?

- What might have gone better?

- Was the decision context appropriately taken into account?

- Did the client and family participate effectively in the decision making including explicit discussion of values and probabilities of desirable and undesirable possible outcomes?

- Was there client consent and ownership of the decision?

- Was effective use made of accurate client and family information?

- Was there appropriate consideration and management of the time dimension such as delaying a decision, care (risk) planning and decision pathways?

- Was a purposeful and effective decision process created?

- Were other professions engaged appropriately?

- Was the decision in accordance with requirements of the law and the social work role (including health and safety, human rights and safeguarding functions)?

- Was there effective use of professional knowledge and models of decision making?

- Was bias avoided through reflective practice and appropriately incorporating best evidence in judgements?

- Was there appropriate use of risk factors, assessment tools and other decision aids?

- Was information presented as well as possible for the decision making?

- Were facts, opinions and knowledge brought together into a cohesive argument?

- Was there a systematic appraisal of the options available?

- Was there clarity about possible benefits and possible harms?

- Were decision outcomes monitored so as to adapt decisions appropriately?

(adapted from Dowie, 1999; O'Sullivan, 1999; and other sources)

Chapter summary

- Sound decision making by frontline professionals requires support by managers and supervisors for reasonable, reasoned decision-making processes. That is the standard by which quality should be judged. No one can foresee the outcomes, but we can use the information that we have to best effect.

- Professional supervision is a central element in managing sound decision making and empowering clients to achieve care (risk, safety) plan goals.

- Organisations need to have decision support systems, policies, training and strategies as well as appropriate engagement in inter-agency working.

- A decision role for managers even more than for practitioners is to *account for resources and priorities* particularly in decisions about allocating scarce public or charitable resources fairly across clients.

- The management of decisions may be viewed within the framework of social care governance, creating a learning organisation (including the evaluation of decision quality), and managing effective risk-taking decision making through learning from good outcomes as well as safeguarding incidents, and including near misses as well as tragedies.

- All professionals have a responsibility to contribute within their own role to sound decision making as an aspect of social care governance.

FURTHER READING

Bostock, L., Bairstow, S., Fish, S. and Macleod, F. (2005) *Managing Risk and Minimising Mistakes in Services to Children and Families: Children and Families' Services Report 6.* London: Social Care Institute for Excellence.

This book develops the term 'safeguarding incident' to include near misses as well as tragedies, and a theory of multiple risk factors coinciding when a tragedy occurs.

Hawkins, P. and Shohet, R. (2000) *Supervision in the Helping Professions.* Buckingham: Open University Press.

This is a well-written book on the essentials of social work supervision.

Simmons, L. (2007) *Social Care Governance: A Practice Workbook.* Belfast: Department of Health, Social Services and Public Safety (Clinical and Social Care Governance Support Team) and London: Social Care Institute for Excellence.

This attractive workbook provides a helpful structure for teams, departments and organisations in developing social care governance arrangements.

Stanley, N. and Manthorpe, J. (eds) (2004) *The Age of the Inquiry: Learning and Blaming in Health and Social Care.* London: Routledge.

This book provides some interesting and useful perspectives on the place of inquiries in social work practice and management.

Conclusion

The journey so far

This book has been about competent social work judgement and decision making. Decisions must be sound from the perspective of our profession and employers who may have statutory safeguarding functions, and roles as custodians of funding provided by the taxpayer or those who give to charitable causes. Many factors need to be considered in making social work decisions: systems; legislation and case law; policy; procedures; standards; principles; professional guidance; opinions of other professions; client choice; family views; neighbours; voluntary and statutory resources; and professional knowledge based on research, theory and many varieties of learning from experience including inquiries, audits and risk and quality governance systems. The pressures of the threat of a legal action for negligence, sanction by a Commission or Inquiry, or interest by the media or a politician create a *wariness of lurking conflict*. Social workers have to manage complex ethical issues, dilemmas and conflicts. Probabilities, values, choices, law, knowledge and skills have to be combined in a complex dynamic interplay in making decisions. Evidence must be incorporated into practice judgements to inform safeguarding decisions, the selection of objectives for social work intervention, the choice of practice method, and advice to clients and families to inform their decision making. Nonetheless, risk-taking decisions are an everyday, inevitable part of being human, and hence are an everyday, inevitable aspect of social work decision making. This creates tensions that are inherent in the professional task. Reasoned, reasonable professional judgement entails support for reasoned, reasonable client decision making including risk-taking, unless safeguarding duties and powers over-ride or the client lacks decisional capacity.

Theoretical sources

There are a number of models of decision making, but no one over-arching model. The professional needs to select an appropriate model, taking into account the type of decision and the types of factors that are important. Our discussion of judgement and decision making has focused on concepts and models that are most readily applied in social work. This has included the main branches of decision study (Bekker *et al.*, 1999; Beresford and Sloper, 2008).

- From *normative decision study* (such as *subjective expected utility theory)*, which focuses on how rational human beings *ought* to make decisions we have developed our thinking about *balancing benefits and harms* (Chapter 7) and in making care (or safeguarding or risk) plans (Chapter 9) to assist in clarifying options, roles, values and responsibilities.

- Our discussion of supporting client decision making (Chapter 2) has encompassed the *naturalistic decision making* school of thought with the *envisioning the future* model to assist in clarifying the voice of the client.

- *Satisficing and decision policy models* have been incorporated into our discussion of safeguarding decisions (Chapter 6) and making decisions on limited information (Chapter 9) due to time and resource pressures.

- Our discussion of heuristics and biases within professional judgement (Chapter 5) has drawn on the school of *descriptive decision study* of real-world decision making as a model to support reflective practice and the use of professional knowledge. The use of multiple cues within professional judgement has drawn on *Brunswick's lens model* and the concepts of learning from experience have parallels in *recognition-primed decision making*.

- We have used *prescriptive decision study* (aiming to improve decision making even if we do not use a specified rational model) in our discussion of assessment tools and the gradual growth of decision support systems (Chapter 8).

Rather than risk getting lost in the detail, our general approach has been to focus on those aspects of theoretical models that are most likely to be useful for social work practice – for *doin' the stuff*, in the memorable words of John Wimber (2004)! In time, we may develop a unified model of decision making in social work such that these models are simplifications of the general model in situations where fewer aspects need to be considered.

The task of engaging and supporting clients and families in decision making is central to effective practice. Clients and families are often in a state of crisis when a social worker enters their lives. There are varying emotions for clients and workers engaging in far-reaching decisions about family and life issues. We can support clients and families in their decision-making processes in various ways such as *envisioning the future* and using tools that assist in exploring issues and clarifying options.

The law provides accountability in a democracy, supporting reasoned, reasonable decision making by professionals. We require an evidence base of professional knowledge to justify our judgements in critical situations. Statutory human rights need to be taken into account explicitly in decision-making processes and in the decision itself. Each professional needs to assure himself or herself that a client consents and has capacity to consent to whatever intervention is proposed unless explicit, justifiable safeguarding powers apply. The touchstone is to ask oneself: *what would a competent professional do?*

Collaborative decision making processes with other professionals and organisations (as well as with clients and families) are a feature of more important decisions. The distinct competence and responsibilities of each profession and organisation must be recognised within a general framework of seeking consensus and thus sharing risk. For *contested decision making*, models can support robust argument in contexts such as child care court proceedings. Timely, focused communication with your line management and professional supervisor are essential in these situations.

Heuristics, or short-cuts, to deal with the complex and varying decisions are an intrinsic component of human judgement but can also lead to bias. Social work practice involves processing large amounts of information, some of it of questionable truth and authority. Reflecting on practice issues in the light of knowledge based on the best available research and theory, individually and through good professional supervision, is central to avoiding bias. We must face the challenges in using the best evidence to inform decisions. When there are limitations of time or resources, professional judgements may be based on information relating to a limited number of key criteria rather than on a comprehensive appraisal of all the factors. Detailed analytic decision making is not possible in every situation.

Trying to predict possible harm on the basis of experience (*clinical prediction*) is prone to more error than using *actuarial* risk factors based on rigorous research. However, even *actuarial* methods are weak at predicting the behaviour of individuals, although they are useful at a population level for planning services. With rigorous research, improved risk factors will become available to better inform our decision making. While actuarial and clinical risk factors should be used where available, their limitations should be recognised and acknowledged. Safeguarding decisions must be taken in the honest recognition that predicting human behaviour will always be prone to error even though we could improve accuracy by using *actuarial* tools. Clarity about thresholds for interventions is required as we make these *criterion-based judgements*.

All of life involves taking risks. Supporting client decision making will involve risk-taking for the client, family, professional and the organisation. We have to support clients to take reasoned, reasonable risks as part of our role in helping them to achieve worthwhile care-related life goals. We need to be able to justify risk-taking in relation to potential benefits and strengths that mitigate the likelihood or seriousness of harm as we *balance benefits and harms*. We also need to fulfil our legal and moral responsibilities to take reasonable care of our own and other people's health and safety.

Assessment tools and other decision support systems are developing steadily to support gathering, collating and analysing information to assist in making a judgement. Assessment tools have become more sophisticated and are beginning to be integrated across professions and organisations, and to integrate specialist assessments into a holistic whole. Perhaps the area where professional decision making in social work could be most obviously improved would be through the increased use of appropriate validated assessment tools in specialist areas, which then contribute to the holistic assessment process. During the past two decades the use of computer systems has become more widespread, providing information to inform decisions. Information systems to manage client data are common even if they lack integration across settings and professions. Passive decision support systems are available in a few places; expert systems are rare. I anticipate that we will see increasing computerised support for our judgements and decision making.

Most research on decision making simplifies the issues to a judgement at a point in time; in social work we need to develop the time dimension of decision study so as to improve the application of decision theory to practice. Sometimes, delaying a decision may be justifiable, but this is in itself also a decision. There are often options at a decision point in social work practice to seek further information or undertake some sort of trial run. Social work practice often involves multiple decisions over time, building up care (risk, decision) pathways. It is salutary to consider what evidence is required to change your mind about a situation! In some social work decisions not only are we lacking full information but also there are time pressures so that *intuitive* models of decision making have their place as well as the *analytic* models that can be applied to weighing options in decisions involving fuller deliberation. Decisions need to be monitored and adapted over time; with appropriate processes for reviewing the implementation of decisions. Monitoring and review points can helpfully be considered as risk-steps, and consideration given to contingency plans and how the situation might be retrieved if it starts to deteriorate.

Organisations have a responsibility to manage more serious decisions in a way that supports front-line professionals in their challenging tasks of supporting reasoned, reasonable client risk-taking decision making and taking safeguarding decisions in emotional, contested situations. Organisations need to take positive steps to counter the blame culture that threatens to undermine professional practice and public confidence in the organisation. *No one* can guarantee good decision outcomes; we *can* set standards for robust, justifiable decision processes which form the proper basis for accountability. There is a pressing challenge in communicating risk and educating the public about the strengths and limitations of predicting harm in a human service field such as social work.

Further learning

The aim of this book is to aid the professional social worker with a robust general framework of concepts to support continuing professional development. You should attend courses or otherwise learn about specific aspects of decisions relevant to your role, in particular:

- child and adult protection knowledge, skills, policies and procedures;
- other protective frameworks for your area of work such as Guardianship, Enduring Power of Attorney, etc;
- Human Rights legislation and recent case law on negligence;
- risk factors, needs and effective helping processes for your own client group;
- decisional capacity and consent to care and treatment;
- your responsibility for health and safety at work; including personal safety for yourself and responsibilities to other staff;
- professional assessment tools embodying sound research and theory; and
- Clinical and Social Care Governance and related policies and procedures (including professional supervision) for the management of decisions.

As you develop your social work career through post-qualifying studies you could:

- explore more detailed aspects of the decision models presented here;
- consider the application of these decision models in more specialised settings;
- explore other decision models;
- develop skills in enabling others in judgement and decision making;

- contribute to organisation development activities such as working groups to develop systems, policies and procedures to support aspects of professional decision making; and

- contribute to developing professional knowledge to inform decision making, through research, audit, service evaluation, and by retrieving, appraising, synthesising and disseminating research by others.

Further research and development

Much further research is required on judgement and decision making in social work (Carroll and Johnson, 1990; Beach and Connolly, 1997; Taylor, 2006a). Some of the key issues for further research and development are:

- describing the way that people make sense of their situation before making a choice between options;

- developing the application of decision models in social work and exploring the connections between these;

- studying the impact of the typical crises encountered in social work referrals for client and family decision making;

- debating the interplay between health and safety regulation, standards of care and social care decisions in areas such as provision of home care services;

- undertaking robust studies of risk factors (including effect size), particularly dynamic risk factors that might be amenable to social work intervention, focused on particular types of harm and at stages in safeguarding decision processes;

- undertaking systematic reviews of the best research on the effectiveness of social work interventions for identifiable types of client problems and on client, family and professional perspectives on care decision processes;

- understanding better how experienced professionals recognise patterns and identify the most important factors for making a decision;

- looking at how types of knowledge such as research, theory, law, service availability and client context are used in various types of social work decisions, and to explore the justifiable and effective use of risk factors;

- developing assessment tools with rigorous tests of validity and reliability, and with increased support for analysis of information to inform decisions;

- exploring the time dimension of decisions, in particular the connection with care (risk) planning and care pathways;

- exploring the potential of various decision support systems, in particular the strengths and limitations of various models of analysing information to inform decisions, such as regression analysis, classification trees, structural equation modelling and neural networks; and

- creating organisation policies that support reasoned, reasonable decision making by practitioners and managers in supporting reasoned, reasonable risk-taking decision making by clients.

Reflection: from novice to expert

Professionals increasingly need to articulate their reasoning in judgements and decision making. Our aim is reasoned and reasonable support for client decision making and sound professional decisions about safeguarding vulnerable people, based on facts considered in the context of values, principles, law, theory, research, policy and procedures. As professionals, we are on a journey where we learn from the interplay between experience and professional knowledge. By reflecting on our practice in the light of professional knowledge – individually, with colleagues, on training courses and in supervision – we will improve our professional judgement and decision making for the ultimate benefit of our clients, their families and our society.

Appendix 1

Pointers in designing or completing an assessment to inform a decision in uncertainty

- Who is the client?

- Who are the key family members and other stakeholders?

- IS it a risk: FROM others? TO others? TO self?

- What is the issue for decision?

- What are the main dangers (the undesirable outcomes to be avoided) for this individual, family, neighbours, other clients, other citizens, care workers, volunteers and the organisation?

- What are the options being considered?

- What are your statutory responsibilities and powers?

- What is the timeframe and degree of urgency, and what is the impact of delaying a decision?

- Clarify the role of the client in the decision process and how this will be supported, including issues of consent and capacity.

- Clarify your role as the social worker in relation to your supervisor, the client, family, other professionals and organisations.

- What are the main vulnerabilities (background hazards, factors that predispose the harm to occur)?

- What are the main trigger factors (situational hazards that might induce the harm to occur)?

- What are the main strengths in the client, family and neighbourhood?

- What are the mitigating factors that might reduce the likelihood or seriousness of harm (perhaps in relation to services that might be provided under each option)?

- What were the outcomes of relevant previous interventions and what has changed since then?

- What value (appreciation, benefit, dread, fear) does the client place on the various options?

- What value does society, the organisation and the profession place on the various options?

- What professional knowledge from research and theory is most useful and what conclusions do you reach?

- What is the likelihood of the benefit being achieved and harm being avoided based on your analysis?

- What are the views of the client and family on the options?

- What are the opinions of other professionals?

- What are the relevant organisational policies and procedures?

- What are the resource implications of each option?

- What is the contingency plan and how will this be initiated?

- What is the proposed monitoring and review arrangement?

(Developed during teaching over the past decade; uses ideas published in
Brearley, 1982; Kelly, 1996; Baron, 2008)

Appendix 2

Supported decision tool (Department of Health, 2007, pp50–1)

1. What is important to you in your life?

2. What is working well?

3. What isn't working so well?

4. What could make it better?

5. What things are difficult for you?

6. Describe how they affect you living your life.

7. What would make things better for you?

8. What is stopping you from doing what you want to do?

9. Do you think there are any risks?

10. Could things be done in a different way, which might reduce the risks?

11. Would you do things differently?

12. Is the risk present wherever you live?

13. What do you need to do?

14. What do staff/organisation need to change?

15. What could family/carers do?

16. Who is important to you?

17. What do people important to you think?

18. Are there any differences of opinion between you and the people you said are important to you?

19. What would help to resolve this?

20. Who might be able to help?

21. What could we do (practitioner) to support you?

Agreed next steps – who will do what

How would you like your care plan to be changed to meet your outcomes?

Record of any disagreements between people involved

Date agreed to review how you are managing

Signatures

When using the tool with the individual, consider carefully the following aspects of the person's life and wishes:

- dignity;
- diversity, race and culture, gender, sexual orientation, age;
- religious and spiritual needs;
- personal strengths;
- ability/willingness to be supported to self care;
- opportunities to learn new skills;
- support networks;
- environment – can it be improved by means of specialist equipment or assistive technology?
- information needs;
- communication needs – tool can be adapted (Braille, photographs, simplified language);
- ability to identify own risks;
- ability to find solutions;
- least restrictive options;
- social isolation, inclusion, exclusion;
- quality of life outcomes and the risk to independence of 'not supporting choice';

Glossary of terms

Actuarial assessment Involves a formal, algorithmic, objective procedure (e.g. equation) to inform a decision (Grove and Meehl, 1996, p293).

Assessing risk The professional task, working with the client and others as far as possible and appropriate, in gathering and analysing information relevant to the possibility of harm and desired goals in order to inform a risk-taking decision about care.

Care planning (Case planning) This term is used here to include plans to safeguard individuals and to support clients to take reasonable, reasoned risks as well as other forms of care planning such as where the focus is decisions about long-term care or provision of public resources for such as home care.

Clinical factors in prediction Factors about a client, family or situation widely recognised by professionals through experience as having an impact on the likelihood of the undesirable harm occurring in similar situations but which have not been tested or measured, and which are therefore not established risk factors.

Clinical social work Professional social work with individuals, particularly where there is a therapeutic or counselling focus rather than, for example, community development, group care or care management.

Dangerousness The seriousness and likelihood of harm being caused by an individual or group to others or to property.

Decision making A conscious process (individually or as a corporate exercise with one or more others) leading to the selection of a course of action among several alternatives.

Decision outcome What happens as a result of a decision, whether intended or not.

Decision policy A rule created by an individual or an organisation so as to standardise the response to future decisions that have similar features.

Hazard Something that may cause harm (Health & Safety Executive, 2006).

Heuristic A mental shortcut to making a particular type of decision, based on previous experience and knowledge that is now part of a person's conceptual framework, as opposed to being consciously considered.

Hindsight error Assuming that because there is an undesirable outcome then the decision process must have been flawed, without taking due account of the information available at the time and the context of the decision.

Integrated assessment system A system of assessment whereby there is more than one level of assessment according to complexity of need and risk, and which co-ordinates specialist assessments into a holistic overview for analysis and decision making (cf McCormack *et al.*, 2007a).

Judgement The considered evaluation of evidence by an individual using their cognitive faculties so as to reach an opinion on a preferred course of action based on available information, knowledge and values.

Likelihood *see Probability*.

Managing risk The professional task, working with the client, family and others as far as possible and appropriate, in reaching a judgement and participating in a decision-making process and its implementation, monitoring and review regarding care planning for this client that involves positive, reasonable risk taking to achieve care plan goals *(see also Risk management)*.

Monitoring Gathering information about the situation at regular time periods after the decision has been taken so as to initiate revision of the care plan if appropriate.

Planning risk *see Taking risk*.

Probability A numerical measure of the strength of a belief that a certain event will occur (adapted from Baron, 2008, p104). Normally the term probability is used where there is data available about how frequently this type of event has occurred in the past and the term likelihood when this event has not occurred before. This distinction depends on the definition of what is a similar event.

Professional judgement When a professional considers the evidence about a client or family situation in the light of professional knowledge to reach a conclusion or recommendation.

Protective factor By contrast with a Risk factor (q.v.) this is a factor that correlates with less probability of harm occurring.

Risk A time-bounded decision-making situation where the outcomes are uncertain and where benefits are sought but undesirable outcomes are possible.

Risk assessment *see Assessing risk*.

Risk factor Factors about a client, family or situation that have been shown through thorough research to correlate with the undesirable harm occurring to a significant extent (i.e. in the majority of cases, but not all).

Risk management The systems and processes of the organisation (including professional, decision-making, policy, procedural, strategic, communication, resource, legal and financial aspects) that support accountable professional judgement and reasonable risk-taking for the benefit of clients and society, and that enable continuing learning from mistakes and near misses as a means to improve safety and performance *(see also Managing risk)*.

Risk planning *see Taking risk*.

Sunk cost bias When a decision maker continues to invest resources in a previously selected course of action even though it is now perceived not to be the best option (Chapman and Elstein, 2000, p194).

Taking risk A positive activity working with the client and others as far as possible to weigh the values and likelihoods of possible harms and benefits of a decision, within professional principles and the frameworks of society and the organisation, to achieve reasoned and reasonable care goals where harm may occur, taking reasonable steps to identify and minimise harm.

Trigger factor A situation that may precipitate the occurrence of an identified undesirable event.

Vulnerability The susceptibility of an individual to suffer from an identified undesirable event.

References

Agathanos-Georgopolou, H. and Browne, K. (1997) The prediction of child maltreatment in Greek families. *Child Abuse and Neglect*, 21 (8): 721–35.

Alaszewski, A. (2000) Risk, trust and nursing: Towards an ethical basis for risk assessment and management in practice (pp157–74), in Alaszewski, A., Alaszewski, H., Ayer, S. and Manthorpe, J. (eds) *Managing Risk in Community Practice: Nursing, Risk and Decision Making*. London: Baillière Tindall & Royal College of Nursing.

Alaszewski, A. (2003) Editorial: Risk, trust and health. *Health, Risk & Society*, 5 (3): 235–9.

Alaszewski, A., Alaszewski, H., Ayer, S. and Manthorpe, J. (2000) *Managing Risk in Community Practice: Nursing, Risk and Decision Making*. Edinburgh: Baillière Tindall.

Alaszewski, A., Harrison, L. and Manthorpe, J. (eds) (1998) *Risk, Health and Welfare*. Buckingham: Open University Press.

Alberg, C., Hatfield, B. and Huxley, P. (1996) *Learning Materials on Mental Health Risk Assessment*. Manchester: Manchester University and the Department of Health.

Austin, C.D. and Seidl, F.W. (1981) Validating professional judgment in a home care agency. *Health and Social Work*, 6: 50–6.

Ball, D. (2007) Risk and the demise of children's play (pp57–76), in Thom, B., Sales, R. and Pearce, J.J. (eds) (2007) *Growing Up with Risk*. Bristol: The Policy Press.

Baltes, P.B. and Baltes, M.M. (1990) Psychological perspectives on successful aging: The model of selective optimisation with compensation (pp1–34), in Baltes, P.B. and Baltes, M.M. (eds) *Successful Aging: Perspectives from Behavioural Sciences*. Cambridge: Cambridge University Press.

Bandolier (2009) *Integrated Care Pathway* **www.medicine.ox.ac.uk/bandolier/booth/glossary/ICP.html**.

Banks, S. (2001) *Ethics and Values in Social Work*. (2nd edn.) Hampshire: Palgrave.

Baron, J. (2008) *Thinking and Deciding*. (4th edn.) Cambridge: Cambridge University Press.

Baumol, W.J. (2004) On rational satisficing, in Augier, M. and March, J.G. (eds) *Models of a Man: Essays in Memory of Herbert A Simon*. Cambridge, MA: MIT Press.

Beach, L.R. and Connolly, T. (1997) *The Psychology of Decision Making: People in Organisations*. California: Sage.

Beaumont, B. (1999) Risk assessment and prediction research (pp69–106), in Parsloe, P. (ed) *Risk Assessment in Social Care and Social Work – Research Highlights in Social Work 36*. London: Jessica Kingsley.

Beck, U. (1992) *Risk Society* (trans. M. Ritter). London: Sage.

Beckett, C. (2008) Risk, uncertainty and thresholds (p46), in Calder, M.C. (ed) *Contemporary Risk Assessment in Safeguarding Children*. Lyme Regis: Russell House.

Bekker, H., Thornton, J.G., Airey, CM., Connelly, J.B., Hewison, J., Robinson, M.B., Lilleyman, J., MacIntosh, M., Maule, A.J., Michie, S. and Pearman, A. (1999) Informed decision making: An annotated bibliography and systematic review. *Health Technology Assessment* 3 (1).

Benner, P. (1984) *From Novice to Expert: Excellence and Power in Clinical Nursing Practice.* Menlo Park, CA: Addison-Wesley (also Commemorative edition published 2001: Upper Saddle River, NJ: Prentice Hall).

Bennett, R. (2009) Khyra Ishaq held captive and starved by her mother and stepfather, *The Times.* **www.timesonline.co.uk/tol/news/uk/crime/article6440362.ece**

Beresford, B. and Sloper, T. (2008) *Understanding the Dynamics of Decision-Making and Choice: A Scoping Study of Key Psychological Theories to Inform the Design and Analysis of the Panel Study.* York: Social Policy Research Unit, University of York.

Boeije, H.R., Janssens, A. and Cecile, J.W. (2004) It might happen or it might not: How patients with multiple sclerosis explain their perception of prognostic risk. *Social Science & Medicine,* 59 (4): 861–8.

Bostock, L., Bairstow, S., Fish, S. and Macleod, F. (2005) *Managing Risk and Minimising Mistakes in Services to Children and Families: Children and Families' Services Report 6.* London: Social Care Institute for Excellence.

Boyd, W. (Chairman) (1996) *Report of the Confidential Inquiry into Homicides and Suicides by Mentally Ill People.* London: Royal College of Psychiatrists.

Brearley, P. (1982) *Risk in Social Work.* London: Routledge & Kegan Paul.

Bridge Child Care Consultancy (1995) *Paul: Death through Neglect.* London: Bridge Child Care Consultancy.

British Association of Social Workers (2008) BASW secures first GSCC appeal win. *Professional Social Work* (05 Nov).

Brown, K. (ed) (2006) *Vulnerable Adults and Community Care.* Exeter: Learning Matters.

Brown, K. and Rutter, L. (2006) *Critical Thinking for Social Work.* Exeter: Learning Matters.

Brown, R. and Barber, P. (2008) *The Social Worker's Guide to the Mental Capacity Act 2005.* Exeter: Learning Matters.

Bunyan, N. (2001) Doctors 'let off hook' in report over ex-Beatle's attacker. *Daily Telegraph,* 24 Oct.

Calder, M.C. (ed) (2008) *Contemporary Risk Assessment in Safeguarding Children.* Lyme Regis, Dorset: Russell House Publishers.

Calman, K.C., Bennett, P.G. and Coles, D.G. (1999) Risks to health: some issues in management, regulation and communication. *Health, Risk and Society,* 1: 107–16.

Cambridge, P. (2004) Abuse inquiries as learning tools for social care organisations (pp231–54), in Stanley, N. and Manthorpe, J. (eds) *The Age of the Inquiry: Learning and Blaming in Health and Social Care.* London: Routledge.

Carroll, J.S. and Johnson, E.J. (1990) *Decision Research: A Field Guide.* London: Sage Publications.

Carson, D. (1988) Risk-taking policies. *Journal of Social Welfare Law,* 5: 328–32.

Carson, D. (1996) Risking legal repercussions (pp3–12), in Kemshall, H. and Pritchard, J. (eds) *Good Practice in Risk Assessment and Risk Management 1.* London: Jessica Kingsley.

Carson, D. and Bain, A. (2008) *Professional Risk and Working with People: Decision-Making in Health, Social Care and Criminal Justice.* London: Jessica Kingsley.

Chapman, G.B. and Elstein, A.S. (2000) Cognitive processes and biases in medical decision making (pp183–210), in Chapman, G.B. and Sonnenberg, F.A. (eds) *Decision Making in Health Care: Theory, Psychology and Applications.* Cambridge: Cambridge University Press.

Cooksey, R.W. (1996) *Judgment Analysis: Theory, Methods and Applications.* New York: Academic Press.

Counsel and Care (1993) *The Right to Take Risks.* London: Counsel and Care.

Covell, N.H., McCorkle, B.H., Weissman, E.M., Summerfelt, T. and Essock, S.M. (2007) What's in a name? Terms preferred by service recipients. *Administration and Policy in Mental Health,* 34: 443–7.

Creighton, S.J. (2004a) *Child Protection Statistics 1: Child Protection in the Community.* London: National Society for the Prevention of Cruelty to Children.

Creighton, S.J. (2004b) *Prevalence and Incidence of Child Abuse: International Comparisons.* London: National Society for the Prevention of Cruelty to Children.

Creighton, S.J. and Tissier, G. (2003) *Child Killings in England and Wales.* London: National Society for the Prevention of Cruelty to Children.

Dalgleish, L. and Drew, E.C. (1989) The relationship of child abuse indicators to the assessment of perceived risk and to the court's decision to separate. *Child Abuse and Neglect,* 13: 491–506.

Darragh, E. and Taylor, B.J. (2008) Research and reflective practice (pp148–60), in Higham, P. (ed) *Post Qualifying Social Work – From Competence to Expertise.* London: Sage.

Dawes, R.M., Faust, D. and Meelh, P.E. (1989) Clinical versus actuarial judgment. *Science,* 243: 1668–74.

DCSF (2009) *Common Assessment Framework: Managers' and Practitioners' Guides.* London: Department for Children, Schools and Families. **www.dcsf.gov.uk/everychildmatters/resources-and-practice/IG00063/**

De Luc, K. (2000) *Developing Care Pathways: The Handbook – Vol. 2: The Toolkit.* London: Radcliffe Publishing for National Pathways Association.

Dempster, M. (2003) Systematic review (pp312–16), in Miller, R. and Brewer, J. (eds) *The A to Z of Social Research.* London: Sage.

Department of Health and Social Services (1998) *Community Care – From Policy to Practice – The Case of Mr Fredrick Joseph McLernon (Deceased).* Belfast. The Stationery Office.

DH (1993) *Risk Management in the NHS.* London: Department of Health, National Health Service Management Executive.

DH (1995) *The Challenge of Partnership in Child Protection.* London: HMSO.

DH (1996) *Building Bridges: A Guide to Arrangements for Inter-Agency Working for the Care and Protection of Severely Mentally Ill People.* London: HMSO.

DH (1998) *Modernising Mental Health Services: Safe, Sound and Supportive.* London: Department of Health.

DH (2001) *Valuing People: A New Strategy for Learning Disability for the 21st Century*. London: Department of Health.

DH (2002) LAC (2002) 13: *Fair Access to Care Services: Guidance on Eligibility Criteria for Adult Social Care*. London: Department of Health.

DH (2007) *Independence, Choice and Risk: A Guide to Best Practice in Supported Decision Making*. London: Department of Health.

DH (2009) *Valuing People Now: A New Three Year Strategy for Learning Disability: Making It Happen Now*. London: Department of Health.

DH and DfEE (Department for Education and Employment) (2000) *Framework for the Assessment of Children in Need and their Families*. London: Home Office.

DH (Social Services Inspectorate) (1993) *Evaluating Performance in Child Protection: A Framework for the Inspection of Local Authority Social Services Practice and Systems*. London: Her Majesty's Stationery Office.

DH, Home Office and DfEE (2006) *Working Together to Safeguard Children: A Guide to Inter-Agency Working to Safeguard and Promote the Welfare of Children*. London: Department of Health.

DHSSPS (2002) Departmental Guidance HSS(PPM) 10/2002 *Governance in the HPSS – Clinical and Social Care Governance: Guidelines for Implementation*. Belfast: Department of Health, Social Services and Public Safety for Northern Ireland.

DHSSPS (2003) *Risk Management: Core Standard*. Belfast: Department of Health, Social Services and Public Safety.

Dimond, B. (1997) *Legal Aspects of Care in the Community*. London: Macmillan Press.

Doel, M and Marsh, P (1992) *Task-Centred Social Work*. Aldershot: Ashgate.

Doueck, H.J. and English, D.J. (1993) Decision making in child protective services: A comparison of selected risk assessment systems. *Child Welfare*, 72 (5): 441–53.

Dowding, D. and Thompson, C. (2002) Decision analysis (pp131–46), in Thompson, C. and Dowding, D. (eds) *Clinical Decision Making and Judgement in Nursing*. Edinburgh: Churchill Livingstone.

Dowie, J. (1993) Clinical decision analysis: Background and introduction, in Llewelyn, H. and Hopkins, A. (eds) *Analysing How We Reach Clinical Decisions*. London: Royal College of Physicians.

Dowie, J. (1999) Communication for better decisions: Not about 'risk'. *Health, Risk and Society*, 1 (1): 41–53.

Doyal, L. and Gough, I. (1991) *The Theory of Human Need*. London: Macmillan Press.

Duffy, J., Taylor, B.J. and McCall, S. (2006) Human rights and decision making in child protection through explicit argumentation. *Child Care in Practice*, 12 (2): 81–95.

Duffy, S. and Sanderson, H. (2008) *Person Centred Planning and Care Management*. **www.helensandersonassociates.co.uk/PDFs/Person%20centred%20planning%20and%20care%20management%20-%20final%20version,%20April%202004.pdf**

Dyckman, K.M. and Carroll, S.J. (1981) *Inviting the Mystic; Supporting the Prophet: An Introduction to Spiritual Direction*. New Jersey: Paulist Press.

Eddy, D.M. (1996) *Clinical Decision Making From Theory to Practice: A Collection of Essays from the Journal of the American Medical Association*. Sudbury, MA: Jones and Bartlett.

Egan, M., Wells, J., Byrne, K., Jaglal, S., Stolee, P., Chesworth, B.M. and Hillier, L.M. (2009) The process of decision-making in home-care case management: Implications for the introduction of universal assessment and information technology. *Health and Social Care in the Community*, 17 (4): 371–8.

English, D. and Pecora, P. (1994) Risk assessment as a practice method in child protective services. *Child Welfare*, LXXIII (5): 451–73.

Farmer, E. and Owen, M. (1995) *Child Protection Practice: Private Risks and Public Remedies*. London: HMSO.

Fisher, M., Qureshi, H., Hardyman, W. and Homewood, J. (2006) *Using Qualitative Research in Systematic Reviews: Older People's Views of Hospital Discharge*. London: Social Care Institute for Excellence.

Flynn, R. (2002) Clinical governance and governmentality. *Health, Risk & Society*, 4 (2): 155–73.

Foster, C. (1998) Bolam: Consolidation and clarification. *Health Care Risk Report*, 4 (5): 5–7.

Freel, K.A. (1995) The guardians of childhood safety: The role of parents in injury prevention. *Dissertation Abstracts International: Section B: The Sciences and Engineering*, 55 (8–B): 3607.

French, S. (1989) *Readings in Decision Analysis: Chapman & Hall Statistics Text Series*. London: Chapman & Hall/CRC.

Gambrill, E.D. (1977) *Behaviour Modification: Handbook of Assessment, Intervention, and Evaluation*. New York: Jossey-Bass (Wiley).

Garson, G.C. (1998) *Neural Networks: An Introductory Guide for Social Scientists*. Thousand Oaks, CA: Sage.

General Social Care Council [England] (2004) *The Post-Qualifying Awards in Social Work*. **www.gscc.org.uk**

Gigerenzer, G. (2002) *Reckoning with Risk: Learning to Live with Uncertainty*. London: Allen Lane The Penguin Press.

Gigerenzer, G. and Goldstein, D.G. (1996) Reasoning the fast and frugal way: Models of bounded rationality. *Psychological Review*, 103 (4): 650–69.

Gilovich, T., Griffin, D. and Kahneman, D. (eds) (2002) *Heuristics and Biases: The Psychology of Intuitive Judgement*. Cambridge: Cambridge University Press.

Goldberg, D. and Huxley, P. (1979) *Mental Illness in the Community: The Pathway to Psychiatric Care*. London: Routledge.

Goodman, R. (1997) The strengths and difficulties questionnaire: A research note. *Journal of Child Psychology and Psychiatry*, 38: 581–6.

Graybeal, C.T. and Konrad, S.C. (2008) Strengths-based child assessment: Locating possibility and transforming the paradigm (pp185–97), in Calder, M.C. (ed) *Contemporary Risk Assessment in Safeguarding Children*. Lyme Regis: Russell House.

Greeno, J.G. (1978) Natures of problem-solving abilities (pp239–70), in Estes, W.K. (ed) *Handbook of Learning and Cognitive Processes, Vol. 5: Human Information Processing*. Mahwah, NJ: Lawrence Erlbaum.

Grice, E. (2008) Hannah Jones: I have been in hospital too much. *Telegraph*, 12 Nov, **www. telegraph.co.uk/health/3444840/Hannah-Jones-I-have-been-in-hospital-too-much.html**

Grove, W. and Meehl, P. (1996) Comparative efficiency of informal (subjective, impressionistic) and formal (mechanical, algorithmic) prediction procedures. *Psychology, Public Policy and Law*, 2: 293–323.

Gunnell, D. (1994) *The Potential for Preventing Suicide – A Review of the Literature on the Effectiveness of Interventions Aimed at Preventing Suicide*. Bristol: University of Bristol Health Care Evaluation Unit.

Hackett, S. (1999) Towards a resilience-based intervention model for young people with harmful sexual behaviours, in Erooga, M. and Masson, H. (eds) *Children and Young People Who Sexually Abuse Others: Challenges and Responses*. London: Routledge.

Hagell, A. (1998) *Dangerous Care: Reviewing the Risks to Children from their Carers*. London: Bridge Child Care Consultancy.

Hammond, K.R. (1996) *Human Judgment and Social Policy: Irreducible Uncertainty, Inevitable Error, Unavoidable Injustice*. New York: Oxford University Press.

Hardman, D. (2009) *Judgment and Decision Making*. London: Oxford University Press.

Hardy, B., Young, R. and Wistow, G. (1999) Dimensions of choice in the assessment and care management process: The views of older people, carers and care managers. *Health and Social Care in the Community*, 7 (6): 483–91.

Hawkins, P. and Shohet, R. (2000) *Supervision in the Helping Professions*. Buckingham: Open University Press.

Health & Social Care Change Agents Team (2003) *Discharge from Hospital: Pathway, Process and Practice*. London: Department of Health.

Heffernan, K. (2006) Social work, new public management and the language of service user. *British Journal of Social Work*, 36: 139–47.

Hollows, A. (2001) The challenges to social work. *Child Psychology & Psychiatry Review*, 6 (1): 11–15.

Hollows, A. (2003) Making professional judgements in the framework for the assessment of children in need and their families (pp61–74), in Calder, M.C. and Hackett, S. (eds) *Assessment in Child Care*. Lyme Regis: Russell House.

Hollows, A (2008) Professional judgement and the risk assessment process (p52–60), in Calder, M.C. (ed) *Contemporary Risk Assessment in Safeguarding Children*. Lyme Regis: Russell House Publishers.

Hood, R. and Shute, S. (2000) *The Parole System at Work: A Study of Risk Based Decision-Making, Home Office Research Study 202*. London: Home Office.

Howarth, J. (2007) *Child Neglect: Identification and Assessment*. Hampshire: Palgrave Macmillan.

HSE (2008) *Myth: Children Need to be Wrapped in Cotton Wool to Keep Them Safe*. London: Health and Safety Executive, **www.hse.gov.uk/myth/nov08.htm**

HSE (2009a) *About the Health and Safety Executive.* London: Health and Safety Executive, **www.hse.gov.uk/aboutus/index.htm**

HSE (2009b) *Health and Safety Law: What You Need to Know.* London: Health and Safety Executive, **www.hse.gov.uk/pubns/law.pdf**

HSE (2009c) *Violence at Work.* London: Health and Safety Executive, **www.hse.gov.uk/statistics/caus-dis/violence/definitions.htm**

HSE (2009d) *The Five Steps to Risk Assessment.* London: Health and Safety Executive, **www.hse.gov.uk/risk/fivesteps.htm**

HSE (2009e) *Evaluate the Risks and Decide on Precautions.* London: Health and Safety Executive, **www.hse.gov.uk/risk/step3.htm**

HSE (2009f) *Principles of Sensible Risk Management,* Speech 9 May 2006 by Tony Bandle, Strategy Division. London: Health and Safety Executive, **www.hse.gov.uk/aboutus/speeches/tbrospa-congress.pdf**

HSE (2009g) *Myth: Health and Safety Rules Take the Adventure Out of Playgrounds.* London: Health and Safety Executive, **www.hse.gov.uk/myth/mar09.htm**

Janis, I.L. (1982) *Groupthink: Psychological Studies of Policy Decisions and Fiascoes.* New York: Houghton Mifflin.

Janis, I.L. and Mann, L. (1977) *Decision Making: A Psychological Analysis of Conflict, Choice and Commitment.* New York: The Free Press.

Jones, D.P.H. (1998) The effectiveness of intervention (pp91–120), in Adcock, M. and White, R. (eds) *Significant Harm: Its Management and Outcome.* (2nd ed.) Croydon: Significant Publications.

Kahneman, D. and Tversky, A. (eds) (2000) *Choices, Values and Frames.* New York: Cambridge University Press.

Kahnemann, D., Slovic, P. and Tversky, P. (1982) *Judgement under Uncertainty: Heuristics and Biases.* Cambridge: Cambridge University Press.

Kane, R.A., Degenholtz, H.B. and Kane, R.L. (1999) Adding values: An experiment in systematic atten-tion to values and preferences of community long-term care clients. *Journal of Gerontology: Social Sciences,* 54b (2): S109–19.

Kane, R.L., Kane, R.A. and Ells, M. (2002) *Assessing Older Persons: Measures, Meaning, and Practical Applications.* New York: Oxford University Press.

Keaney, F., Strang, J., Martinez-Raga, J., Spektor, D., Manning, V., Kelleher, M., Wilson-Jones, C., Wanagaratne, S. and Sabater, A. (2004) Does anyone care about names? How attendees at substance misuse services like to be addressed by professionals. *European Addiction Research,* 10: 75–9.

Kelly, G. (1996) Competence in risk analysis (pp108–23), in O'Hagan, K. (ed) *Competence in Social Work Practice.* London: Jessica Kingsley.

Kelly, N. and Milner, J. (1996) Child protection decision-making. *Child Abuse Review,* 5: 91–102.

Kemshall, H. (2008) Actuarial and clinical risk assessment: Contrasts, comparisons and collective usages (pp198–205), in Calder, M.C. (ed) *Contemporary Risk Assessment in Safeguarding Children.* Lyme Regis, Dorset: Russell House Publishing.

Kemshall, H. and Pritchard, J. (eds) (1996) *Good Practice in Risk Assessment and Risk Management 1 and 2*. London: Jessica Kingsley.

Killick, J.C. (2008) *Factors Influencing Judgments of Social Care Professionals on Adult Protection Referrals*. Thesis (PhD). Coleraine, Northern Ireland: University of Ulster.

Kitzinger, J. and Reilly, J. (1997) The rise and fall of risk reporting: Media coverage of human genetics research, 'false memory syndrome' and 'mad cow disease.' *European Journal of Communication*, 12 (3): 319–50.

Klein, G. (1996) *Sources of Power: The Study of Naturalistic Decision Making*. Mahwah, NJ: Lawrence Erlbaum.

Laming, H. (2003) *The Victoria Climbié Inquiry Report*. London: HMSO.

Lawhead, S. (1989) *Arthur*. London: Lion Publishing.

Lipsky, M. (1980) *Street-Level Bureaucracy: Dilemmas of the Individual in Public Services*. New York: Sage.

Littlechild, B. and Reid, J. (2007) Assessment (pp149–64), in Tovey, W. (ed) *The Post-Qualifying Handbook for Social Workers*. London: Jessica Kingsley.

Lloyd, C., King, R., Bassett, H., Sandland, S. and Saviage, G. (2001) Patient, client or consumer: A survey of preferred terms. *Australasian Psychiatry*, 9: 321–4.

Luft, J. (1969) *Of Human Interaction*. Palo Alto, CA: National Press.

Macdonald, G. (2001) *Effective Interventions for Child Abuse and Neglect: An Evidence-Based Approach to Planning and Evaluating Interventions*. Chichester: Wiley.

Macdonald, G. and Sheldon, B. (1998) Changing one's mind: The final frontier? *Issues in Social Work Education*, 18 (1): 3–25.

Macdonald, K.I. and Macdonald, G.M. (1999) Perceptions of risk (pp17–52), in Parsloe, P. (ed) *Risk Assessment in Social Care and Social Work*. Aberdeen: Research Highlights.

Manthorpe, J. and Alaszewski, A. (2000) Service users, informal carers and risk (pp47–70), in Alaszewski, A., Alaszewski, H., Ayer, S. and Manthorpe, J. (eds) *Managing Risk in Community Practice: Nursing, Risk and Decision Making*. London: Bailliere Tindall and Royal College of Nursing.

Manthorpe, J., Walsh, M., Alaszewski, A. and Harrison, L. (1997) Issues of risk practice and welfare in learning disability services. *Disability & Society*, 12 (1): 69–82.

Marsh, J. and Soulsby, J. (1994) *Outlines of English Law*. Cheltenham: Stanley Thornes.

Marsh, P. and Fisher, M. in collaboration with Mathers, N. and Fish, S. (2005) *Developing the Evidence Base for Social Work and Social Care Practice: Using Knowledge in Social Care, Report 10*. London: Social Care Institute for Excellence.

Maslow, A. (1943) A theory of human motivation. *Psychological Review*, 50: 370–96.

Maung, N.A. and Hammond, N. (2000) *Risk of Re-offending and Needs Assessments: The Users' Perspective, Home Office Research Study 216*. London: Home Office.

McCormack, B.G., Taylor, B.J., McConville, J.E., Slater, P.F. and Murray, B.J. (2007a) *The Validity of the Core Component of the Northern Ireland Single Assessment Tool (NISAT) for the Health and Social Care of Older People.* Belfast: Department of Health, Social Services and Public Safety.

McCormack, B.G., Taylor, B.J., McConville, J.E., Slater, P.F. and Murray, B.J. (2007b) *The Reliability of the Core Component of the Northern Ireland Single Assessment Tool (NISAT) for the Health and Social Care of Older People.* Belfast: Department of Health, Social Services and Public Safety.

McCormack, B.G., Taylor, B.J., McConville, J.E., Slater, P.F. and Murray, B.J. (2008a) *The Northern Ireland Single Assessment Tool (NISAT) for the Health and Social Care of Older People.* Belfast: Department of Health, Social Services and Public Safety.

McCormack, B.G., Taylor, B.J., McConville, J.E., Slater, P.F. and Murray, B.J. (2008b) *Guidance Document for the Northern Ireland Single Assessment Tool (NISAT) for the Health and Social Care of Older People.* Belfast: Department of Health, Social Services and Public Safety.

McCormack, B.G., Taylor, B.J., McConville, J.E., Slater, P.F. and Murray, B.J. (2008c) *The Usability of the Northern Ireland Single Assessment Tool (NISAT) for the Health and Social Care of Older People.* Belfast: Department of Health, Social Services and Public Safety.

McCormack, B.G., Taylor, B.J., McConville, J.E., Slater, P.F. and Murray, B.J. (2008d) *The Reliability of the Complex Component of the Northern Ireland Single Assessment Tool (NISAT) for the Health and Social Care of Older People.* Belfast: Department of Health, Social Services and Public Safety.

McGrath, B.J. (2007) Identifying health and safety risks for childcare workers. *American Association of Occupational Health Nurses' Journal,* 55 (80): 321–6.

McKillop, C. (2007) *Assessing Child Neglect: An Exploration into the Usefulness of the Graded Care Profile (GCP) for the Assessment of Child Neglect by Social Work Staff Directly Involved in the Assessment Process.* Report (Application of Research Methods in Social Work Programme). Coleraine, Northern Ireland: University of Ulster.

Meehl, P.E. (1954) *Clinical Versus Statistical Prediction: A Theoretical Analysis and a Review of the Evidence.* Minneapolis: University of Minnesota Press.

Middleton, S., Barnett, J. and Reeves, D. (2001) What is an integrated care pathway? *Evidence Based Medicine,* 3 (3): 1–8, **www.medicine.ox.ac.uk/bandolier/painres/download/whatis/What_is_an_ICP.pdf**

Monahan, J. (1981) *Predicting Violent Behaviour: An Assessment of Clinical Techniques.* Beverley Hills, CA: Sage.

Monahan, J. (1993) Limiting therapist exposure to Tarasoff liability: Guidelines for risk containment. *American Psychologist,* 48 (3): 242–50.

Monahan, J., Steadman, H.J., Silver, E., Appelbaum, P.S., Robbins, P.C., Mulvey, E.P., Roth, L.H., Grisso, T. and Banks, S. (2001) *Rethinking Risk Assessment: The MacArthur Study of Mental Disorder and Violence.* Oxford: Oxford University Press.

Morgan, S. (2000) *Clinical Risk Management: A Clinical Tool and Practitioner Manual.* London: The Sainsbury Centre for Mental Health.

Moriarty, J., Rapaport, P., Beresford, P., Branfield, F., Forrest, V., Manthorpe, J., Martineau, S., Cornes, M., Butt, J., Iliffe, S., Taylor, B. and Keady, J. (2007) *Practice Guide 11: The Participation of Adult Service Users, Including Older People, in Developing Social Care.* London: Social Care Institute for Excellence.

Morrison, T. (1998) Partnership, collaboration and change under the Children Act (pp121–48), in Adcock, M. and White, R. (eds) *Significant Harm: Its Management and Outcome*. (2nd ed.). Croydon: Significant Publications.

Morrison, T. and Henniker, J. (1999) Building a comprehensive interagency assessment and intervention system for young people who sexually harm, in Erooga, M. and Masson, H. (eds) *Children and Young People Who Sexually Harm Others: Current Developments and Practice Responses*. London: Routledge.

Munro, E. (1996) Avoidable and unavoidable mistakes in child protection work. *British Journal of Social Work*, 26 (6): 793–808.

Munro, E. (1999) Common errors of reasoning in child protection work. *Child Abuse and Neglect*, 23 (8): 745–58.

Munro, E. (2005) A systems approach to investigating child abuse deaths. *British Journal of Social Work*, 35 (4): 531–46.

Munro, E. (2008) *Effective Child Protection*. (2nd ed.) London: Sage.

National Commission of Inquiry into the Prevention of Child Abuse (1996) *Childhood Matters: Report of the National Commission of Inquiry into the Prevention of Child Abuse: Volume 1: The Report*. London: HMSO.

Neill, M., Allen, J., Woodhead, N., Reid, S., Irwin, L. and Sanderson, H. (2008) *A Positive Approach to Risk Requires Person Centred Thinking*. **www.dhcarenetworks.org.uk/_library/Resources/ Personalisation/Personalisation_advice/A_Person_Centred_Approach_to_Risk.pdf**

Newell, A. and Simon, H.A. (1972) *Human Problem Solving*. Englewood Cliffs, NJ: Prentice Hall.

Newhill, C.E. (1996) Prevalence and risk factors for client violence toward social workers. *Families in Society*, 77 (8): 488–95.

Newman, T., Moseley, A., Tierney, S. and Ellis, A. (2005) *Evidence Based Social Work: A Guide for the Perplexed*. Lyme Regis: Russell House.

NISRA (2007) *Statistics Press Notice – Mortality Statistics for Northern Ireland (2006)*. Belfast: Northern Ireland Statistics and Research Agency.

Nolan, M., Davies, S. and Grant, G. (eds) (2001) *Working with Older People and Their Families: Key Issues in Policy and Practice*. Buckingham: Open University Press.

Norman, A.J. (1980) *Rights and Risk*. London: Centre for Policy on Ageing.

Northern Ireland Post Qualifying Education and Training Partnership (2007) *Requirements and Guidance for Accreditation in NI PQ Framework*. **www.nipqetp.com/NI_framework/ nidownloads/07_05_16_%20AP_Req_Guide_for_Accreditation_in_NIPQ_FW.pdf**

Novaco, R.W. (1994) *Novaco Anger Scale and Provocation Inventory (NAS-PI)*. Los Angeles, CA: Western Psychological Services.

Office of Public Sector Information (2009) *Dependent Children*. **www.statistics.gov.uk/cci/ nugget.asp?id=1163**

O'Hagan, K. (1991) Crisis intervention in social work (pp138–56), in Lishman, J. (ed) *Handbook of Theory for Practice Teachers in Social Work*. London: Jessica Kingsley.

O'Sullivan, T. (1999) *Decision Making in Social Work*. London: Macmillan.

Osmo, R. and Landau, R. (2001) The need for explicit argumentation in ethical decision-making in social work. *Social Work Education*, 20 (4): 483–92.

Parton, N., Thorpe, D. and Wattam, C. (1997) *Child Protection – Risk and the Moral Order*. London: Macmillan.

Pascoe-Watson, G. and Wilson, G. (2008) Baby P gets the justice you demanded. *The Sun*, London (1 December 2008).

Pattison, S. (2006) *Medical Law and Ethics*. (2nd ed.) London: Sweet and Maxwell.

Payne, M. (1996) *What is Professional Social Work?* Birmingham: Venture Press.

Perry, J. and Sheldon, B. (1995) *Richard Phillips Inquiry Report*. London: City of Westminster, and Kensington & Chelsea & Westminster District Health Authority.

Peter, L. (1980) *Quotations for Our Time*. London: Methuen.

Petticrew M. and Roberts, H. (2006) *Systematic Reviews in the Social Sciences: A Practical Guide*. Oxford: Blackwell.

Pfister, H.-R., and Bohm, G. (2008) The multiplicity of emotions: A framework of emotional functions in decision making. *Judgment and Decision Making*, 3 (1): 5–17.

Plous, S. (1993) *The Psychology of Judgment and Decision Making*. New York: McGraw-Hill.

Porter, D. (1986) *Children at Risk*. Sussex: Kingsway.

Post Qualifying Consortium for Social Work in Scotland (2005) *Post Qualifying Award in Social Work – Part 1 & 2*. **www.sssc.uk.com/NR/rdonlyres/3BEEE02B-465F-425E-B8FE-1DADA03E6631/ 0/GuidancePQPart1010405.pdf**

Pritchard, C. (1992) Children's homicide as an indicator of effective child protection: A comparative study of Western European statistics. *British Journal of Social Work*, 22 (6): 663–84.

Raynor, P., Kynch, J., Roberts, C. and Merrington, S. (2000) *Risk and Need Assessment in Probation Services: An Evaluation, Home Office Research Study 211*. London: Home Office.

Reder, P. and Duncan, S. (2004) From Colwell to Climbié: Inquiring into fatal child abuse (pp92–115), in Stanley, N. and Manthorpe, J. (eds) *The Age of the Inquiry: Learning and Blaming in Health and Social Care*. London: Routledge.

Reith, M. (1998) *Community Care Tragedies: A Practice Guide to Mental Health Inquiries*. Birmingham: Venture Press.

Reynolds, B.C. (1942) *Learning and Teaching in the Practice of Social Work*. New York: Macmillan.

Righthand, S., Kerr, B. and Drach, K. (2003) *Child Maltreatment Risk Assessments: An Evaluation Guide*. New York: The Hawthorne Maltreatment and Trauma Press.

Roberts, A.R. (2000) *Crisis Intervention Handbook*. New York: Oxford University Press.

Roberts, A.R. and Greene, G.J. (2002) *Social Workers' Desk Reference*. New York: Oxford University Press.

Robertson, C. (ed) (1996) *The Wordsworth Dictionary of Quotations*. Ware, Hertfordshire: Wordsworth Editions.

Rogers, W.V.H. (2006) *Winfield and Jolowicz on Tort*. London: Sweet & Maxwell.

Ross, L. and Waterson, J. (1996) Risk for whom? Social work and people with physical disabilities (pp80–92), in Kemshall, H. and Pritchard, J. (eds) *Good Practice in Risk Assessment and Risk Management 1*. London: Jessica Kingsley.

Ryan, M., Scott, D.A., Reeves, C., Bate, A., van Teijlingen, E.R., Russell, E.M., Napper, M. and Robb, C.M. (2001) Eliciting public preferences for healthcare: A systematic review of techniques. *Health Technology Assessment*, 5 (5).

Ryan, T. (ed) (1999) *Managing Crisis and Risk in Mental Health Nursing*. Cheltenham: Stanley Thornes.

Schaffer, H.R. (1998) *Making Decisions About Children*. (2nd edn.) Oxford: Blackwell.

Schon, D.A. (1983) *The Reflective Practitioner*. Aldershot: Arena.

Schon, D.A. (1996) *Educating the Reflective Practitioner: Toward a New Design for Teaching and Learning in the Professions*. San Francisco, CA: Jossey Bass.

Scott-Jones, J. and Raisborough, J. (eds) (2007) *Risk, Identities and the Everyday*. Hampshire: Ashgate.

Seal, M. (2008) *Not About Us Without Us: Client Involvement in Supported Housing*. Dorset: Russell House.

Senge, P. (1990) *The Fifth Discipline*. New York: Doubleday.

Seymour, C. and Seymour, R. (2007) *Courtroom Skills for Social Workers*. Exeter: Learning Matters.

Sheppard, D. (2004) Mental health inquiries 1985–2003 (pp165–212), in Stanley, N. and Manthorpe, J. (eds) *The Age of the Inquiry: Learning and Blaming in Health and Social Care*. London: Routledge.

Shulman, L. (1999) *The Skills of Helping Individuals, Families, Groups and Communities*. Itasca, Illinois: FE Peacock.

Simmonds, J. (1998) Making decisions in social work – persecuting, rescuing or being a victim (pp175–96), in Adcock, M. and White, R. (eds) *Significant Harm: Its Management and Outcome*. (2nd ed.). Croydon: Significant Publications.

Simmons, L. (2007) *Social Care Governance: A Practice Workbook*. Belfast: Department of Health, Social Services and Public Safety (Clinical and Social Care Governance Support Team) and London: Social Care Institute for Excellence.

Slovic, P. (1999) Trust, emotion, sex, politics, and science: Surveying the risk-assessment battlefield. *Risk Analysis*, 19 (4): 689–701.

Social Exclusion Task Force (2008) *Think Family: Improving the Life Chances of Families at Risk*. London: Cabinet Office.

Social Services Inspectorate (1993) *Evaluating Performance in Child Protection*. London: Department of Health.

Spratt, T. (2001) The influence of child protection orientation on child welfare practice. *British Journal of Social Work*, 31 (6): 933–54.

Srivastava, O.P., Fountain, R., Ayre, P. and Stewart, J. (2003) The Graded Care Profile: A measure of care, in Calder, M. and Hackett, S. (eds) *Assessment in Child Care*. Lyme Regis: Russell House.

Stanley, N. and Manthorpe, J. (2004) Introduction: The Inquiry as Janus (pp1–16), in Stanley, N. and Manthorpe, J. (eds) *The Age of the Inquiry: Learning and Blaming in Health and Social Care*. London: Routledge.

Stoner, J. (1968) Risky and cautious shifts in group decision: The influence of widely-held values. *Journal of Experimental Social Psychology*, 4: 442–59.

Taylor, B.J. (1999) Developing partnership between professions in implementing new children's legislation in Northern Ireland. *Journal of Inter-Professional Care*, 13 (3): 249–59.

Taylor, B.J. (2003) Literature searching (pp171–6), in Miller, R. and Brewer, J. (eds) *The A to Z of Social Research*. London: Sage.

Taylor B.J. (2006a) Factorial surveys: Using vignettes to study professional judgement. *British Journal of Social Work*, 36 (7): 1187–207.

Taylor, B.J. (2006b) Risk management paradigms in health and social services for professional decision making on the long-term care of older people. *British Journal of Social Work*, 36 (8): 1411–29.

Taylor, B.J. and Devine, T. (1993; latest reprint 2005) *Assessing Needs and Planning Care in Social Work*. Aldershot: Ashgate.

Taylor, B.J. and Donnelly, M. (2006a) Risks to home care workers: Professional perspectives. *Health, Risk & Society*, 8 (3): 239–56.

Taylor, B.J. and Donnelly, M. (2006b) Professional perspectives on decision making about the long-term care of older people. *British Journal Social Work*, 36 (5): 807–26.

Taylor, B.J. and Zeller, R.A. (2007) Getting robust and valid data on decision policies: The factorial survey. *Irish Journal of Psychology*, 28 (1–2): 27–42.

Taylor, B.J., Dempster, M. and Donnelly, M. (2003) Hidden gems: Systematically searching electronic databases for research publications for social work and social care. *British Journal of Social Work*, 33 (4): 423–39.

Taylor, B.J., Dempster, M. and Donnelly, M. (2007) Grading gems: Appraising the quality of research for social work and social care. *British Journal of Social Work*, 37 (2): 335–54.

Thom, B., Sales, R. and Pearce, J. (eds) (2007) *Growing Up with Risk*. Bristol: The Policy Press.

Thompson, C. (2002) Human error, bias, decision making and judgement in nursing – The need for a systematic approach (pp21–46), in Thompson, C. and Dowding, D. (eds) (2002) *Clinical Decision Making and Judgement in Nursing*. Edinburgh: Churchill Livingstone.

Thompson, C. and Dowding, D. (eds) (2002) *Clinical Decision Making and Judgement in Nursing*. Edinburgh: Churchill Livingstone.

Tooth, G. (2009) Decision-making (pp66–83), in Mantell, A. (ed) *Social Work Skills with Adults*. Exeter: Learning Matters.

TOPSS (2005) *National Occupational Standards for Social Work in England*. London: Training Organisation for Personal Social Services.

Toulmin, S.E. (1958) *The Uses of Argument*. Cambridge: Cambridge University Press.

Turnbull, J. and Paterson, B. (eds) (1999) *Aggression and Violence: Approaches to Effective Management*. Hampshire: Macmillan.

Tweedie, N. (2008) Why did Khyra Ishaq's neighbours not come to her aid? *Daily Telegraph* (24 May) **www.telegraph.co.uk/news/uknews/2017378/Khyra-Ishaq-Why-did-her-neighbours-not-come-to-her-aid.html**

Urgent Care Pathway Working Group, Department of Health (2007) *Urgent Care Pathways for Older People with Complex Needs (Guidance)*. Gateway reference: 7817 London: Department of Health **www.dh.gov.uk/en/Publicationsandstatistics/Publications/PublicationsPolicyAndGuidance/DH_08 0135**

Varma, V. (1997) *Violence in Children and Adolescents*. London: Jessica Kingsley Publishers.

Walter, I., Nutley, S., Percy-Smith, J., McNeish, D. and Frost, S. (2004) *Improving the Use of Research in Social Care Practice (Knowledge Review 7)*. London: Social Care Institute for Excellence.

Walters, H. (2008) *Gillick Competency or Fraser Guidelines: An Overview*. London: National Society for the Prevention of Cruelty to Children, Library and Information Service. **www.nspcc.org.uk/Inform/ resourcesforprofessionals/InformationBriefings/gillick_wda61289.html**

White, C. (2008) *Northern Ireland Social Work Law*. West Sussex: Tottel Publishing.

White, R., Broadbent, G. and Brown, K. (2007) *Law and the Social Work Practitioner*. Exeter: Learning Matters.

Whyte, S. and Campbell, A. (2008) The strengths and difficulties questionnaire: A useful screening tool to identify mental health strengths and needs in looked after children and inform care plans at looked after children reviews? *Child Care in Practice*, 14 (2): 193–206.

Wimber, J. (2004) *Doin' the Stuff: The Ministry and Teachings of John Wimber*. **www.doin-the-stuff.com/WelcomePage.htm**

Wood, J., Ashman, M., Davies, C., Lloyd, H. and Lockett, K. (1966) *Report of the Independent Inquiry into the Care of Anthony Smith*. Derbyshire: Southern Derbyshire Health Authority and Derbyshire County Council.

Wood, J.M. (1996) Weighing evidence in sexual abuse evaluations: An introduction to Bayes Theorem. *Child Maltreatment*, 1 (1): 25–36.

Woods, D., Johannesen, L., Cook, R. and Sarter, N. (1993) *Behind Human Error: Cognitive Systems, Computers and Hindsight. State-of-the-Art Report*. Dayton, Ohio: Crew System Ergonomics Information Analysis Centre.

World Health Organisation (2002) *Active Aging: A Policy Framework*. Noncommunicable Disease and Mental Health Cluster, Noncommunicable Disease Prevention and Health Promotion Department, Aging and Life Course. Geneva: World Health Organisation.

Wynne-Harley, D. (1991) *Living Dangerously: Risk-taking, Safety and Older People*. London: Centre for Policy on Ageing.

Young, W.P. (2008) *The Shack*. London: Hodder & Stoughton.

Index